北京联合大学教材资助项目

跨文化交际

迟红 ◎ 主编

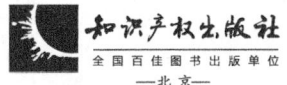
知识产权出版社
全国百佳图书出版单位
—北京—

图书在版编目（CIP）数据

跨文化交际/迟红主编．—北京：知识产权出版社，2022.9
ISBN 978-7-5130-8101-6

Ⅰ.①跨… Ⅱ.①迟… Ⅲ.①文化交流 Ⅳ.①G115

中国版本图书馆 CIP 数据核字（2022）第 048054 号

内容提要

跨文化交际课程于 2019 年在中国大学慕课平台上成功上线，本教材是在该慕课课件的基础上，根据教育部颁布的《大学英语教学指南》精神编写而成的。本教材以培养具有"家国情怀，国际视野"的高素质人才为己任，在借鉴和吸收国内外优秀教材的基础上，一方面选取具有代表性的英语国家的主流文化现象进行描述、阐释和讨论，另一方面有机融入了中国传统文化，帮助学生掌握必要的跨文化交际知识，培养学生对目的语文化的兴趣和理解力。同时引导学生对中西方文化进行主动观察、分析比较，从而拓宽国际视野，提高跨文化交际意识，增强跨文化交际能力。

本教材由 9 个单元构成，围绕什么是文化、文化的特征、语言与文化的关系、跨文化交际的历史发展、跨文化交际障碍以及如何培养跨文化交际能力等内容展开。

责任编辑：张水华	责任校对：王　岩
封面设计：臧　磊	责任印制：孙婷婷

跨文化交际
迟　红　主编

出版发行：知识产权出版社有限责任公司	网　　址：http://www.ipph.cn
社　　址：北京市海淀区气象路 50 号院	邮　　编：100081
责编电话：010-82000860 转 8389	责编邮箱：46816202@qq.com
发行电话：010-82000860 转 8101/8102	发行传真：010-82000893/82005070/82000270
印　　刷：北京九州迅驰传媒文化有限公司	经　　销：新华书店、各大网上书店及相关专业书店
开　　本：720mm×1000mm　1/16	印　　张：20.5
版　　次：2022 年 9 月第 1 版	印　　次：2022 年 9 月第 1 次印刷
字　　数：350 千字	定　　价：89.00 元
ISBN 978-7-5130-8101-6	

出版权专有　侵权必究
如有印装质量问题，本社负责调换。

前 言
PREFACE

跨文化交际课程于2019年在中国大学慕课平台成功上线,选课人数超过万人。本教材是在慕课课件的基础上,根据教育部颁布的《大学英语教学指南》编写而成的。语言是文化的载体,同时也是文化的重要组成部分,学生学习英语这一交流工具,除了学习、交流先进的科学技术和专业信息,还要了解国外的社会与文化,增进对不同文化的理解、对中外文化异同的认识,培养跨文化交际能力。人文性的核心是以人为本,弘扬人的价值,注重人的综合素质培养和全面发展,应将社会主义核心价值观有机地融入大学英语教学中。因此,要充分挖掘大学英语课程丰富的人文内涵,实现工具性和人文性的有机统一。

本教材以培养具有"家国情怀,国际视野"的高素质人才为己任,在借鉴国内外优秀教材的基础上:一方面选取具有代表性的英语国家的主流文化现象进行描述、阐释和讨论;另一方面有机地融入了中国传统文化,帮助学生掌握必要的跨文化交际知识,培养学生对目的语文化的兴趣和理解力,同时引导学生对中西方文化进行主动观察、分析比较,从而拓宽国际视野,增强跨文化交际意识,提高跨文化交际能力。

本教材由9章构成,围绕什么是文化、文化的特征、语言与文化的关系、跨文化交际的历史发展、跨文化交际的障碍以及如何培养跨文化交际能力等内容展开。

每章均有导读,设定教学目标,根据主题配有预热练习,并以图片、话题讨论等形式来设置练习。按照慕课讲授形式分为课前、课中、课后三个环节展开:一种是基于学生掌握的基本理论;另一种是讨论式的,学生通过头脑风暴、小组讨论、小组展示等方式来完成。为便于学生掌握章节内容,我们在每一节后面都列出了重点词汇,并对课文中提到的重要人物及代表作予以介绍。案例分析之后配有阅读材料，帮助学生在中西方文化对比中培养思辨能力。

课后练习是对课上所学内容的巩固和提高。我们设计了单选题、填空题、判断对错题、阅读题和翻译题，旨在进一步夯实学生的语言基础，同时帮助学生在实践中学会运用单元所学的重点知识。本教材是跨文化交际教学团队集体研究成果，由各位参与者共同完成。具体分工如下：迟红负责全书的设计、统稿，并撰写了前言和第1~3章；姜君负责第4章；封婧超负责第5章；彭慧负责第6章；韩杨负责第7章；石文静负责第8章；苗苗负责第9章。

本教材为北京联合大学2020年资助出版的教材。此外，本教材还配有附录、课后练习的答案，供教师和学生参考使用。

目 录

Chapter 1　Intercultural Communication ······· 001
　1.1　Introduction of Intercultural Communication ······· 003
　1.2　History of Intercultural Communication ······· 005
　　　1.2.1　Intercultural Communication in America ······· 005
　　　1.2.2　Intercultural Communication in China ······· 006
　1.3　Classifications of Intercultural Communication ······· 007
　　　1.3.1　International Communication ······· 008
　　　1.3.2　Interethnic Communication & Interracial Communication ··· 008
　　　1.3.3　Inter-ethnic Communication ······· 008
　　　1.3.4　Inter-regional Communication ······· 009
　　　1.3.5　Intracultural Communication ······· 009
　Further Reading ······· 017
　Exercises ······· 025

Chapter 2　Communication ······· 028
　2.1　Definitions of Communication ······· 029
　　　The Function of Communication ······· 032
　2.2　Components of Communication ······· 034
　2.3　The Models of Communication ······· 037
　　　2.3.1　Linear Model ······· 037
　　　2.3.2　Circular Model ······· 038
　　　2.3.3　Contextualized Model ······· 038
　2.4　Communication Skills ······· 039
　　　2.4.1　Speaking Skills ······· 040
　　　2.4.2　Writing Skills ······· 040

i

2.4.3 Reading Skills ……………………………………… 040
    2.4.4 Listening Skills ……………………………………… 041
2.5 Characteristics of Communication ……………………………………… 042
    2.5.1 Communication Is Symbolic ……………………………………… 042
    2.5.2 Communication Is Dynamic ……………………………………… 043
    2.5.3 Communication Is Interpretive ……………………………………… 044
    2.5.4 Communication Is Contextual ……………………………………… 044
    2.5.5 Communication Is Irreversible（不可逆的）……………………………………… 046
    2.5.6 Communication Is Shared ……………………………………… 047
Further Reading ……………………………………… 056
Exercises ……………………………………… 061

Chapter 3 Culture and Language ……………………………………… 064

3.1 Definitions and Classification ……………………………………… 065
3.2 The Nature of Culture ……………………………………… 067
    3.2.1 Culture Is like an Iceberg（冰川）……………………………………… 067
    3.2.2 Culture Is Like an Onion ……………………………………… 068
    3.2.3 Culture is Our Software ……………………………………… 069
    3.2.4 Culture Is like the Water a Fish Swims In ……………………………………… 069
    3.2.5 Culture Is the Grammar of Our Behavior ……………………………………… 069
3.3 Characteristics of Culture ……………………………………… 070
    3.3.1 Culture Is Learned ……………………………………… 071
    3.3.2 Culture Is Dynamic ……………………………………… 076
    3.3.3 Culture Is Based on Symbols ……………………………………… 076
    3.3.4 Culture Is Integrated ……………………………………… 077
    3.3.5 Culture Is Adaptive ……………………………………… 077
3.4 Classification of Culture ……………………………………… 078
3.5 Language ……………………………………… 080
    3.5.1 The Relationship Between Language and Culture ……………………………………… 081
    3.5.2 The Relationship Between Language and Communication ……………………………………… 081
    3.5.3 The Relationship Between Culture and Communication ……………………………………… 082
Further Reading ……………………………………… 090

Exercises 095

Chapter 4 Cultural Patterns 098
 4.1 Introduction 099
 4.2 Definition of Cultural Patterns 100
 4.3 Components of Cultural Patterns 102
  4.3.1 Beliefs 102
  4.3.2 Values 102
  4.3.3 Norms 103
  4.3.4 Social Practices 104
 4.4 Edward T. Hall's Context-Culture Theory 105
  4.4.1 High Context 106
  4.4.2 Low Context 106
 4.5 Kluckhohn and Strodtbeck's Value Orientation 108
  4.5.1 Human-Nature Orientation 110
  4.5.2 Man-Nature Orientation 111
  4.5.3 Time Orientation 112
  4.5.4 Activity Orientation 112
  4.5.5 Relational Orientation 113
 4.6 Hofstede's Dimensions of Cultural Variability 114
  4.6.1 Individualism and Collectivism 114
  4.6.2 Power Distance 116
  4.6.3 Masculinity versus Femininity 117
  4.6.4 Long-Term Orientation versus Short-Term Orientation 117
  4.6.5 Indulgence versus Restraint 118
 Further Reading 124
 Exercises 129

Chapter 5 Verbal Communication 132
 5.1 Significance of Verbal Communication 133
 5.2 Language and Thought 135
 5.3 Language and Culture 137

    5.3.1 Language as a Reflection of the Environment ⋯⋯⋯⋯⋯ 137
    5.3.2 Language as a Reflection of Values ⋯⋯⋯⋯⋯⋯⋯⋯⋯ 138
  5.4 Language and Identity ⋯⋯⋯⋯⋯⋯⋯⋯⋯⋯⋯⋯⋯⋯⋯⋯⋯⋯ 139
    5.4.1 Social identity ⋯⋯⋯⋯⋯⋯⋯⋯⋯⋯⋯⋯⋯⋯⋯⋯⋯⋯ 140
    5.4.2 National identity ⋯⋯⋯⋯⋯⋯⋯⋯⋯⋯⋯⋯⋯⋯⋯⋯⋯ 140
    5.4.3 Ethnic identity ⋯⋯⋯⋯⋯⋯⋯⋯⋯⋯⋯⋯⋯⋯⋯⋯⋯⋯ 141
  5.5 Verbal Communication Styles ⋯⋯⋯⋯⋯⋯⋯⋯⋯⋯⋯⋯⋯⋯⋯ 142
    5.5.1 Direct vs. Indirect Communication Styles ⋯⋯⋯⋯⋯⋯ 142
    5.5.2 Self-enhancement and Self-effacement ⋯⋯⋯⋯⋯⋯⋯⋯ 144
    5.5.3 Elaborate, Exacting and Succinct styles ⋯⋯⋯⋯⋯⋯⋯ 144
    5.5.4 Personal and Contextual Styles ⋯⋯⋯⋯⋯⋯⋯⋯⋯⋯⋯ 145
    5.5.5 Instrumental Styles and Affective Styles ⋯⋯⋯⋯⋯⋯⋯ 145
  5.6 Language Diversity ⋯⋯⋯⋯⋯⋯⋯⋯⋯⋯⋯⋯⋯⋯⋯⋯⋯⋯⋯ 146
    5.6.1 Dialects and Sociolects ⋯⋯⋯⋯⋯⋯⋯⋯⋯⋯⋯⋯⋯⋯⋯ 146
    5.6.2 Taboo and Euphemism ⋯⋯⋯⋯⋯⋯⋯⋯⋯⋯⋯⋯⋯⋯⋯ 148
    5.6.3 Pidgin and Lingua Franca ⋯⋯⋯⋯⋯⋯⋯⋯⋯⋯⋯⋯⋯ 152
    5.6.4 Idioms ⋯⋯⋯⋯⋯⋯⋯⋯⋯⋯⋯⋯⋯⋯⋯⋯⋯⋯⋯⋯⋯⋯ 154
  Further Reading ⋯⋯⋯⋯⋯⋯⋯⋯⋯⋯⋯⋯⋯⋯⋯⋯⋯⋯⋯⋯⋯⋯⋯⋯ 161
  Exercises ⋯⋯⋯⋯⋯⋯⋯⋯⋯⋯⋯⋯⋯⋯⋯⋯⋯⋯⋯⋯⋯⋯⋯⋯⋯⋯⋯ 164

Chapter 6 Nonverbal Communication ⋯⋯⋯⋯⋯⋯⋯⋯⋯⋯⋯⋯⋯ 166

  6.1 Definition of Nonverbal Communication ⋯⋯⋯⋯⋯⋯⋯⋯⋯ 167
  6.2 Significance of Nonverbal Communication ⋯⋯⋯⋯⋯⋯⋯⋯ 168
  6.3 Functions of Nonverbal Communication ⋯⋯⋯⋯⋯⋯⋯⋯⋯⋯ 169
    6.3.1 Repeating ⋯⋯⋯⋯⋯⋯⋯⋯⋯⋯⋯⋯⋯⋯⋯⋯⋯⋯⋯⋯ 169
    6.3.2 Complementing ⋯⋯⋯⋯⋯⋯⋯⋯⋯⋯⋯⋯⋯⋯⋯⋯⋯⋯ 170
    6.3.3 Substituting ⋯⋯⋯⋯⋯⋯⋯⋯⋯⋯⋯⋯⋯⋯⋯⋯⋯⋯⋯ 170
    6.3.4 Regulating ⋯⋯⋯⋯⋯⋯⋯⋯⋯⋯⋯⋯⋯⋯⋯⋯⋯⋯⋯⋯ 171
    6.3.5 Contradicting ⋯⋯⋯⋯⋯⋯⋯⋯⋯⋯⋯⋯⋯⋯⋯⋯⋯⋯⋯ 171
  6.4 Categories of Nonverbal Communication ⋯⋯⋯⋯⋯⋯⋯⋯⋯⋯ 171
    6.4.1 Paralanguage ⋯⋯⋯⋯⋯⋯⋯⋯⋯⋯⋯⋯⋯⋯⋯⋯⋯⋯⋯ 172
    6.4.2 Body Language ⋯⋯⋯⋯⋯⋯⋯⋯⋯⋯⋯⋯⋯⋯⋯⋯⋯⋯ 174

6.4.3	Time	180
6.4.4	Space	180
6.4.5	Chromatics	182
6.4.6	Attire	183

Further Reading ………………………………………………… 188
Exercises ………………………………………………………… 193

Chapter 7 Intercultural Communication Barriers …………… 196

- 7.1 Emotional Problems ………………………………………… 197
  - 7.1.1 Anxiety and Uncertainty ………………………… 197
  - 7.1.2 Assuming Similarity ……………………………… 199
- 7.2 Attitudinal Problems ………………………………………… 200
  - 7.2.1 Ethnocentrism …………………………………… 200
  - 7.2.2 Stereotyping ……………………………………… 202
- 7.3 Translation Problems ……………………………………… 211
  - 7.3.1 Lack of Vocabulary Equivalence ……………… 213
  - 7.3.2 Lack of Idiomatic Equivalence ………………… 214
  - 7.3.3 Lack of Grammatical-Syntactical Equivalence … 215
  - 7.3.4 Lack of Experiential Equivalence ……………… 216
  - 7.3.5 Lack of Conceptual Equivalence ……………… 217

Further Reading ………………………………………………… 228
Exercises ………………………………………………………… 235

Chapter 8 Intercultural Adaptation ……………………………… 239

- 8.1 Introduction ………………………………………………… 240
- 8.2 Acculturation ……………………………………………… 240
  - 8.2.1 Assimilation ……………………………………… 241
  - 8.2.2 Integration ……………………………………… 241
  - 8.2.3 Separation ……………………………………… 242
  - 8.2.4 Marginalization ………………………………… 242
- 8.3 Culture Shock ……………………………………………… 243
  - Factors of Culture Shock ………………………………… 244

8.4 Intercultural Adaptation ⋯ 247
   8.4.1 Honeymoon Period ⋯ 248
   8.4.2 Crisis Period ⋯ 248
   8.4.3 Adjustment Period ⋯ 248
   8.4.4 Biculturalism Period ⋯ 249
8.5 Strategies of Intercultural Adaptation ⋯ 249
Further Reading ⋯ 256
Exercises ⋯ 261

Chapter 9 Intercultural Communication Competence ⋯ 264

9.1 Imperative for Intercultural Communication Competence ⋯ 265
   9.1.1 Economic Concern ⋯ 265
   9.1.2 Demographic Concern ⋯ 266
   9.1.3 Social Justice Concern ⋯ 267
   9.1.4 Cultural Transmission Concern ⋯ 267
9.2 Communication Competence vs. Intercultural Communication Competence ⋯ 267
   9.2.1 Communication Competence ⋯ 267
   9.2.2 Intercultural Communication Competence ⋯ 269
9.3 Byram's Model of ICC ⋯ 271
   9.3.1 Attitudes ⋯ 272
   9.3.2 Knowledge ⋯ 273
   9.3.3 Skills of Interpreting and Relating ⋯ 273
   9.3.4 Skills of Discovery and Interaction ⋯ 274
   9.3.5 Critical Cultural Awareness ⋯ 275
9.4 Components of Intercultural Communication Competence ⋯ 276
   9.4.1 Individual Components ⋯ 276
   9.4.2 Contextual Components ⋯ 280
9.5 How to Achieve Intercultural Communication Competence ⋯ 281
   9.5.1 Desire to Learn and Adjust ⋯ 282
   9.5.2 Decentering ⋯ 282

  9.5.3 Cognitive Complexity ……………………………………… 283
  9.5.4 High Self-esteem and Confidence …………………………… 283
  9.5.5 Innovativeness ………………………………………………… 283
  9.5.6 Respect for People …………………………………………… 284
9.6 Intercultural Communication Toward a Community with
  a Shared Future for Mankind ………………………………………… 285
  9.6.1 The Connotation of the Thought of "a Community with
     a Shared Future for Mankind" ……………………………… 285
  9.6.2 Political Concern ……………………………………………… 286
  9.6.3 Secure Concern ………………………………………………… 286
  9.6.4 Economic Concern …………………………………………… 287
  9.6.5 Cultural Concern ……………………………………………… 287
  9.6.6 Ecological Concern …………………………………………… 288
Further Reading ……………………………………………………………… 297
Exercises ……………………………………………………………………… 302

Key to Exercises …………………………………………………………… 305

References ………………………………………………………………… 313

Chapter 1

Intercultural Communication

> Whenever people interact, they communicate. To live in societies and to maintain their culture they have to communicate.
>
> ——Smith
>
> 只要人们有接触就有交际的存在。只要人们生活在一定的社会群体中并保持其社会文化发展，他们就需要交际。
>
> ——史密斯

本章导读

我们所生活的时代，技术、旅游、经济与政治的逐步发展、人口迁移更加频繁，人口密度的增大都迫使我们越来越多地与具有不同文化背景的人交往。随着全球化进程的加快，跨文化交往将会越来越频繁。正如休斯顿·史密斯所说："当历史学家回首我们这个世纪，最激动人心的事不是太空旅行或核能的应用，而是整个世界上的人们可以真诚相待，互相理解。"而文化又包罗万象，无处不在，它潜移默化地支配着人们的行为表现，并深刻地影响着人们的处世态度。本章从刘洋的案例引入，帮助学习者理解跨文化交际的概念，了解中西方文化的差异，认识到跨文化交际的重要性，从而帮助学习者全面理解跨文化交际的形式。

Learning Objectives

In this chapter, students will learn how to: define intercultural communication, evaluate the history of intercultural communication, understand the classification of intercultural communication, and describe the importance of intercultural communication.

Liu Yang and Her Book

Liu Yang was born in 1976 in Beijing. After studying at the Berlin University of the Arts (UdK), she worked as a designer in Singapore, London, Berlin and New York. In 2004 she founded her own design studio, which she continues to run today. In 2010 she was appointed as a professor at the BTK University of Applied Sciences in Berlin. Her works have won numerous prizes in international competitions and can be found in museums and collections all over the world. *East Meets West*, a series of **infographics** (信息图表) drawing on her personal bicultural experience has been exhibited worldwide, and the corresponding book has become an instant bestseller.

Liu Yang lives and works in Berlin. On November 4, 2016, this Berlin-based artist and designer Liu Yang gave a presentation of her award-winning cultural pictograms at New York University Shanghai. Drawn from her experiences of growing up in China and Germany, Liu's *East Meets West*—an infographic portrait—**juxtaposes** (把……并列) eye-catching infographics that were cleverly **distilled** (提取) from her observations of the two cultures.

"I had a wonderful childhood growing up in Beijing," Liu said, "but at age 13—that impressionable age for building one's personality—my parents convinced me to move to Germany. I came to make these images as a result of that move, constantly comparing every aspect of life between the two countries."

With Western customs depicted on a blue background and Eastern ones on red, the series **succinctly** (简洁地) captures different perceptions and attitudes through a single image: In Liu's vision, the complexities of self-expression, problem-solving, and memory-making become a path between two points, a set of footprints confronting an obstacle, and a single eye versus a camera.

The infographics started as a set of posters but quickly became a **viral** (病毒) hit on social media leading her to publish the series as a book, *East Meets West*. Liu's other work explores perceived differences between men and women, and observations of the modern age—contrasting the old 9 to 5 working day to **round-the-clock** (全天候的) email checking.

"When I first saw Liu Yang's series of infographics on the differences between Eastern and Western culture, I reacted similarly to how millions of others around the world did: I shared it. The simple graphics reveal an **ineffable** (妙不可言的) understanding and witty and take on the cultural differences of people on opposite sides of the globe. I am glad to be able to share it again, this time with the creator in person and to the NYU Shanghai community," said host and moderator assistant arts professor Antonius Wiriadjaja. Liu's work has been shown in solo and group exhibitions around the world including Germany, US, Japan, France and Poland.

(选自 http://shanghai.nyu.edu/news/east-meets-west-artists-captures-cultural-differences.)

Questions for Discussion

1. Why did her parents convince Liu Yang to move to Germany?

2. What's the difference between Eastern culture and Western culture in Liu's eyes?

3. What's the influence of Liu Yang's book: *East Meets West*?

1.1 Introduction of Intercultural Communication

Warm-up Activities

(1) What are the major differences between Chinese culture and Western culture?

(2) Use some examples to explain intercultural communication.

Intercultural communication, as you might suspect, is not new. Since the dawn of civilization, when the first humans formed tribal groups, intercultural contact occurred whenever people from one tribe encountered members of another tribe and discovered that they were different. Sometimes, these differences, in the absence of multicultural awareness and tolerance, **elicited** (引出, 探出) the human prosperity to respond **malevolently** (恶意地; 伤害地). However, in the pursuit of political alliances, knowledge, or commercial trade, these differences were more often recognized and accommodated.

Spices, silk, tea and coffee made their way to Europe from China, Southeast Asia, and the Middle East via the Silk Road trade routes. Guns, modern medicine, and even bread were brought to the Far East by traders sailing from Western Europe on the voyages of discovery.

Intercultural communication occurs when a member of one culture produces a message for consumption by a member of another culture. To put it simply, intercultural communication means the communication between people from different cultural backgrounds. Intercultural communication is not something new, but something that has always taken place, sometimes without us knowing it. Wandering **nomads** (流浪者; 游牧生活), religious missionaries, and conquering warriors have encountered people different from themselves since the beginning of time.

The term cross-cultural is typically used to refer to the study of a particular idea or concept within many cultures. The goal of such investigation is to conduct a series of intracultural analyses in order to compare one culture to another on the attributes of interest. For example, someone interested in studying the marriage rituals in many cultures would be considered as a cross-cultural researcher. Scholars who study self-disclosure patterns, child-rearing practices, or educational methods as they exist in many different cultures are doing cross-cultural comparisons. Whereas intercultural communication involves interactions among people from different cultures, cross-cultural communication involves a comparison of interactions among people from the same culture to those from another culture.

Intercultural communication focuses on what is happening when people from different culture have contact with each other. Cross-cultural communication emphasizes the differences of different cultural communities or groups. Since many scholars do not distinguish between these two terms, we prefer to use intercultural communication in this book. Intercultural communication may be understood as a practice, called "跨文化交际" in Chinese , which focuses on the pragmatics or language teaching. It can also be regarded as a discipline called "跨文化交际学" which implies it is a multidisciplinary course. Finally it can also be generally called "跨文化交际" without, any distinction. As a phenomenon, intercultural communication is really universal, and it takes place everywhere. In your academic life, when you talk with a foreign lecturer; in business environment, when you correspond with a Western customer through e-mail; in your everyday life, when you watch a French film or read an American novel, you're experiencing intercultural communication.

Edward T. Hall simply defines intercultural communication as communication between persons of different cultures. **Hu Wenzhong,** a well-known professor of intercultural communication in China, defines intercultural communication as communication between people of different cultural backgrounds. Intercultural communication is the exchange of information between individuals who are unalike culturally.

In a broad sense, intercultural communication occurs when a member of one culture produces a message to be understood by a member of another culture. In a narrow sense, it is communication between people whose cultural perception and symbol system are distinct enough to alter the communication event. As a discipline, intercultural communication should focus on the mainstream of a nation or a country; intercultural communication in this course will mainly deal with the communication between people from different national cultures.

Intercultural communication is a form of global communication. It is used to describe wide range of communication problems that naturally appear within an organization made up of individuals from different religious, social, ethnic, and educational backgrounds. Intercultural communication is sometimes used **synonymously** (同义) with cross-cultural communication. In this sense, it seeks to understand how people from different countries and cultures act, communicate and perceive the world around them. Many people in intercultural business communication argue that culture determines how individuals encode messages, what mediums they choose for transmitting them, and the way messages are interpreted. As a separate notion, it studies situations where people from different cultural backgrounds interact. Aside from language, intercultural communication focuses on social attributes, thought patterns, and the cultures of different groups of people.

It also involves understanding the different cultures, languages, and customs of people from other countries. Intercultural communication plays a role in social sciences such as anthropology, cultural studies, linguistics, psychology, and communication studies. Intercultural communication is also referred to as the base for international businesses.

1.2 History of Intercultural Communication

1.2.1 Intercultural Communication in America

As a newly developed discipline, intercultural communication started in America in the 1960s. This term was first coined by Edward T. Hall in 1959. In its most general sense, intercultural communication occurs when a member of one culture produces a message for consumption by a member of another culture. More precisely, intercultural communication is a communication between people whose cultural perceptions and symbol systems are distinct enough to alter the communication event.

Intercultural communication looks at how people from different cultural backgrounds try to communicate. Intercultural communication tries to bring together such relatively unrelated areas as cultural anthropology and established areas of communication. Its core is to establish and understand how people from different cultures communicate with each other. Its change is also to produce some guidelines under which people from different cultures can better communicate with each other. For example, how does a person from China communicate with a person from Turkey? Furthermore, what underlying mental constructs appear from both parties that allow for constructive communication?

1.2.2 Intercultural Communication in China

As we mentioned, intercultural communication is not a brand-new thing. We have many famous cases of intercultural communication in Chinese ancient times. Can you think of some in history? The Silk Road, Zhang Qian, Jian Zhen, Xuan Zang, Zheng He, Marco Polo, etc. These are all cases of communication between people from different cultures. Take "Silk Road" in Chinese history for example: people in Asia, Africa, and Europe interacted with each other through the "Road". The Silk Road was an ancient network of trade routes, formally established during the Han Dynasty of China, which linked the regions of the ancient world in commerce.

The history of intercultural communication in China is comparatively shorter. Many foreign language teachers, linguists, psychologists and people engaged in management are interested in this field, and their study focuses on the following aspects: the relationship between language and culture; nonverbal communication; comparison between Chinese and Western customs and traditions; comparison between business management in China and Western countries and so on. So why do we need to study intercultural communication? It is often thought that people can communicate effectively if they have mastered the basic communication skills in a foreign language. However, it is not the case. Quite often, one polite behavior in a culture may be impolite or even rude in another one.

《礼记·曲礼上》中说:"入境而问禁,入国而问俗,入门而问讳。"苏轼在《密州谢上表》中说:"入境问俗,又复过于所期。"The main idea of the two quotations is that when you enter into a new culture, you'd better get to know their customs and taboos in case you may offend people, which may hinder the communication. Therefore, it is of vital importance to know "how to say" than "what to say" in intercultural communication. Hopefully the study of this course will help us take a positive and understandable attitude towards other cultures, understand Chinese culture better from new perspectives, and make effective intercultural communication in a global environment.

In order to be successful in intercultural communication, people should learn about both cultural similarities and cultural differences. To some degree, it is more important to learn about cultural differences, for understanding cultural differences will help people know where communication barriers lie and how to solve the problems. In general, there are two ways to learn about the target culture: intellectual approach and experiential approach. There is no doubt that for foreign language learners, the best way to learn about foreign culture is to experience it. Only through experiencing foreign culture can we really understand the target culture and find out how native speakers use their languages. Unfortunately, many of us may not have the chance to go abroad, but we can still read foreign novels or watch foreign movies. The process of understanding it is in effect a complicated intercultural communication.

1.3 Classifications of Intercultural Communication

Warm-up Activities
Identify what kind of communication it is.
(1) Chinese president communicates with American president.
(2) A Tibetan communicates with a Han.
(3) An Afro-American interacts with a white American.
(4) A northerner interacts with a southerner.

In general sense: intercultural communication occurs when a member of one culture produces a message to be understood by a member of another culture. In precise sense: intercultural communication is a communication between people whose cultural **perception** (感知) and symbol system are distinct enough to alter the communication event. Usually there are five forms of intercultural communication: international communication, interracial communication, inter-ethnic communication, inter-regional communication and intracultural communication.

1.3.1 International Communication

International communication occurs between nations and countries rather than individuals; so it is quite formal and **ritualized** (仪式化的). The dialogue at the United Nations, for example, would be termed as an international communication. Scholars who compare and analyze nations' media usage also use this term. Certainly, communication among people from different countries is likely to be intercultural communication, but that is not always true.

1.3.2 Interethnic Communication & Interracial Communication

Interracial communication is a communication between people of the same race but different ethnic background. Physical differences frequently do influence communication and it is often in the form of strong prejudices and leads to **stereotyping** (模式化) and **discrimination** (歧视). For example, the communication between African Americans and European Americans is often referred to as **interracial communication**.

1.3.3 Inter-ethnic Communication

Inter-ethnic communication is a communication between different ethnic groups. Ethnic groups usually form their own communities in a country or culture. These groups share a common origin or heritage that **is apt to** (倾向于) influence family names, language, religion, values, and the like. As you know, there are 56 ethnic groups which compose our big Chinese ethics.

Just as race and ethnic group are terms commonly used to refer to cultures, interethnic and interracial communication are two labels commonly used as substitutes for intercultural communication event. Usually, these terms are used to explain the differences in communication between members of racial and ethnic groups who are all members of the same nation-state.

A large number of people of Latino origin who work and live with people of European ancestry produce communication characterized as interethnic. Sometimes the terms are also used to refer to communication between people from various ethnic or racial groups who are not part of the same nation but live in specific geographic areas. Although it may be useful in some circumstances to use the terms **interethnic and interracial,** we believe these types of communication are most usefully categorized as subsets of intercultural communication. Both ethnicity and race contribute to the perceived effects of cultural differences on communication, which moves that communication toward the most intercultural ‖ end of the continuum.

1. 3. 4 Inter-regional Communication

Inter-regional communication refers to the exchange of messages between members of the dominant culture within a country. They share common messages and experiences over a long period of time, but live in different regions of the same country. For example, a northern in China interacts with a southerner. People living in eastern areas communicate with people from western regions.

1. 3. 5 Intracultural Communication

Intracultural communication is defined as a communication between or among members of the same culture. In intracultural communication, speakers rely on their prior knowledge rooted in cultural models, core common ground, shared knowledge, and common beliefs of a relatively definable speech community. This knowledge is privatized and adjusted to actual situations by individuals belonging to that speech community.

The term intercultural used to describe one end point of the continuum, denotes the presence of at least two individuals who are culturally different from each other on such important attributes as their value orientations, preferred communication codes, role expectations, and perceived rules of social relationships. We now would like to relabel the least intercultural end of the continuum, which is used to refer to communication between culturally similar individuals as intracultural. Both intercultural and intracultural are comparative terms. That is, each refers to differences in the magnitude and importance of expectations that people have about what constitutes competent communication behaviors.

Key Terms

intercultural communication	跨文化交际
international communication	跨国交际
interethnic communication	跨民族交际
interracial communication	跨种族交际
interregional communication	跨地区交际
intracultural communication	同文化交际

Notes

1. **Edward T. Hall,** an author usually mentioned as the first to write explicitly about intercultural communication. His book, *The Silent Language*, published in 1959 and generally listed as the first work in the field, has been influential in setting the agenda for the field of intercultural communication. He expounded the relationship between culture and language as well as nonverbal communication. In the 1960s, communication scholars mainly focused on the conceptualization of the field. From then on, intercultural communication has been developing more and more rapidly with a lot of books and periodicals published.

   爱德华·T.霍尔是第一位明确阐述跨文化交际的作者。他的著作《无声语言》出版于1959年，被公认为是该领域的第一部著作，在跨文化交际领域的议程制定方面具有重要影响。他阐述了文化与语言及非语言交际的关系。20世纪60年代，传播学界的研究主要集中在传播领域的概念化上。此后，跨文化交际得到了迅猛发展，出版了大量的书籍与刊物。

2. **Fred E. Jandt,** *An Introduction to Intercultural Communication* was written by Fred E. Jandt. Fred E. Jandt was born of second-generation German immigrants and lived in the multicultural south-central region of Texas. After graduation, he received his doctoral degree in communication from Bowling Green State University. He has taught intercultural communication for more than 40 years, developing his experience through travel and international training and research projects. Meanwhile, intercultural communication has become a compulsory or

optional course in many of the universities and colleges in the states.

《跨文化交际导论》是由弗雷德·E. 詹特写的。弗雷德·E. 詹特出生于德克萨斯州中南部多元文化地区，他是第二代德国移民。毕业后，他获得博林格林州立大学传播学博士学位。他从事跨文化交际的教学和研究已有40多年，通过旅游和国际培训及研究项目积累了丰富的经验。与此同时，跨文化交际已经成为美国许多大学的必修课或选修课。

3. **Hu Wenzhong,** the president of China Association for Intercultural Communication. His works include *Teaching and Learning of English*, *A collection of Australian Short Stories*, *Foreign Language Teaching and Culture*, and *Encountering the Chinese*.

   胡文仲，曾任中国跨文化交际协会会长。他的著作包括《英语的教与学》《澳大利亚短篇小说集》《外语教学与文化》《与中国人交际》等。

4. **Everett M. Rogers,** a professor and head of the Department of Communication and Journalism at the University of New Mexico. He lived in Albuquerque, New Mexico. His works include *Silicon Valley Fever*, *Diffusion of Innovation*, *History of Communication*, *History of Communication Research*, *Communication Skills* and so on.

   埃弗雷特·M. 罗杰斯，新墨西哥大学传播学与新闻学系教授，系主任，居住在新墨西哥州阿尔伯克基。著有《硅谷热》《创新的扩散》《传播学史》《传播研究史》《传播技巧》等。

5. **Thomas M. Steinfatt,** a professor of speech communication at Auburn University, Auburn, Alabama.

   托马斯·M. 斯坦法特，美国阿拉巴马州奥本市奥本大学的言语交际学教授。

6. *The Book of Rites (Liji),* a collection of descriptions of ritual matters written during the late Warring States and Western Han periods. It is one of the Five Classics (*The Book of Songs, The Book of History, The Book of Rites, The Book of Changes and The Spring and Autumn Annals*) and one of the Three Rituals (*Rites of the Zhou, The Book of Etiquette and Ceremonial, and The Book of Rites*).

   《礼记》是战国晚期和西汉时期所写的关于礼事的描述。它是儒家"五经"（《诗经》《尚书》《礼记》《周易》和《春秋》）之一和"三礼"（《周礼》《仪礼》和《礼记》）之一。

Case 1

The International Language of Gestures
Paul Ekman, Wallace V. Friesen, and John Bear

On his first trip to Naples, a well-meaning American tourist thanks his waiter for a good meal well-served by making the "okay" gesture with his thumb and forefinger. The waiter pales and heads for the manager. They seriously discuss calling the police and having the hapless tourist arrested for obscene and offensive public behavior.

What happened? Most travelers wouldn't think of leaving home without a phrase book of some kind, enough of a guide to help them say and understand "Ja", "Nein", "Gmzie" and "Uù se trouvent les toilettes?" And yet, while most people are aware that gestures are the most common form of cross-cultural communication, they don't realize that the language of gestures can be just as different, just as regional and just as likely to cause misunderstanding as the spoken word.

Consider our puzzled tourist. The thumb-and-forefinger-in-a-circle gesture, a friendly one in America, has an insulting meaning in France and Belgium: "You're worth zero," while in Greece and Turkey it is an insulting or vulgar sexual invitation.

There are, in fact, dozens of gestures that take on totally different meanings as you move from one country or region to another. Is "thumbs up" always a positive gesture? Absolutely not. Does nodding the head up and down always mean "Yes"? No!

To make matters even more confusing, many hand movements have no meaning at all, in any country.

（选自杨利民，徐克荣. 现代大学英语精读 3（第 2 版）. 北京：外语教学与研究出版社，2016.）

Questions for Discussion

1. Why did the waiter want to call the police?
2. What is the most common form of cross-cultural communication?

3. Is "thumbs up" always a positive gesture?

4. Does nodding the head up and down always mean "Yes"?

5. What does the gesture "a thumb-and-a forefinger-in-a-circle" mean in different countries?

Case 2

Taboos of Chinese New Year

The events that occurred during New Year's Day may impact your life for the rest of the year. Be careful in your actions. Certain **precautions** (预防) are taken to ensure that the New Year will be a good one.

The entire house should be cleaned before New Year's Day. On New Year's Eve, all brooms, brushes, dusters, **dustpans** (簸箕) and other cleaning equipment are put away. Sweeping or dusting should not be done on New Year's Day for fear that good fortune will be swept away. After New Year's Day, the floors may be swept. At no time should the rubbish in the corners be trampled upon. In sweeping, there is a **superstition** (迷信) that if you sweep the dust and dirt out of your house by the front entrance, you sweep away the good fortune of the family; it must always be swept inwards and then carried out, then no harm will follow. All dirt and rubbish must be taken out the back door.

Shooting off firecrackers on New Year's Eve is the Chinese way of sending out the old year and welcoming in the new. On the stroke of midnight on New Year's Eve, every door in the house, or even windows, has to be open to allow the old year to go out. Nothing should be lent on New Year's Day, as anyone who does so will be lending all the year. All debts have to be paid by New Year's Eve.

Everyone should refrain from using **foul** (污秽) language and bad or unlucky words. Negative terms and the word "four", or "si" in Chinese which sounds like the word for death are not to be uttered. Death and dying are never mentioned and ghost stories are totally taboo.

Hair must be cleaned and set **prior** (先前的) to the holiday, for doing so during the New Year season would invite financial ruin. On New Year's Day, hair should not be washed because it would mean washing away good luck for the New Year. Care must be taken not to break any dishes or other things on the first day of the year.

The use of knives and **scissors** (剪子) as well as any sharp instrument is to be avoided, for these things could **augur** (预兆) bad luck in the coming year. Wear brand-new clothes—preferably in red. Children should wear new clothes and new shoes. Red is considered a bright, happy color, sure to bring the wearer a sunny and bright future. It is believed that appearance and attitude during New Year's Day set the tone for the rest of the year.

(选自 http://m.kekenet.com/read/201001/95451.shtml/.)

Questions for Discussion

1. Why do Chinese people like to give a thorough clean before New Year's Day?
2. Why can't you sweep the dust and dirt out of your house by the front entrance?
3. What kind of terms or words can't you say during New Year's Day?
4. Why can't you wash your hair on New Year's Day?
5. What does red symbolize on New Year's Day?

Case 3

A: Matthew, do you know much about body language in countries around the world?

B: Sure, I've picked up a few things from travelling around for work. Why?

A: Well, I had a meeting today with a woman from Japan and she wouldn't stop bowing! I didn't know what to do!

B: Did you bow back?

A: No, I tried to shake her hand, but her hand was so limp I was a bit offended.

B: Well, Japanese businessmen and women typically bow to greet each other in Japan. She might have been offended by your strong handshake.

A: But she was in America! Shouldn't she have known that strong handshakes in America signify confidence and respect?

B: Things are different in Japan. You know, in some countries, making eye contact with others is considered rude.

A: Is that why she wouldn't look at me in the meeting?

B: I think it's highly possible, yes.

A: The meeting really didn't go down well at all. I think I need to read up about intercultural communication before I have another meeting with someone from another country.

B: That's a good idea. When you don't know much about other cultures, the simplest thing can offend someone.

A: That's so true. It's great that we see eye to eye on this.

 Questions for Discussion

1. Did Matthew know much about body language in countries around the world?
2. Did Matthew bow back when the Japanese woman wouldn't stop bowing?
3. What did Matthew assume the woman should do?
4. Did the Japanese woman look at Matthew in the meeting?
5. Did Matthew draw a lesson from his meeting with the Japanese woman?

Case 4

A: There is something I can never puzzle out! The other day a Chinese friend who has helped me a lot was celebrating his birthday and I asked him what he would like for a birthday present. Do you know what he said? "No, no, no! Don't give me anything. Don't be polite! " Can you believe it?

B: (Laughs) Actually, I can well believe it. It's a slight misunderstanding because of difference in culture, and also because of faulty language. What he said was a word for word translation from Chinese, but even if he had phrased his idea more idiomatically, you still would have misunderstood him.

A: What did he mean by refusing a present from me then?

B: I don't think he was actually refusing to accept a present from you. It was just his way of being "polite", just as you would say "That's very kind of you." He didn't mean to be rude and certainly he didn't mean to offend you.

A: Well, how do you like that? And what was I supposed to do or say in such a situation?

B: You just insist, and if your friend is an elderly gentleman, you probably have to insist several times, but even then I doubt if he will ever give you a direct answer. By the way, do you always ask people what they would like for presents in the West?

A: As a matter of fact, we don't usually. We might among very intimate friends, and also we sometimes ask children what they would like. Otherwise we just go by the standard items, such as ties or tie-pins for men, pipes or lighters for smokers, household articles for housewives and toys for children. And if we are invited to dinner, we usually take a bottle of table wine with us or some flowers for the hostess.

B: We also have our standard items. Chinese tonics such as ginseng or swallow nest are most suitable gifts for elderly people. Chinese spirits and Chinese tea-leaves can also be regarded as standard items, and now with modern people instant coffee is taking the place of Chinese tea. For birthdays and weddings, cash wrapped in red paper is the standard gift.

A: We don't give cash as presents, but book tokens are sometimes given.

B: Ready cash as a form of gift has its advantages. For the donor, it saves you from racking your brains thinking of something suitable, and especially for the newly-weds, a large sum of money really helps to start a new home.

A: I see what you mean. I've never thought of it that way. There is another thing that puzzled me. The other day another Chinese friend gave me a present. When I unwrapped it and thanked him and praised the gift, he went all red in the face, apparently very disgruntled.

B: (Laughs) That's another point where we differ. We don't usually unwrap or comment on a present in the presence of the donor. Your friend felt very embarrassed—probably because it was only a small gift so no wonder he felt very uncomfortable when you thanked him and praised the gift.

A: Oh dear! I certainly did not mean to offend him. It's our custom to unwrap a present in the donor's presence. A gift, however small, represents the donor's good will, and it is only appropriate that you should show your appreciation.

Questions for Discussion

1. Why did the Westerner puzzle out when he wanted to give a present to his Chinese friend?

2. What caused the misunderstanding here?

3. What was the Westerner supposed to do or say in such a situation?

4. What would the Westerners like to give during birthday celebrations?
5. What would Chinese people like to give during birthday celebrations?

Further Reading

Passage 1

The Silk Road

The Silk Road, which referred to both the **terrestrial** (陆地的) and the maritime routes, was an ancient network of trade routes that connected the East and West. It also acted as the role of cultural interaction between the regions for many centuries. Trade on the Road played a significant role in the development of the civilizations, and opened long-distance political and economic relations between the civilizations.

From the second century BC to the end of the fourteenth century AD, a great trade route originated from Chang'an (now Xi'an) in the east and ended at the Mediterranean in the west, linking China with the Roman Empire. Because silk was the major trade product which travelled on this road, it was named the Silk Road in 1877 by Ferdinand von Richthofen—a well-known German geographer. This ancient route not only circulated good but also exchanged the splendid cultures of China, India, Persia, Arab, Greece and Rome.

This route was opened up by Zhang Qian in the Western Han Dynasty and the routes were gradually formed throughout the Han Dynasty. This trade route spent its childhood and gradually grew up in this dynasty. With the establishment of the Tang Dynasty, which saw rapid development of economy and society, this famous trade route reached its most thriving stage in history. During the **reign** (君主统治时期) of Yuan Dynasty, it experienced its last flourishing period.

In the history of the Silk Road, many renowned people left their footprints on this most historically important trade route, including outstanding diplomats, generals and great monks, such as Zhang Qian, Xuan Zang, and Marco Polo.

Zhang Qian

Zhang Qian was born in Chenggu (the present Chenggu County of Shaanxi Province) of Western Han Dynasty. He was an outstanding envoy and explorer in Chinese history, opening up the ancient Silk Road and bringing reliable information about the Western Regions.

During the reign of the Emperor Wudi of the Han Dynasty (206 BC–AD 220), the Huns (Xiongnu) often intruded into the northern borders of the Han Empire, so the emperor was making preparations to fight against the Huns. When he knew Da Yuezhi (an ancient state in Amu Darya) had a **feud** (有仇) with the Huns, because its king was killed by the Huns' Chanyu (the headman of Hunnish tribes) and the head was made into a goblet, he decided to unite with this state to combat their common enemy. Therefore, Zhang Qian was sent as a diplomatic **envoy** (使节) to the Western Regions.

In 139 BC, with about 100 people, Zhang Qian departed from Longxi (in Gansu Province). Unfortunately, he and the delegation were captured by the Huns when they reached the Hexi Corridor and detained for ten years as **hostage** (人质). Finally, they found a chance to flee. They crossed deserts and the Gobi, and went over the snow-covered **Pamirs** (帕米尔高原). After about ten days, they arrived in Dawan (in Fergana Basin). Under the help of a Dawan's guide, they went through Kangju (between Balkhash Lake and the Aral Sea) and reached Da Yuezhi.

To Zhang's surprise, satisfied with their life, the Da Yuezhi people refused to make an alliance against the Huns. Besides, they thought it was impossible to resist the Huns together because they were far away from the Han Dynasty. Zhang Qian made an on-the-spot investigation in Daxia (Balkh) and other countries for more than one year. In 128 BC, He decided to return to Chang'an (the ancient name of Xi'an). On their return journey, they were captured by the Huns again and **detained** (耽搁) for more than one year. In 126 BC, Zhang seized the opportunity provided by internal disorder among the Huns. He escaped and reached Chang'an. Although he failed to finish the mission to make a military alliance with Da Yuezhi, he obtained a great deal of knowledge about the people, geography, culture and customs of 36 states in the Western Regions.

In 119 BC, Zhang Qian set off on his second journey to the Western Regions, in order to ally with Wusun (in Ili Valley) against the Huns. At that time, the Huns had been expelled from the Hexi Corridor, so Zhang Qian reached Wusun easily.

Then he sent other envoys to Dawan, Kangju, Da Yuezhi, Anxi (Parthia, in now Iran), Juandu (present India), Yutian (Hetian) and other countries. In 115 BC, the king of Wusun put an interpreter and a guide at Zhang's **disposal** (任凭处置). Moreover, Wusun's ten envoys convoyed Zhang to Chang'an. He died there in 114 BC. Then the diplomatic envoys he sent came back in droves. Finally, the Han Dynasty was able to build good relationships with states of the Western Regions.

Xuan Zang

An influential Buddhist monk of the Tang Dynasty (AD 618-907), Xuan Zang not only brought Indian **sutra** (佛经) to China, but also brought Chinese culture to the West and contributed to the spread of other cultures throughout the world.

Xuan Zang's family was very poor and his parents died early, so he became a monk at thirteen years old. In the following years, he studied sutras earnestly, went to many places to call on Buddhist masters, and gradually became accomplished in religious works. However, he found there was much **divergence** (分歧) in Buddhist theories and it was difficult to get one authoritative and credible theory, so he decided to go to India for his further study of Buddhism.

In the early years of the Tang Dynasty, most regions of the Silk Road were under the control of the Turks (a minority in ancient China), so the government prohibited people from going to the Western Regions. Xuan Zang departed **stealthily** (偷偷摸摸地) from Chang'an (the present Xi'an), traveled along the Hexi Corridor and reached Liangzhou (Wuwei in Gansu Province). He escaped the toll-gates at the frontier and arrived in Guazhou (now Anxi in Gansu Province) near the Yumenguan Pass, which was at the western end of the Great Wall. Under the help of a Tartar, he went out of Yumenguan Pass, traversed deserts for a few days, passed through Yiwu (Hami), and reached Gaochang (Turpan). The King of Gaochang respected Xuan Zang very much. He sent Xuan Zang 25 people and 30 horses. Then Xuan Zang continued his westbound journey by crossing the snow-covered Pamir Plateau and passing Qiuci (Kuche), Suiye (in Kirghizia), Tashkent, and Samarkand. After four years of painstaking travel, he finally reached India.

In an ancient temple called the Nalanda Temple, Xuan Zang studied India's sutras for five years under the guidance of the Master Jie Xian. Afterwards, he traveled across India to exchange ideas with other religious leaders and to give sermons. In 645 AD, he returned to Chang'an with more than 600 sutras. The Tang Emperor Taizong (Li Shimin) gave him a right royal welcome. In the rest of his life, he committed himself to translating the sutras he brought back in Big Wild Goose Pagoda.

***Pilgrim** (朝圣者) to the West in the Tang Dynasty*: a book Xuan Zang and Bian Ji compiled. It recorded geography, people, customs, history, religions, languages and cultures of about 140 countries, which provided precious data for studying history and geography. It is another big travelogue after *Records of the Buddhist Kingdoms* written by Fa Xian, a respectable monk in Jin Dynasty (AD 265 – 420). In *Pilgrim to the West in the Tang Dynasty*, besides the descriptions of many Buddhist sites such as Bamiyan's Buddha and Nalanda Temple, dozens of Buddhist legends were also recorded. Due to its comprehensive and vivid content, it was translated into English, German, French and Japanese and widely spread. It is the precious document for the research of China and the world cultural exchange, Buddhism history and national history. In archaeological **excavation** (古迹), experts referred to the clues provided in the book and successfully discovered the sites of many famous temples such as Nalanda Temple, Rajagaha and Sarnath Temple, which fully shows that a great deal of information was accurately placed on record.

Marco Polo

Marco Polo (1254–1324) was an Italian merchant believed to have journeyed across Asia at the height of the Mongol Empire. A well-known traveler and explorer, Marco Polo headed for China along the Silk Road in the Yuan Dynasty (1271–1368). *The Travels of Marco Polo*, dictated by him, described Chinese politics, economy, and culture in detail, which greatly aroused the desire of Westerners to go to China and had a great effect on the European navigation.

Marco Polo was born in a merchant family in Venice in 1254. His father and uncle often traded into the west coast of Mediterranean Sea. On one **fortuitous** (偶然发生的) occasion, they went to China and met with Kublai Khan, an emperor of the Yuan Dynasty. In 1269, they returned to Venice with a letter Kublai Khan had written to Pope Clement IV. In fact, Clement IV had died the year before, and a new pope had not yet been appointed.

Young Marco Polo was very interested in listening to the stories of their travels and made up his mind to go to China. In 1271, when he was 17 years old his dream came true. With a letter in reply from the new Pope Gregory X, and with valuable gifts, the Polos set out eastwards from Venice on their second trip to China. They crossed over the Mediterranean and Black Sea, passed through the land of **Euphrates** (幼发拉底河) and Tigris Rivers, and reached the age-old city of Middle East-Baghdad. They headed south and eastwards to the prosperous seaport of Ormuz at the mouth of the Persian Gulf. From there, they journeyed towards north and then east, successively crossing the desolate Iran Plateau and the snow-covered Pamirs. Overcoming the trials of illness, hunger and thirst, escaping bandits and wild animals, they finally reached Xinjiang. Marco Polo was attracted by beautiful Kashgar and Hetian famed for its jade. Then they traversed Taklimakan Desert, arrived in Dunhuang and visited the Mogao Grottoes, noted for Buddhist sculptures and **frescos** (壁画). They continued on their journey along the Hexi Corridor and reached Shang Du in Inner Mongolia (the summer palace of Kublai Khan) in 1275. Kublai Khan gave them a hospitable reception there and took them to Da Du (now Beijing).

Clever Marco Polo quickly learned Mongolian, Chinese and became familiar with the Chinese customs. Soon he became a confidant of Kublai Khan. He was appointed to high posts in the court and was sent on many special diplomatic missions to many places in China, India and some kingdoms of Southeast Asia, such as Vietnam, Burma and Sumatra. Astonished at the wealth of China, luxurious imperial palace and prosperous cities, he **assiduously** (勤勉地) investigated the customs, geography, people and culture of all places he visited. Then he reported to Kublai Khan in detail.

In 1292, Kublai Khan agreed to let Marco Polo, his father and uncle return home, after they convoyed a Mongolian princess Kokachin to marry a Persian king. In 1295, they finally reached Venice by sea via the Black Sea and **Constantinople** (君士坦丁堡). The information about China and some Asian states they brought back aroused great interest among the Venetians. In 1298, Marco Polo joined in the war between Venice and Genoa. Unfortunately, he was captured and put into a Genoese prison, where he met a writer, Rustichello da Pisa. The writer recorded the story of his travels, well-known as *The Travels of Marco Polo*. The book has detailed descriptions of the wealth of China and Japan filled with gold, and the exotic custom of Central Asia, West Asia, and Southeast Asia soon made it a bestseller. Afterwards, the book became very popular in Europe and paved the way for the arrivals of countless Westerners in the following centuries.

(节选自 http://www. travel china guide. com/silk – rood/history/western – han. htm.)

 Questions for Discussion

1. What does the ancient "Silk Road" refer to?
2. Can you identify any famous travelers on the ancient Silk Road?
3. Who opened up this ancient trade road?

Passage 2

Sino-Indian cultural exchange: From ancient to modern times

China and India have long held important positions in Asia and have a history of cultural exchange. In recent years, the two countries have deepened this aspect of their relations with exchanges in a variety of cultural fields including literature, film and travel.

History of cultural exchange

China and India are both ancient civilizations boasting a long history and rich culture. The earliest reference to India in Chinese historical documents is the "Records of the Historian" during the Han Dynasty (202 BC—8 AD), known as "Shi Ji" in Chinese. According to the record, India was called "Sindhu" or "Tintu" at that time.

According to another book "The First Spring: The Golden Age of India, " Buddhism originated in ancient India and spread through much of Asia. Historically, Buddhism was introduced to China around 57 AD—75 AD, during the Eastern Han Dynasty, and has since been an important religion in China. It all shows that the cultural exchanges and influences between China and India have a long history.

Literature

The cultural tie between China and India is still influencing people in modern times. There are many Indian writers, artists and musicians are influenced by Chinese culture, with **Rabindranath Tagore** (泰戈尔) being one of the most famous ones.

Tagore was born into a well-educated family in Calcutta, India in 1861. He was a poet, philosopher, musician, artist, and the first Asian to win the Nobel Prize in Literature in 1913. He visited China in 1924 and had a great friendship with Chinese writers. He also had a Chinese name "Zhu Zhendan," which he mentioned multiple times in his book.

While visiting China, Tagore once said, "I do not know why coming to China seems to me like returning to my native soil. I always feel that India has been one of China's extremely close relatives, and China and India have been enjoying time-honored and affectionate brotherhood."

Yoga in China

Like many other parts of the world, China has been influenced by yoga, a physical and spiritual practice that originated in ancient India. Yunnan Minzu University, located in Kunming, the capital city of Yunnan Province in southwest China, founded Sino-Indian Yoga College, the first yoga college in China. Students here have the opportunity to go to India to learn the practice of yoga.

Yoga can help to relieve low back pain and stress, and also has a meditative and spiritual core. With millions of practitioners and more than 10 000 main yoga schools nationwide, China is transforming into another yoga superpower.

(选自 https://news.cgtn.com/news/2019-10-12/Sino-India-cultural-exchange-From-ancient-to-modern-times--KJC8AVTzyw/index.html.)

 Questions for Discussion

1. In which areas will China and India deepen their relations with exchanges?

2. What are the two major books marking the history of cultural exchanges between the two countries?

3. What is yoga?

Passage 3

The Red Phone Box, a British Icon, Stages a Comeback

Sometimes it's hard to let go. For many British people, that can apply to institutions and objects that represent their country's past—age-old castles, splendid homes ... and red phone boxes.

Beaten first by the march of technology and lately by the terrible weather in **junkyards** (废品场), the phone boxes representative of an age are now making something of a comeback. Adapted in imaginative ways, many have reappeared on city streets and village greens housing tiny cafes, cellphone repair shops or even **defibrillator machines** (除颤器).

The original iron boxes with the round roofs first appeared in 1926. They were designed by Giles Gilbert Scott, the architect of the Battersea Power Station in London. After becoming an important part of many British streets, the phone boxes began disappearing in the 1980s, with the rise of the mobile phone sending most of them away to the junkyards.

About that time, Tony Inglis' engineering and transport company got the job to remove phone boxes from the streets and sell them out. But Inglis ended up buying hundreds of them himself, with the idea of repairing and selling them. He said that he had heard the calls to preserve the boxes and had seen how some of them were listed as historic buildings.

As Inglis and later other businessmen, got to work, repurposed phone boxes began reappearing in cities and villages as people found new uses for them. Today, they are once again a familiar sight, playing roles that are often just as important for the community as their original purpose.

In rural areas, where ambulances can take a relatively long time to arrive, the phone boxes have taken on a lifesaving role. Local organizations can adopt them for 1 pound, and install defibrillators to help in emergencies.

Others also looked at the phone boxes and saw business opportunities. Love Fone, a company that advocates repairing cellphones rather than abandoning them, opened a mini workshop in a London phone box in 2016.

The tiny shops made economic sense, according to Robert Kerr, a founder of Love Fone. He said that one of the boxes generated around $13 500 in revenue a month and cost only about $400 to rent.

Inglis said phone boxes called to mind an age when things were built to last. "I like what they are to people, and I enjoy bringing things back," he said.

(选自 https://www.tingclass.net/show-7804-412869-1.html.)

 Questions for Discussion

1. Why did the phone boxes begin to go out of service in the 1980s?

They lost to new technologies.

2. Why the phone boxes are becoming more and more popular?

Because in rural areas, where ambulances can take a relatively long time to arrive, the phone boxes have taken on a lifesaving role.

3. Why did Inglis say that the phone boxes called to mind an age when things were built to last?

To remind people of a historical period.

Exercises

I. True or False

Directions: *Decide whether the statements are true (T) or false (F).*

1. Intercultural communication is the exchange of information between individuals.
2. In intracultural communication, speakers rely on their prior knowledge rooted in cultural models, core common ground, shared knowledge, common beliefs of a relatively definable speech community.
3. Zheng He opened up the ancient "Silk Road" in Chinese history.
4. The Silk Road referred to both the terrestrial and the maritime routes connecting the East and West.
5. "One Belt, One Road" strategy was proposed by Chinese President Xi Jinping in 2015.
6. Zhang Qian was sent as a diplomatic envoy to the Western Regions.

7. International communication takes place between nations and countries rather than individuals.
8. The ancient route not only circulated goods, but also exchanged the splendid cultures of China, India, Persia, Arab, Greece and Rome.
9. Cross-cultural communication emphasizes the differences of different cultural communities or groups.
10. In order to be successful in intercultural communication, people should learn only cultural differences.

II. Matching

Directions: *Match the following words and expressions with the correct Chinese.*

1. Maritime Silk Road   A. 底格里斯河
2. Silk Road Economic Belt   B. 欧亚国家
3. Tea Road   C. 海上丝绸之路
4. Eurasian countries   D. 丝绸之路经济带
5. Tigris Rivers   E. 茶马古道
6. Euphrates   F. 波斯湾
7. Persian Gulf   G. 帕米尔高原
8. Constantinople   H. 日本群岛
9. Pamirs   I. 幼发拉底河
10. Japanese archipelago   J. 君士坦丁堡

III. Translation

A. Directions: *Translate the following paragraph into Chinese.*

The term cross-cultural communication is typically used to refer to the study of a particular idea or concept within many cultures. The goal of such investigations is to conduct a series of intercultural analysis in order to compare one culture to another on the attributes of interests.

Intracultural communication is defined as communication between and among members of the same culture. Generally, people who are of the same race, political persuasion, and religion or who share the same interests communicate intraculturally.

B. Directions: *Translate the following paragraph into English.*

丝绸之路（Silk Road）是我国古代一条连接中国和欧亚大陆（Eurasia）的交通线路，由于这条商路以丝绸贸易为主，故称"丝绸之路"。作为国际贸易的通道和文化交流的桥梁，丝绸之路有效地促进了东西方经济文化交流和发展，对世界文明进程有着深远影响。当前，在新的历史条件下，我国提出"一带一路"倡议（the Belt and Road Initiative）（即"丝绸之路经济带"和"21世纪海上丝绸之路"）。"一带一路"以合作共赢为核心，强调相关各国的互利共赢和共同发展。这一倡议一经提出即受到沿线各国的积极响应。

Chapter 2

Communication

> Nature and man are united as one. 天人合一。
> Good communication is as stimulating as black coffee, and just as hard to sleep after.
> ——Anne Morrow Lindbergh
>
> 愉悦的交流如同一杯黑咖啡,事后都会令我彻夜难眠。
> ——安妮·莫罗·林德伯格

本章导读

根据《孟子·万章下》:"敢问交际,何心也?"朱熹集注:"际,接也。交际,谓人以礼仪币帛相交接也。"交际通常指两人或两人以上通过语言、行为等表达方式进行意见、情感、信息交流的过程,是人们运用一定的工具传递信息、交流思想以达到某种目的的社会活动。交际是人类在相互交往中使用符号创造意义和反射意义的动态、系统过程。交际受语境制约,信息交流总是在特定的地点发生。本章从交际的概念入手,通过介绍中西方对交际的不同定义,帮助学习者认识到构成交际的要素、交际的功能以及交际的特点,从而帮助学习者全面理解交际模式,提高跨文化交际能力。

Learning Objectives

In this chapter, students will learn how to: understand the definition of communication, describe the function of communication, evaluate the components of communication, identify the characteristics of communication, and evaluate the model of communication.

Warm-up Activities

1. How many Chinese words can you think of in terms of communication?

2. Define communication in your own words.

3. List the Chinese characters that are usually employed to translate communication.

Culture and communication, although two different concepts, are directly linked. They are **inextricably** (形影不离地) bound that some anthropologists believe the terms are virtually **synonymous** (同义). As Smith notes, "whenever people interact they communicate. To live in societies and to maintain their culture, they have to communicate." Culture is learned, acted out, transmitted, and preserved through communication. Although the concepts of communication and culture work in **tandem** (串联), we separate them here for the purpose of our discussion. We begin by examining communication because to understand intercultural interaction, we must first recognize the role of communication in that process.

Communication—our ability to share our ideas and feelings—is the basis of all human contact. Wherever we live, we all participate in the same activity when communicating. The results and the methods might be different, but the process is the same: all five and a half billion of us communicate so that we can share our realities with other human beings.

2.1 Definitions of Communication

It is difficult to find a single definition of human communication. For example, over twenty years ago, Dance and Larson reviewed literature on communication and found 126 definitions of communication; since then, countless others have been added to their list. The same is true in Chinese. How many Chinese words can you think of concerning communication? (传播、通讯、联络、交流、对话、传报、交际、沟通，还有传达等等。) From these expressions, we can see it is difficult to define "communication" because it has been used in a variety of ways for varied purposes. Up till now, there are as many as over 100 definitions of communication, yet none of them has been universally agreed on. For example, in Chinese, "duihua" is a compound character combining "dui", or an element of mutuality and face-to-face contacts, with "hua" meaning a word or a talk. This term refers to the face-to-face contact among two or more persons; it can also be used to refer to the interactions where one uses other channels of communication including the Internet, television, magazines, radio, and other electronic means.

In fact, the word "communication" is derived from the Latin word *communicare*, meaning to share with or to make common, as in giving to another a part or share of your thoughts, hopes, and knowledge.

According to *Webster Dictionary*, communication is a process by which the information is exchanged between individuals through a common system of symbols, signs, or behavior. According to *Oxford English Dictionary*, communication means the imparting or exchanging of information by speaking, writing, or using some other medium. It means the successful conveying or sharing ideas and feelings. As this definition makes clear, communication is more than simply the transmission of information. The term requires an element of success in transmitting or imparting a message, whether it is the information, ideas, or emotions.

Mac Arthur defines communication as the transmission of a message between a sender and a receiver by using the signaling system. Samovar & Portion defines that communication occurs whenever meaning is attributed to behavior or the **residue** (残余物) of behavior. Zhang Guoliang interprets communication as the act and process of sending and receiving messages among people.

Charles Cooley considers communication as the **mechanism** (机制) through which human relations exist and develop—all the symbols of the mind, together with the means of conveying them through space and preserving in time. It is a process in which a person, through the use of signs, (natural, universal) symbols (by human convention), verbally or non-verbally expressions, and consciously or unconsciously but intentionally motives, conveys meaning to another person in order to affect change.

We might say that communication consists of transmitting information from one person to another. In fact, many scholars of communication take this as a working definition and use Lasswell's maxim, "who says what to whom in what channel with what effect," as a means of **circumscribing** (划定……范围) the field of communication theory.

Human communication is a subtle and **ingenious** (设计独特的) set of processes. It is always thick with a thousand ingredients—signals, codes, meanings—no matter how simple the message or transaction is. Communication becomes even more complex when we add cultural dimensions. Although all cultures use symbols to share their realities, the specific realities and the symbols employed are quite different. In one culture you may smile in a causal manner as a form of greeting, whereas in another you may bow formally in silence, and in yet another you may acknowledge your friend with a full embrace.

There are two schools of thought on whether communication behavior is intentional or unintentional. As Miller and Steinberg put it, "communication is the process whereby one person deliberately attempts to convey meaning to another." We intentionally send messages to change or modify the behavior of other people, and therefore we select our words or actions with some degree of consciousness. For Miller and Steinberg, communication is not a random activity that happens by chance, but rather a systematic and planned event. The planning might be **protracted** (拖延的) or **instantaneous** (瞬间的), but in either case it is conscious.

The second school of thought proposes that the concept of intentionality is too limiting and fails to account for all the circumstances in which messages are conveyed unintentionally. Scholars who support that approach believe that communication takes place whenever people attach meaning to behavior, even if the sender of the message does not expect his or her actions to be communicated. They contend that communication can influence other people whether or not such influence is intended. Those who hold this broader approach to communication believe that communication, much like culture, often takes place "without awareness."

Different cultures have different views towards communication: in Western cultures, communication is studied as a means of transmitting ideas; Western cultures emphasize the instrumental function of communication, while Eastern cultures stress harmony and emphasize the relationship between the communicators.

The way Westerners communicate tends to be relatively explicit(直率的) and direct. In other words, Westerners tend to put most of their ideas and feelings into words, and then state these ideas and feelings clearly and openly. It is generally considered a good thing to "get to the point" and "say what you mean," and it is largely the speaker's responsibility to ensure that his/her message is stated in a way that is clear and easy to understand.

In contrast, Chinese people tend to communicate in a way that is more indirect and subtle. They often view direct, explicit communication as unsophisticated(不成熟的) or even rude. They are more likely to preserve good feelings and relationships by not saying something that might upset or offend another person. If a Westerner makes a request and a Chinese person responds by saying something like "I'll think it over", the Westerner may assume that there is a good chance that the answer will be "yes". In fact, there is a better chance that the implied answer is "no".

The Function of Communication

Warm-up Activities

Look at these examples and try to identify what kind of communication does it belong to?

(1) Information is sent through TV, radio, newspapers or magazines.

(2) Your company sends circulars and messengers to other companies.

(3) You send an email message to an American friend.

(4) A girl is talking to herself while flourishing her doll.

The importance and influence of communication on human behavior are dramatically understood by Keating when she writes, "Communication is powerful: it brings companions to our side or scatters our rivals, reassures or alerts children, and forges consensus or battle lines between us." What she is saying is that communication—our ability to share our beliefs, values, ideas and feelings—is at the heart of all human contact. Whether people live in a city in China, in a village in India, on a farm in Israel, or in the Amazon rainforests of Brazil, they all employ the same activity when they attempt to share their thoughts and feelings with others. While the results when sending messages might be different, the reasons people communicate tend to what folllows.

According to Maslow's need hierarchy, our basic needs are about food, shelter and sex. Just above that come the needs of safety—knowing that one belongs to some group like family. Then there are the social needs for things like love and friendship, which urge us into building relationships. These are followed by our ego and esteem needs, which are about us as individuals wanting self-respect, recognition, even power. Finally, at the top of the triangle comes the most sophisticated need—for self-actualization.

Chapter 2 Communication

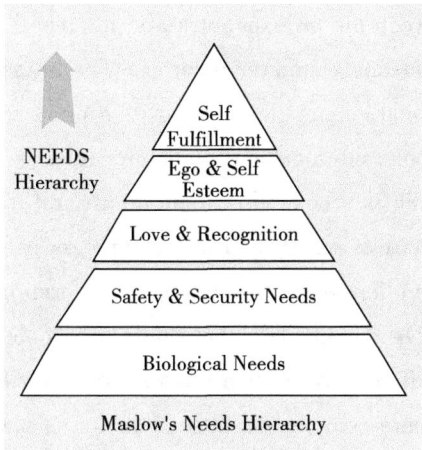

Maslow's Needs Hierarchy

People communicate for a number of important reasons: we buy food, rent an apartment, secure job, maintain our health and safety in order to meet our practical needs. We establish ties, maintain friendships, and develop intimate relationships to fulfill our social needs. We chat with our classmates, friends, colleagues or partners in order to obtain information. The more information we receive, the better the decisions we make. Through self-expression and feedback from others, we define and confirm who we are, we feel appreciated and successful, and therefore increase our level of self-awareness. We expose ourselves to challenging new experiences. As a result, we grow up and promote our personal growth.

There is a variety of forms of communication, including interpersonal communication, intrapersonal communication. mass communication, and organizational communication.

When people talk to each other, they are engaging in interpersonal communication. In this simplest form, interpersonal communication is a communication between two people physically located in the same place. It can occur, however, if they are physically separated but emotionally connected, like lovers on cell phones.

Interpersonal communication includes exchanges in which two or more people take part, but the term is usually reserved for situations in which just two people are communicating. Having a face-to-face conversation over lunch and writing a letter to a friend are everyday examples. When interpersonal communication is electronically mediated, as in a telephone conversation, the term point-to-point communication is sometimes used.

The difference between the prefixes intra-and inter-is the key difference between intrapersonal and interpersonal communication. Just as intrasquad athletic games are within a team, intrapersonal communication is within one's self. Just as intercollegiate games are between schools, interpersonal communication is between individuals. Intrapersonal communication is a communication within and to the self.

Mass communication can be defined as the process of using a mass medium to send messages to large audiences for the purpose of informing, entertaining or persuading. Crafting an effective message for thousands of people of diverse backgrounds and interests requires different skills than chatting with a friend across the table. Encoding the message is more complex because a device is always used-for example, a printing press, a camera or a recorder. Capable of reaching thousands, even millions, of people is mass communication, which is accomplished through a mass medium like television or newspapers.

Organizational communication is a communication within groups of people and by groups of people to others. There comes a point when the number of people involved reduces the intimacy of the communication process. That's when the situation becomes group communication. A club meeting is an example. So is a speech to an audience in an auditorium.

2.2 Components of Communication

Warm-up Activities

(1) Try to identify six components of communication.

(2) Work out as many components or steps involved in communication as you can.

There are at least six key components of communication: sender, message, channel, receiver, noise, and feedback. From the literal meaning, the sender refers to the person who sends the message. The receiver is a person who performs the inverse operation done by the transmitter, reconstructing the message from the signal. Let's think of this situation: when you talk to your teacher, sing a song to your daughter, or send a letter to your customer, you are the individual who originates a message, so you are the sender who begins the communication process. When you speak to someone face-to-face, listen to your voice mail, talk on the phone, send an e-mail to your friend, or deliver a speech, you are sending messages to them.

A message refers to any signals that trigger the response of a receiver. It is composed of a set of symbols either verbal or nonverbal. A verbal message includes both oral messages and written ones. A nonverbal message has more uncertainties than the verbal one. Consequently, whether you smile, listen, renew a magazine subscription, watch a particular TV program, or turn away from a person, you are communicating some message, and your message will have some effect.

Let's suppose you are the sender, you have to tell your subordinate that she'll be fired by your company. What would you say to her? In this case, you may choose certain words or nonverbal methods to send the message. This process is called encoding. As your subordinate listens to your words and observes your nonverbal symbols, she is trying to attach meaning to the words or symbols. This process is called decoding. Both are of special importance because the communication is achieved by encoding a message into a signal and by decoding this signal at the receiving end. In the process of message decoding, noise along the channel may interfere with the receiver's interpreting of the signal from the sender. It can distort or destroy the signal. As long as the message decoded is identical to the message encoded, successful communication is guaranteed.

The channel (media) is the method by which we used to deliver a message. We may send our message to receivers through a variety of sensory channels. We may use sound, sight, smell, taste, touch, or any combination of these to carry a message. Some channels are more effective at communicating messages than others, and the nature of the channel selected affects the way a message processed. Selecting the appropriate channel becomes more important as the importance or sensitivity of a message increases. For example, if you wanted to resign, which channel would you choose? Would you prefer to make a phone call to your boss or just write a letter of resignation to him?

The response of a receiver to a sender's message is called **feedback** . Feedback can be both nonverbal and verbal, you may say "yes" and smile to your customer or say "no" and frown on your screen. Feedback can be further divided into two pairs: positive feedback vs. negative feedback; internal feedback vs. external feedback.

Remember that any response, even no response, is a feedback.

Feedback returns information to the sender of a message, thereby enabling the sender to determine whether the message is received or correctly understood. There are at least three ways to look at feedback.

Firstly, it can be positive or negative. Positive feedback encourages sources to continue sending similar messages. In contrast, negative feedback discourages sources from encoding similar messages.

Secondly, feedback can be immediate or delayedly; and thirdly, it can be free or limited. In an immediate and free feedback condition, the reactions of the receiver are directly and freely communicated to and perceived by the source. For example at a political rally, a speaker knows immediately whether the audience in the hall is friendly or not. In contrast, if you want to communicate your opinion of a newspaper article with the editor, before your views are received and printed by the intended party, several days or perhaps even weeks might elapse.

Feedback serves useful functions for both the senders and receivers: it provides senders with the opportunity to measure how they are coming across, and it provides receivers with the opportunity to exert some influence over the communication process.

In the process of message decoding, noise along the channel may interfere with the receiver's interpreting of the signal from the sender. It can distort or even destroy the signal. As long as the message decoded is identical to the message encoded, successful communication is guaranteed.

Noise refers to the factors that interfere with the exchange of messages. In general, there are four types of noises: external noise, physiological noise, psychological noise, and semantic noise. The most obvious type of noise is **external noise** (also called physical noise), which refers to the environmental distractions such as poorly heated rooms, startling sounds, the appearances of things, music playing somewhere else, and someone talking really loudly near you.

Physiological noise refers to the biological influences that distract you from communicating competently. For example, when you speak in public, you may become nervous, your palms will be sweaty, your heart will be pounding, and you may have a butterfly in your stomach.

Psychological noise is the forces within the sender or receiver that interfere with understanding. Psychological noise is the preconception bias and assumptions such as thinking someone who speaks like a valley girl is dumb, or someone from a foreign country can't speak English well so you speak loudly and slowly to them.

Semantic noise means that the receiver does not derive the meanings intended by the sender. It occurs when people choose confusing and distracting words. For example, someone are talking at length in Vietnamese but you simply do not understand the language. Or a speaker may make incorrect assumptions about how much shared knowledge you both possess—he may assume you know all about uncle John's recent fall but dctually you do not—and then the communication potentially breaks down.

In short, noise is inevitable; all communication contains some kind of noise. It can function as a communication barrier. As the noise increases, the chances for effective communication usually decrease, and as the noise decreases, the chances for effective communication usually rise. Therefore, we should try to reduce the noise and its effect as much as possible even though we may not get rid of them completely.

2.3 The Models of Communication

There are three commonly used models: the linear model, the circular model and the contextualized model.

2.3.1 Linear Model

One of the earliest and most useful models aims to describe the communication process in separate parts which was made by Harold in 1948. For example, if you say "I love you" to your husband, you may put words into your feelings that "I love you!" and speak the words in the hope that they will be suitably understood by your husband. This is a very famous model and has been used by a lot of communication scholars. It's a linear model, laying out parts of the process in a line, as if communication is all about sending messages from A to B. In fact, communication is not that simple. What the sender through what message through what channel to what the receiver with what effect? The disadvantages in this model lie in that there is no feedback in this model. It seems like a one-way communication.

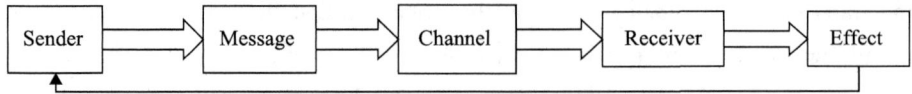

2.3.2 Circular Model

He or she puts what he means into a particular kind of code. It's called encoding. The person who encodes it is called an encoder. So he encodes his meaning into a message, and it goes to the second person, who gets the message and has to decode it, that is, he has to understand it. If it's an English message, he has to read and decode the English message. After he has got this message, he decides to send back some feedback. This time he himself becomes an encoder. And he sends a message back to the first person, who has become a decoder this time. So here we have a circular. The first person can then send the second message and goes through the same channel. So this seems to be a more desirable model of communication. This is an exchange model, indicating that communication is at least a two-way process and that everyone is a decoder and an encoder. That is to say, we have to find some ways of putting together and expressing what we have to say, as well as some ways of taking in what the other person says.

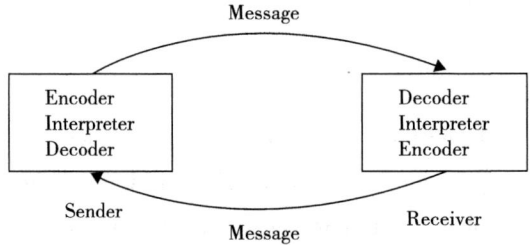

2.3.3 Contextualized Model

This model adds the dimension of situations or surroundings. Context always affects the act of communication. What is a context? All communication takes place within a setting or situation which is called a context. As **Hall** puts it, "Context is the information that surrounds an event, and bounds up with the meaning of the event." In other words, it is the broad circumstances or situations in which communication occurs. The context includes the physical, social, and interpersonal settings within which messages are exchanged.

Physical context includes the actual location of the communicators: indoors or outdoors, crowded or quiet, public or private, close together or far apart, warm or cold, bright or dark. For example, if we are talking to someone in our living room, we'd better speak in a low voice.

Social context refers to the widely shared expectations people have about the kinds of interactions that normally occur in different kinds of social events. This might be a group of friends in a club or a family meal or a group of mourners at a funeral. For example, we would communicate differently in the situation of a formal dinner with our boss, and a casual hangout with our friends, eating fish and chips in the kitchen.

Cultural context refers to an even broader set of circumstances and beliefs, which still may affect how we talk.

Interpersonal context refers to the expectations people have about the behaviors of others as a result of differences in the relationships between them.

In conclusion, every communication takes place in some context or setting. Sometimes, the context is so natural that we fail to notice it; at other times, the context makes such an impression on us that we make a conscious effort to control our behaviors. For example, consider the extent to which our behavior would change if we were to move from a park to a political rally, to a movie theatre, or to a funeral home. Every context provides us with rules or norms for interaction. Sometimes the place, time, and the people with us affect us unconsciously and consciously.

2.4 Communication Skills

Being able to communicate effectively is perhaps most important of all life skills. It is what enables us to pass information to other people and to understand what is said to us. We only have to watch a baby listening intently to its mother and try to repeat the sounds that she makes to understand how fundamental the urge to communicate is.

Communication, at its simplest, is the act of transferring information from one place to another. It may be vocally (voice), written (printed or digital media such as books, magazines, websites or emails), visually (logos, maps, charts or graphs) or nonverbally (body language, gestures, tone and pitch of voice). In practice, it is often a combination of several of these.

When we discuss communication skills, we generally mean reading, listening, nonverbal, speaking and writing skills. As you know, communication skills are regarded as "soft skills". As **Beverly Amer** puts it, soft skills refer to those attitudes and behaviors that relate to critical thinking, problem solving, communication, collaboration, and presentation skills. It not only helps us get a job in the market, but also is essential to the long-term success in our workplace. We have two means by which to send messages and two means by which to receive messages. To send messages, We speak and write. To receive messages, We read and listen.

2.4.1 Speaking Skills

The way we send your messages by using oral skills over a period of time creates an image. The image is a key to your success. Think twice before you speak once. When conversing with someone, remember that you need to take time to think before reacting to what is being said. It is an excellent communication skill to take a few moments and process all the information before you respond. When you speak, you have to employ the right kind of body language to improve your communication skills. Maintain eye contact as you speak; sit and stand in an **erect** (直立的) position, and have a firm handshake; do not give wrong signals by crossing your arms or legs; and avoid moving your body or playing with small things frequently. Always remember that your gestures say a lot about your personality as an individual.

2.4.2 Writing Skills

Though it is the least used form of communication, it receives a great deal of attention in schools. In an educational setting, writing is required extensively. You have to do a lot of assignment or hand in your paper before the deadline; otherwise you may fail in the exam. In your personal life, your ability to write an effective letter can deepen a relationship, earn the respect of a friend, and reflect your attitude.

2.4.3 Reading Skills

In this age of exploding information, you must read continually in order to stay current. Reading is a means of gaining culture and enriching your knowledge in different areas. It can help you have a great imagination and makes things easier when it comes to making compositions on different themes. It gives you the possibility to speak about science, even if you don't work in this area, or you can express your opinion about a political aspect, just because you have read something connected to that.

2.4.4 Listening Skills

Though listening is the most frequently used means of communication, it is the least taught. Listening is more than just hearing: it requires understanding. Communication is not just about speaking effectively and in an impressive manner, you also need to be a good listener. It is important to be a good listener in order to understand what the other person is saying, and reply accordingly. So try to be a patient listener and employ all your communication skills while listening to others.

During communication, "words" express only 7% of meanings between people. About 23% of meanings are from the "tone of voice" and 70% of meanings comes from "body language". So next time when you want to draw someone's attention—try your body language instead.

Nonverbal communication means that messages are sent without words such as the appearance and the accuracy of written messages. The main areas of nonverbal communication are body language, touching, space, time, voice, and paralanguage.

Developing your communication skills can help you in all aspects of your life, from your professional life to social gatherings and everything in between. Professionally, if you are applying for jobs or looking for a promotion with your current employer, you will almost certainly need to demonstrate your good communication skills. Communication skills are needed to speak appropriately with a wide variety of people whilst maintaining good eye contact, demonstrate a varied vocabulary and tailor your language to your audience, listen effectively, present your ideas appropriately, write clearly and concisely, and work well in a group. Many of these are essential skills that most employers seek.

In your personal life, good communication skills can improve your personal relationships by helping you understand others and be understood. It is almost a **cliché**

(陈词滥调) that personal relationships need communication. Failure to talk has been blamed for the breakdown of large numbers of partnerships and relationships—but the ability to listen is also an important element. Communication is vital in wide family relationships, whether you want to discuss the arrangements for holidays, or ensure that your teenage children are well and happy.

Communication skills can also ensure that you are able to manage interactions with businesses and organisations. Over the course of your lifetime, you are likely to interact with a wide range of organisations and institutions, including shops, businesses, government offices and schools. Good communication skills can ease these interactions, and ensure that you are able to get your points.

2.5 Characteristics of Communication

To understand intercultural communication events, we must first study the more general processes involved in all human communication transactions. All communication events, including intercultural ones, are made up of a set of basic characteristics. Once these characteristics are known, they can be applied to intercultural interactions in order to analyze the unique ways in which intercultural communication differs from other forms of communication.

Six characteristics of the definition of communication require further elaboration. Our definition asserts that communication is symbolic, dynamic, interpretive, contextual, irreversible, and shared. Let's examine each of these characteristics more closely.

2.5.1 Communication Is Symbolic

Symbols are central to the communication process because they represent the shared meanings that are communicated. A symbol is a word, an action, or an object that stands for or represents a unit of meanings. Meaning, in turn, is a perception, a thought, or the feeling that a person experiences and might want to communicate to others. These meaningful experiences could include the sensations resulting from a room's temperature, thoughts about a teacher in a particular course, or the feelings of happiness or anger shared directly with others. They can become shared and understood only when they are interpreted as a message. A message, then, refers to a package of symbols used to create shared meanings.

People's behaviors are frequently interpreted symbolically as an external representation of feelings, emotions, and internal states. To many people in the United States, for example, raising an arm with the hand extended and moving the hand and arm up and down symbolize saying goodbye.

As you know, humans are symbol-making creatures. It is this symbol-making ability that allows for our everyday interaction. Other animals may participate in the communication process, but none of them has the unique communication capability. Symbols are vehicles by which the thoughts and ideas of one person can be communicated to another person. In terms of intercultural communication, it is significant for us to keep in mind that the symbols we use are **discretionary** (任意的) and subjective. We employ symbols to share our internal states. Two sets of symbols, words and actions, help us let other human beings know how we experience the world. Today we have very different types of symbols at hand to conduct communication with sound, light, a mark, a statue, **braille** (盲人用点字法), or a painting, etc.

2.5.2 Communication Is Dynamic

Firstly, as the Greek philosopher **Heraclitus** (赫拉克利特) says, "There is nothing permanent except change." **Wang Fuzhi,** a famous philosopher in Ming Dynasty, puts it, "太极动而生阳, 动之动也。静而生阴, 动之静也……一动一静". Communication is an ongoing activity. It is like a motion picture, not a single snapshot. A word or an action does not stay frozen when we communicate; it is immediately replaced with yet another word or action. When we communicate, we interact with each other. We are constantly affected by other people's messages and, as a consequence, are always changing.

Secondly, as the proverb goes in China, "Once the arrow has been shot it cannot be recalled." which means once a word or an action is employed, it cannot be retracted. Once an event takes place, we cannot have it over; perhaps we can experience a similar event, but not an identical one.

Thirdly, the word dynamic also testifies to the idea that all the elements of communication constantly interact with each other. We send words, create actions, watch the response of those around us, and listen to our partners all at the same time.

Fourthly, communication is dynamic because inattention pervades communication behavior. As the Buddha says, "The mind is fickle and flighty, it flies after fancies wherever it likes: it is difficult indeed to restrain." We often shift topics in the middle of a sentence, and a research shows that when we listen, our attention span is brief.

2.5.3　Communication Is Interpretive

Messages do not have to be consciously or purposefully created with the specific intention of communicating a certain set of meanings for others to be able to make sense of those symbols forming the message. Rather, communication is always an interpretive process. Whenever people communicate, they must interpret the symbolic behaviors of others and assign significance to some of those behaviors in order to create a meaningful account of the other's actions. This idea suggests that each person in a communication transaction may not necessarily interpret the messages in exactly the same way. Indeed, during episodes involving intercultural communication the likelihood is high that people will interpret the meaning of messages differently.

Humans are meaning-seeking creatures. Throughout our life, we have accumulated various meanings as the outside world has sent us trillions of messages. In each communication event, participants attribute meaning to a behavior. Then meaning exchange is more obvious.

Nonverbal communication has to do with gestures, movements and closeness of two people when they are talking. The scientists say that those gestures and movements have meaning which words do not carry. For example, the body distance between two speakers can be important. North Americans often complain that South Americans are unfriendly because they tend to stand close to the North American when speaking, while the South American often considers the North American to be "cold" or "distant" because he keeps a greater distance between himself and the person he is speaking to.

2.5.4　Communication Is Contextual

We interact with others not in isolation but in a specific setting. Setting and environment help us determine how we communicate with others. It is our culture's role to help us discover these meanings. Communication takes place within a certain setting or situation such as the actual location and the types of social relationships. Can you think of some of the elements associated with the contextual nature of communication? Cultural context, envionmental context, occasion, time, and the number of people. For example, the time after the death or passing away of a person in India is given a lot of importance. The basic idea behind the Indians' following all these funeral traditions is to show **reverence** (尊敬) to the deceased person. Normally during this time, all the family members share each other's sorrows and pray, so the soul of the deceased person rests peacefully.

(1) Cultural Context

All communication has a context; communication happens for a reason. Communication can fail because one or more of the participants overlook the context. To help us avoid misunderstandings, and to communicate more effectively, it is important that the context of the communication be understood by all. Why is the communication happening? It is important that all participants be on the same **"wavelength"** (波长) so that they understand why the communication is occurring. It may be useful to start a larger conversation by explaining why it is happening.

The largest contextual component is the cultural setting in which the communication is taking place. This framework governs all the other environments since it includes the learned behaviors and rules that the participants bring to a communication event. For example, if we were raised in a culture in which people touch each other as a greeting, and out of politeness during an introduction, if we touch a woman from a non-touch culture, we may have violated the rules of a particular cultural context by accident.

Firstly, communication rules prescribe proper behaviors by establishing appropriate responses to communication stimuli for the various social contexts found within the larger culture. Communication rules cover both verbal and nonverbal behaviors and specify not only what should be said but also how it should be said. The rules differ depending on the context. Secondly, the context specifies the appropriate rules. Thirdly, the rules are culturally diverse. Although cultures have many of the same social settings or contexts, they frequently abide by different rules. Consequently, the concepts of dress, time, language, manners, nonverbal behavior, and the control of communication ebb and flow can differ significantly among cultures.

(2) Occasion

The occasion of a communication encounter also controls the behavior of the participants. The same auditorium can be the occasion for a graduation ceremony, pre-rally, **convocation** (正式集会), play, dance, or memorial service. Each of these occasions calls for distinctly different forms of behaviors. It should be fairly obvious that the communication is going to be less effective if it is conducted in a noisy, uncomfortable or busy place. Such places may have many distractions and often lack privacy.

(3) Time

The influence of time on communication is so subtle that it is often ignored. Every communication event takes place on a time-space continuum, and the amount of time allotted, whether it is of social conversation or a formal speech, affects that event. Cultures as well as people use time to communicate. Timing is fundamental to a successful communication. Considering a suitable time to hold a conversation, we should make sure that there is enough time to cover all that is needed, including the time to clarify and negotiate. Talking to employees about a strategic decision five minutes before they have to leave the office for the day, for example, would probably not be as successful as having the same conversation in the following morning.

(4) Number of People

The number of people with whom you communicate also influences the flow of communication; we'll feel and act differently if you are speaking with one person, in a group, or in front of a great many people. Cultures also respond to changes in number. For example, Japanese prefer small-group interaction, yet they often feel extremely uncomfortable when they have to give a formal public speech in front of a large group of people.

2.5.5 Communication Is Irreversible(不可逆的)

As the proverb goes, in Asia, "Once the arrow has been shot it cannot be recalled." Once the information has been sent and received by others, it cannot be taken back. Once an event takes place, you cannot have it again; perhaps we can experience a similar event, but not an identical one. The words are spoken, and they cannot be unspoken.

2.5.6 Communication Is Shared

Meanings are invented by participants in the communication that form the context for common interpretations. The interpretive and transactional nature of communication suggests that correct meanings are not just out there to be discovered. Rather, meanings are created and shared by groups of people as they participate in the ordinary and everyday activities that form the context for common interpretations. The focus, therefore, must be on the ways that people attempt to make sense of their common experiences in the world.

Communication is the process of attempting to suggest information from a sender to a receiver with the use of a medium. Communication requires that all parties have an area of communicative commonality. There are auditory means, such as speaking, singing and sometimes tone of voice, and nonverbal, physical means, such as body language, sign language, paralanguage, touch, eye contact, or the use of writing. Communication is defined as a process by which we assign and convey meaning in an attempt to create shared understanding. This process requires a vast repertoire of skills in intrapersonal and interpersonal processing, such as listening, observing, speaking, questioning, analyzing, and evaluating. Use of these processes is developmental and transfers to all areas of life: home, school, community, work, and beyond. It is through communication that collaboration and cooperation occur.

Communication is the articulation of sending a message through different media, whether it is verbal or nonverbal, so long as it can transmit a thought provoking idea, gesture, action, etc. Communication is a learned skill. Most people are born with the physical ability to talk, but they must learn to speak well and communicate effectively. Speaking, listening, and our ability to understand verbal and nonverbal meanings are the skills we develop in various ways. We learn basic communication skills by observing other people and modeling our behaviors based on what we have seen. We are also taught some communication skills directly through education, and we practise those skills and have them evaluated.

 Key Terms

    practical function   实用功能

social function	社交功能
decision-making function	决策功能
personal growth function	个人成长功能
interpersonal communication	人际交流
mass communication	大众传媒
organizational communication	机构交流
intrapersonal communication	自我传播
sender	信息发出者
receiver	信息接收者
feedback	反馈
message	信息
noise	干扰
context	语境
decode	解码
encode	编码
linear model	线性模型
circular model	环形模型
contextualized model	语境化模型
channel	渠道
external noise	外部干扰
physiological noise	生理干扰
psychological noise	心理干扰
semantic noise	语义干扰
physical context	物理语境
social context	社交语境
interpersonal context	人际语境
cultural context	文化语境
semiotic rules	符号学规则
syntactic	句法的
pragmatic	实用主义的
semantic	语义的

Notes

1. **Charles Horton Cooley** (1864–1929), an American sociologist and social psychologist, pioneer of American communication studies. He was born in Ann Arbor, Michigan. His works include *Human Nature and Social Order*, *Social Organization*, *Social Process*, etc.

   查尔斯·霍顿·库利(1864—1929)，美国社会学家和社会心理学家，美国传播学研究的先驱。出生于美国密歇根州安娜堡市。他的作品包括《人性和社会秩序》《社会组织》《社会过程》等。

2. **Larry A. Samovar**, an associate professor of speech-communication at San Diego State College. He obtained his Ph. D. degree from Purdue University in 1962. He is the co-author of *Oral Communication: Message and Response*, (1967); and co-editor of *Small Group Communication: A Reader*, to be published 1969. Dr. Samovar is also an associate editor for the *Journal of Communication*.

   拉里·A. 萨莫瓦尔是圣地亚哥州立大学言语交际专业副教授。于1962年在普渡大学获得博士学位。他与人合著了《口头交流：信息与回应》(1967)；于1969年主编了《小团体交流：读者》。萨莫瓦尔博士还是《传播学报》的副主编。

3. *The Book of Changes*, one of the important Confucian classics, also known as *The Book of Yijing*, including two parts: classics and biographies. "Jing" is mainly 64 hexagrams and 384 lines, and the hexagrams and lines have their own instructions (hexagrams, lines), as the use of divination. "Biography" contains seven kinds of words explaining hexagrams and lines, collectively known as "Ten wings". *The Book of changes* is the theoretical root of natural philosophy and humanistic practice in Chinese traditional ideology and culture, the crystallization of ancient Han thought and wisdom, known as the "source of the road", and an outstanding representative of Chinese traditional culture. It is also the source of Chinese civilization. *The Book of Changes* includes a wealth of knowledge, such as astronomy, geography, military, science, literature, agriculture, and so on, and has had an extremely profound impact on China's political, economic, cultural, and other fields for thousands of years. Being the first in the group of Yi, poetry,

books, etiquette, music, Spring and Autumn, *The Book of Changes* sets up the book of education, and enjoys a high position in the cultural history of our country.

《周易》为儒家重要经典之一,又称《易经》,包括《经》和《传》两部分。《经》主要是64卦和384爻,卦和爻各有说明(卦辞、爻辞),作为占卜之用。《传》包含解释卦辞和爻辞的七种文辞,共十篇,统称《十翼》。《周易》是中国传统思想文化中自然哲学与人文实践的理论根源,是古代汉民族思想、智慧的结晶,被誉为"大道之源",是华夏传统文化的杰出代表,亦是中华文明的源头活水。《周易》囊括了天文、地理、军事、科学、文学、农学等丰富的知识内容,对中国几千年来的政治、经济、文化等各个领域都产生了极其深刻的影响,为易、诗、书、礼、乐、春秋群经之首,设教之书,在我国文化史上享有崇高的地位。

4. **Harold Lasswell**, (1902-1978), an influential political scientist known for seminal studies of power relations and personality and politics and for other major contributions to contemporary behavioral political science. He authored more than 30 books and 250 scholarly articles on diverse subjects, including international relations, psychoanalysis, and legal education.

哈罗德·拉斯韦尔(1902—1978),是一位有影响的政治学家,以对权力关系、人格和政治的开创性研究以及对当代行为政治学的其他重大贡献而闻名。他撰写了30多本书,发表了250多篇学术文章,内容涉及国际关系、精神分析和法律教育等多个领域。

5. **Herakleitos** (544 BC-483 BC), an ancient Greek philosopher. He is a legendary philosopher and the founder of Orpheus school. He was born in the city of Orpheus in Ionia. In today's royal family near Izmir, Turkey. He should have inherited the throne, but he gave it up to his brother and went to live in seclusion near the temple of the goddess aldimes. It is said that Darius, King of Persia, once wrote a letter inviting him to go to the Persian court to teach Greek culture. He is the author of *The Book on Nature*, and the remaining chapters of the book are preserved.

赫拉克利特(公元前544—483),古希腊哲学家,是一位富有传奇色彩的哲学家,爱菲斯学派的创始人。他出生在伊奥尼亚地区的爱菲斯城邦(土耳其伊兹密尔附近)的王族家庭里。他本应继承王位,但却将王位让给了他的兄弟,自己跑到女神阿尔迪美斯庙附近隐居起来。据说,波斯国王大流士曾经写信邀请他去波斯宫廷教授希腊文化。著有《论自然》一书，现有残篇留存。
6. **Wang Fuzhi** (1619−1692), a native of Hengyang County, Hengzhou Prefecture, Huguang (now Hengyang, Hunan province). He, Gu Yanwu and Huang Zongxi were known as the three great thinkers in the Ming and Qing Dynasties. His works include *Zhouyi Waizhuan, Huangshu, Shangshu Yinyi, Yongli Shilu, Chunqiu Shilun, Menggu, Dutongjian* and *Songlun*.

王夫之(1619—1692)，湖广衡州府衡阳县（今湖南衡阳）人。他与顾炎武、黄宗羲并称"明清三大思想家"。其著有《周易外传》《黄书》《尚书引义》《永历实录》《春秋世论》《噩梦》《读通鉴论》《宋论》等书。

Case 1

Movements Betray Who You Are

If you've seen the film *Inglourious Basterds*, you will know that German and British people indicate the number THREE with their fingers in different ways. Germans raise their thumbs and first two fingers; Britons pin the little finger with their thumb and raise the rest. Most never realise that this difference exists until they see the alternative, which, to them, looks strange. Some signals may be random quirks that happened to catch on. Others may have served a purpose. Vladimir Putin is said to display his KGB weapons training in the way he walks, with his "gun arm" hanging motionless by his side. Since their initial discovery, Marsh and Elfenbein have detected more of these "nonverbal accents"—physical ways in which we show where we come from without realising. Americans, for example, can spot Australians from the way they smile, wave or walk.

More recent research supports their findings. A team at the University of Glasgow has now trained a computer to recognise and then generate more than 60 different nonverbal accents on a simulated face. Subtle, almost indecipherable differences in the way a nose wrinkles and a lip is raised were often all that differentiated them. But when East Asians were shown these artificial "East Asian" expressions, they recognised them much more easily than "Western" ones.

The presence of these subtle cues might help to explain the bias that can creep into our thinking about people from different backgrounds. As we've seen, nonverbal accents often have the effect of making outsiders more difficult to understand.

At the very least, when people really want to understand each other, nonverbal accents show us that it's good to talk.

(节选自 http://language.chinadaily.com.cn/a/202009/21/ws5F6849a8a31024adoba7acd3.html.)

 Questions for Discussion

1. How did Britons and Germans indicate the number THREE with their fingers?

2. How can Americans spot Australians?

3. What did the team at the University of Glasgow do?

4. What does "nonverbal accents" mean?

5. Was it difficult to distinguish the differences between the way a nose wrinkles and a lip raised?

Case 2

One of the world's oldest shared traditions, New Year's celebrations take many forms, but most cultures have one thing in common—letting one's hair down after a long, hard year. For much of the globe, this involves sipping bubbly with friends until the sun comes up, seeing out the old year with bonfires and flares and off-key renditions of Auld Lang Syne.

But others have rather more curious habits, often steeped in superstition. In Finland, people pour molten lead into cold water to divine the year ahead from the shape the metal sets in. If the blob represents a ship it is said to foretell travel; if it's a ball, good luck. In Denmark, people stand on chairs and jump off in unison as the clock strikes midnight, literally leaping into the New Year.

The Danes also throw plates at their friends' homes during the night, the more shards you find outside your door in the morning, the more popular you are said to be.

The Dutch build massive bonfires with their Christmas trees and eat sugary donuts—one of many cultures to consume round New Year's foods traditionally believed to represent good fortune.

Spaniards, in turn, **gobble** (狼吞虎咽地吃) a dozen grapes before the stroke of midnight, each fruit representing a month that will either be sweet or sour. In the Philippines, **revelers** (狂欢者) wear polka dots for good luck, while in some countries of South America people wear brightly colored underwear to attract fortune—red for love and yellow for financial success.

Despite regional and cultural differences, for most the New Year's festivities are a chance to let off steam before the annual cycle starts all over again.

Questions for Discussion

1. How do people celebrate the New Year in Finland?

2. Why do people in Denmark stand on their chairs and jump off in unison as the clock strikes midnight?

3. What kind of New Year's food do the Dutch eat? Why?

4. What do most revelers in the Philippines wear?

5. What kind of fruit do Spaniards eat during New Year's Day?

Case 3

A: What Chinese customs of politeness are traditional?

B: I think you've heard this one before; you fight with a friend over the bill in a restaurant.

A: Yeah, that's a part of Chinese culture. You can see that in other cultures too, but not so much in American culture.

B: My friends and I sometimes split the cost equally instead of shouting, let my pay!…No, let me pay!

A: In the U.S., it is common for people to split the bill after a meal. They call this habit "going Dutch". For example, after a meal, I would turn to you and say: "Let's go Dutch." Do you know any other polite customs related to eating or drinking?

B: In my hometown in Inner Mongolia, people like to drink a lot at mealtimes, especially when guests are over. If you visit me at my place, I'll try my best to get you as drunk as possible.

A: Really? That's very funny.

B: Yeah, that's our way of being polite. If you drink so much that you pass out at my place, you would make my parents very happy.

A: Very interesting.

B: I actually don't like it very much. It pleases the family but sometimes makes the guests feel uncomfortable.

 Questions for Discussion

1. What's the difference between Chinese people and American people in terms of paying the bill?

2. What's the custom in Inner Mongolia in China?

3. What does "go Dutch" mean in English?

4. How do Japanese pay the bill?

5. Why do you think there is such a cultural difference for paying the bill?

Case 4

Qixi Festival, the Chinese equivalent of Valentine's Day, was not only a disappointment for forgotten lovers, but also for businessmen who left with empty pockets.

The cold reception has prompted cultural experts to seriously worry that the lovers' festival, marked for generations since the Han Dynasty (206 BC-AD 220), is dying out. Some have even called for legislation to make the festival a legal "Chinese Lovers' Day," which falls on the seventh day of the seventh month of the lunar year.

But the effectiveness of such a measure is in doubt, although efforts to preserve traditional festivals are highly commendable. A growing number of traditional Chinese festivals, such as the Dragon Boat Festival and Mid-Autumn Festival share the same fate as the Qixi Festival.

Young people are showing less interest in traditional culture as symbolized by these festivals. Even if all traditional festivals are finally made legal, the risk of them becoming purely formalized celebrations with little meaning is not removed. If the younger generation fails to identify with the cultural significance of these holidays, there is little that can be done.

While complaining about traditional festivals' fading appeal, decision-makers should reflect on cultural protection. Undeniably our country has done a bad job of preserving culture and traditional festivals in the past, compared to neighbouring Japan and the Republic of Korea (ROK).

The 2,500-year-old Dragon Boat Festival falls on the fifth day of the fifth lunar month. The traditional customs and rituals of the occasion which originated in China, have been better preserved in the ROK.

Only a few years ago did China begin to realize the significance of preserving intangible cultural heritage when the ROK planned to apply to the United Nations Educational, Scientific and Cultural Organization (UNESCO) its version of the Dragon Boat Festival as an important example of intangible culture.

Concern about traditional holidays also reminds people of the growing influence of foreign cultures as the country opens wider to the outside world. With traditional festivals waning and imports such as Christmas and Valentine's Day gaining widespread popularity, the public including cultural professionals have tended to measure traditional Chinese festivals in economic terms.

Business rather than culture has begun to play a dominant role. More and more people are preoccupied with how much money can be generated during the holidays. In fact, what makes traditional festivals unique and what keeps them alive are their cultural elements. After all, it is unique culture that contributes to the world's diversity amid globalization.

(选自 http://easylearn.baidu.com/edu-page/tiangong/guestiondetai/?id=1735172955038489575αfr=search.)

 Questions for Discussion

1. What's the Chinese equivalent festival for Valentine's Day?
2. What other Chinese festivals are dying out? Can you name some?
3. Why do young people show less interest in traditional Chinese festivals?
4. What should decision-makers do to deal with this phenomenon?
5. What makes the traditional festivals unique and what keeps them alive?

Further Reading

Passage 1

Communication

As the basic building blocks of communication, words communicate meaning, but as we have seen, the meanings of words are very much influenced by culture. Meaning is in the person, not in the word, and each person is the product of a particular culture that passed on shared and appropriate meanings. Thus, if we want to learn to communicate well in a foreign language, we must understand the culture that gives that language meaning. In other words, culture and communication are inseparably linked; we can't have one without the other. Culture gives meaning and provides the context for communication, and the ability to communicate allows us to act out our cultural values and to share our language and our culture.

But our own native language and culture are so much a part of us that we take them for granted. When we travel to another country, we carry, along with our passports, our own culturally designed lenses through which we view the new environment. Using our own culture as the standard by which to judge other cultures is called **ethnocentrism** (民族优越感), and although unintentional, our ethnocentric ways of thinking and acting often get in the way of our understanding of other languages and cultures. The ability and willingness to change **lenses** (透镜, 镜头) when we look at a different culture is both the cure for and the prevention of such cultural blindness. Studying a new language provides the opportunity to practice changing lenses when we also learn the context of the culture to which it belongs.

When linguists study a new language they often compare it to their own, and consequently they gain a better understanding of not only the new language but of their own language as well. Students who study a foreign language will also learn more about their mother tongue by comparing and contrasting the two languages. You can follow the same comparative method in learning more about culture—

your own, as well as others'. Remember that each culture has developed a set of patterns that are appropriate for that culture. If people do things differently in another culture, they are not "wrong"; they are just different! Always thinking that "culturally different" means "culturally wrong" will only promote intercultural misunderstanding.

The clothes we wear, the way we decorate our homes, the car we drive, the way we address people, and the jobs we choose, and the mates we choose—all these things communicate different things to different people, and they may communicate more, or less, than we intend to. It depends on how the receiver of the message sees, thinks, and feels as much as on what the sender says, thinks, and feels. Communication is a very complex process, even among people from the same culture who speak the same language. The potential problems and the **likelihood** (可能性) of communication **multiply** (增加) when communication takes place between people from different cultures.

Intercultural communication occurs whenever a person from one culture does something that is given meaning by a person from another culture. Communicating across cultures is made difficult by each person's ethnocentric tendencies to perceive objects, events, and behavior through lenses designed in the person's own culture. But an honest desire to communicate with people from other cultures, coupled with an attempt to understand cultural differences, will go a long way in helping you become a successful intercultural communicator.

Communicating in a new culture means learning what to say (words, phrases, meaning, structure), who to communicate with (the role and status of the person), who you are (how you perceive yourself), how you communicate the message (emotional components, nonverbal cues, intonation), why you communicate in a given situation (intentions, values, assumptions), when to communicate (time), and where you can or should communicate. This sounds like an impossible task—but remember, you learned to do all these things in your own native language and culture, mostly without thinking about them. The difference is that now as an adult, you must think about the process, learning a second language and culture.

(选自 http://www.1010jiajiao.com/gzyy/shiti_ id834002cobdfcaceaea3cb3a49ee21817.)

Questions for Discussion

1. Why do we say the meanings of words are very much influenced by culture?
2. What is ethnocentrism?
3. What will promote intercultural misunderstanding?
4. What will help you become a successful intercultural communicator?
5. What does communicating in a new culture mean?

Passage 2

Communication Skills for Workplace Success

Do you want to stand out from the competition? These are some of the top communication skills that recruiters and hiring managers want to see in your resume and cover letter. Highlight these skills and demonstrate them during job interviews, and you'll make a solid first impression. Continue to develop these skills once you're hired, and you'll impress your boss, teammates, and clients.

1. Listening

Being a good listener is one of the best ways to be a good communicator. No one likes communicating with someone who cares only about putting in her two cents and does not take the time to listen to the other person. If you're not a good listener, it's going to be hard to comprehend what you're being asked to do.

Take the time to practice active listening. Active listening involves paying close attention to what the other person is saying, asking clarifying questions, and rephrasing what the person says to ensure understanding ("So, what you're saying is..."). Through active listening, you can better understand what the other person is trying to say, and can respond appropriately.

2. Nonverbal Communication

Your body language, eye contact, hand gestures, and tone of voice all color the message you are trying to convey. A relaxed, open **stance** (站姿) (arms open, legs relaxed), and a friendly tone will make you appear approachable and will encourage others to speak openly with you. Eye contact is also important; you want to look the person in the eye to demonstrate that you focus on them and the conversation. (However, be sure not to stare at the person, which can make him or her uncomfortable.) Also, pay attention to other people's nonverbal signals while you are talking. Often, nonverbal cues convey how a person is really feeling. For example, if the person is not looking you in the eye, he or she might be uncomfortable or hiding the truth.

3. Clarity and Concision(简洁)

Good verbal communication means saying just enough: don't talk too much or too little. Try to convey your message in as few words as possible. Say what you want clearly and directly, whether you're speaking to someone in person, on the phone, or via email. If you **ramble on** (漫谈), your listener will either tune you out or be unsure of what exactly you want.

4. Friendliness

Through a friendly tone, a personal question, or simply a smile, you will encourage your co-workers to engage in an open and honest communication with you. It's important to be polite in all your workplace communications.

This is important in both face-to-face communication and written communication. When you can personalize your emails to co-workers or employees—a quick "I hope you all had a good weekend" at the start of an email can personalize a message and make the recipient feel more appreciated.

5. Confidence

It is important to be confident in your interactions with others. Confidence shows your co-workers that you believe in what you're saying and will follow through. **Exuding** (使渗出) confidence can be as simple as making an eye contact or using a firm but friendly tone. Avoid making statements that sound like questions. Of course, be careful not to sound arrogant or aggressive. Be sure you are always listening to and empathizing with the other person.

6. Empathy(移情作用)

Using phrases as simple as "I understand where you are coming from" demonstrates that you have been listening to the other person and respected their opinions. Active listening can help you tune in to what your conversational partner is thinking and feeling, which will in turn, make it easier to display empathy.

7. Open-Mindedness

A good communicator should enter into any conversation with a flexible, open mind. Be open to listening to and understanding the other person's point of view, rather than simply getting your message across. By being willing to enter into a dialogue, even with people with whom you disagree, you will be able to have more honest, productive conversations.

8. Respect

People will be more open to communicate with you if you convey respect for their ideas. Simple actions like using a person's name, making an eye contact, and actively listening when a person speaks will make the person feel appreciated. On the phone, avoid distractions and stay focused on the conversation.

Convey respect through email by taking the time to edit your message. If you send a **sloppily** (草率地) written, confusing email, the recipient will think that you do not respect her enough to think through your communication with her.

9. Feedback

Being able to give and receive feedback appropriately is an important communication skill. Managers and supervisors should continuously look for ways to provide employees with constructive feedback, be it through emails, phone calls, or weekly status updates.

Similarly, you should be able to accept and even encourage feedback from others. Listen to the feedback you are given, clarify questions if you are unsure of the issue, and make efforts to implement the feedback.

10. Picking the Right Medium

An important communication skill is to simply know what form of communication to use. For example, some serious conversations (layoffs, resignation, changes in salary, etc.) are almost always best done in person.

You should also think about the person with whom you wish to speak. If they are very busy (such as your boss, perhaps), you might want to convey your message through email. People will appreciate your thoughtful means of communication and will be more likely to respond positively to you.

(选自 http://www.thebalancecaneer.com/communication-skills-list-2063779.)

 Questions for Discussion

1. What kind of skills do you need to highlight and demonstrate during job in-

terviews?

2. What kind of nonverbal communication can make others feel uncomfortable?

3. What does good verbal communication mean?

4. What should managers and supervisors continuously look for ways to do?

5. Can you list some of the serious conversations which are almost done in person?

Exercises

I. True or False

Directions: *Decide whether the statements are true (T) or false (F).*

1. Physical context refers to the widely shared expectations people have about the kinds of interactions that normally should occur in different kinds of social events.
2. Semantic noise refers to that the receiver does not derive the meanings intended by the sender.
3. Verbal communication means that messages are sent without words.
4. There are three commonly used models of communication: the linear model, the circular model and the contextualized models.
5. "One Belt, One Road" strategy was proposed by Chinese President Xi Jinping in 2015.
6. Semantics refers to the study of relationships between signs and symbols and what they represent.
7. Nonverbal communication has to do with gestures, movements and closeness of two people when they are talking.
8. Symbols are central to the communication process because they represent the shared meanings that are communicated.
9. The receiver is a person who performs the inverse operation done by the transmitter, reconstructing the message from the signal.
10. The occasion of a communication encounter doesn't control the behavior of the participants.

II. Matching

Directions: *Match the following words and expressions with the correct Chinese.*

1. linear model
2. contextualized model
3. circular model
4. physical context
5. empathy
6. interpersonal context
7. cultural context
8. social context
9. physiological noise
10. psychological noise

A. 心理干扰
B. 物理语境
C. 人际语境
D. 移情作用
E. 直线模式
F. 圆形模式
G. 语境化模式
H. 身体干扰
I. 文化语境
J. 社会语境

III. Translation

A. Directions: *Translate the following paragraph into English.*

没有网络，就没有网络语言。以传播学的视角来看，任何一种新的传播方式都会产生与之相适应的语言表现形式，如平面报纸、有声广播、声像兼备的电视，构成媒体语言家族。网络传播以键盘输入、屏幕阅读，完全不同于日常口耳相传、白纸黑字的交际形式；网络交际的非现场性，使得一笑一颦、喜怒哀乐无从表现，于是各种鲜活的表情符号应运而生，生动传递着交际双方的心态与情感。

B. Directions: *Translate the following paragraph into Chinese.*

The main categories of business communication are critical for performing basic operations and for effectively running and managing a business. Without effective communication processes and tools, operating a business would be inherently difficult. The business world is highly competitive, and most companies stay on the cutting edge of communication technology to ensure that they are receiving and delivering clear messages both internally and externally, to their audience or customers. Businesses have internal communication processes, external communication processes, marketing and sales communications, formal communications, informal communications and a variety of different styles for communicating in different roles and levels of the business. The way in which a business communicates has evolved dramatically, with the inventions and mainstream acceptance of postal mail, telephones, the Internet and mobile phones. Specifically, the Internet and mobile phones are responsible for broad-sweeping changes in business communication models internally and externally.

Chapter 3

Culture and Language

> The study, practical or theoretical, of a language, native or second, cannot be divorced from the cultural context in which that study takes place.
>
> ——Douglas A. Chibby
>
> 语言研究,无论是实践性的还是理论性的,无论是母语还是第二语言,都不能与该研究发生时的文化语境相分离。
>
> ——道格拉斯·A. 奇比

本章导读

文化是天地万物的信息产生、融汇和渗透的过程。我们很难给它下一个严格且精确的定义,因为文化是一个非常宽泛的概念。正如费孝通所说:"文化的深处时常并不是在典章制度之中,而是在人们洒扫应对的日常起居之间。一举手,一投足,看似那样自然,不加做作,可是事实上却全没有任意之处,可说是都受着一套从小潜移默化中得来的价值体系所控制。在什么场合之下,应当怎样举止,文化替我们早就安排好,不必我们临时考虑,犹豫取决的。愈是基本的价值,我们就愈是不假思索。行为时最不经意的,也就是最深入的文化表现。"

本章主要阐述了有关文化的概念,分别从人类学、社会学、跨文化等不同学科领域对文化的定义进行了具体的描述,这些定义既有相同性也有差异性。文化具有习得性、动态性、普遍性、整体性和适应性等特点。中华文化又称中国传统文化、华夏文化和中华古文化,包含民俗、戏曲、棋艺、茶道、中国传统乐器、文人字画等。中华文明绵延五千年,璀璨多姿、博大精深。本章介绍了一些代表人物:杜甫、齐白石、梁启超;中国古代的四大发明以及现代的四大发明。

人们往往有意识地把自己归为人类某一群体的成员并形成文化身份。本章对文化与身份的关系，以及文化身份的定义、形成过程及其特点给予了描述，还对亚文化和共文化进行了比较分析。

Learning Objectives

In this chapter, students will learn how to: define the term of culture, understand the classification of culture, identify the function of culture, describe the characteristics of culture, summarize the process of the formation of cultural identity, and evaluate the cultural diversity.

Warm-up Activities

1. How important is culture to us human beings?
2. How often are we aware of its existence around us?
3. When do you think you will be aware of it? Why?

3.1 Definitions and Classification

Historically, the word "culture" derives from the Latin word "Colere", which could be translated as "to build", "to care for", "to plant" or "to cultivate". Thus, "culture" usually refers to something that is derived from, or created by the intervention of humans—"culture" is cultivated.

With this definition in mind, the word "culture" is often used to describe something refined, especially "high culture", or to describe the concept of selected valuable and **cultivated** (耕作) **artifacts** (手工制品) of a society.

According to *Concise Oxford Dictionary*, culture is "the arts and other **manifestations** (体现) of human intellectual achievement regarded collectively". It refers to intellectual perspective, such as music, an exhibition, dance, etc. When you talk about Qi Baishi, Du Fu, you are talking about Chinese culture.

Culture is the core of communication. It is a very large, complicated concept. Man is the producer of culture and the product of culture. Usually we can define the term "culture" from these four perspectives: anthropological, psychological, sociological and intercultural perspectives.

Culture is a complex and multidimensional. It is in fact too complex to define in a simple term. **Kroeber and Kluckhohn** (1952) identified over 160 different definitions of culture. One of the earliest widely cited definitions by **Tylor** (1887) defines culture as "that complex whole which includes knowledge, belief, art, morals, law, custom, and any other capabilities and habits acquired by man as a member of society."

In this century, culture has been defined by different authors as follows: According to **Mahatma Gandhi**, "No culture can live, if it attempts to be exclusive." **Ruth Benedict** says, "What really binds men together is their culture-the ideas and the standards they have in common." In **Andre Malraux's** view, "Culture is the sum of all the forms of art, of love, and of thought, which, in the course of centuries, have enabled man to be less enslaved."

(1) Anthropological perspective: According to **Kroeber and Kluckhohn,** culture consists of patterns, explicit and **implicit** (含蓄的), of and for behavior acquired and transmitted by symbols, constituting the distinctive achievement of human groups, including their embodiments in artifacts; the essential core of culture consists of traditional ideas and especially their achieved values. For example, we have Greek culture, Chinese culture and Egyptian culture, etc. When we talk about Chinese culture; we mean the customs, civilizations and achievements of China with 5000 years history.

(2) Psychological perspective: According to **Geert Hofstede,** culture is the collective programming of the mind which distinguishes the members of one category of people from another. Culture is "the software of the mind".

(3) Sociological perspective: Culture is defined as a pattern of learned, group-related perception-including both verbal and nonverbal language, attitudes, values, belief systems, disbelief systems and behavior. **Edward Sapir** defined culture **as** what a society does and thinks.

(4) Intercultural perspective: According to **Samovar,** culture is the **deposit** (集合) of knowledge, experience, beliefs, values, attitudes, meanings, **hierarchies** (阶级), religion, notions of time, roles, **spatial relations** (空间观), concepts of the universe, and material objects and possessions acquired by a group of people in the course of generations through individual and group striving.

In conclusion, culture is so large and inclusive that it is really difficult to define. In its broad sense, culture is a set of human-made objective and subjective elements that in the past have increased the probability of survival, resulted in satisfaction for people in an ecological place, and thus become shared among persons who communicate with each other through a common language and lived at the same time. In its narrow sense, culture refers to the acquired knowledge that people use to interpret experience and generate behavior. Culture provides the guidelines that determines the way we think, feel, and behave in society.

3.2 The Nature of Culture

Warm-up Activities

Can you identify three **similes**（明喻）and two **metaphors**（暗喻）to describe the nature of culture?

3.2.1 Culture Is like an Iceberg（冰川）

Culture can be viewed as an iceberg. Nine-tenths of an iceberg is out of sight (below the water line). Likewise, nine-tenths of culture is outside of conscious awareness. The part of the cultural iceberg that is above the water is easy to be noticed, such as food, dress, music, visual arts, drama, crafts, dance, literature, language, celebrations and games. The out-of-awareness part is sometimes called "deep culture": **Courtesy**（礼貌）, contextual conversational patterns, concept of time, personal space, rules of conduct, facial expressions, nonverbal communication, body language, touching, eye contact, and notions of leadership. This part of the cultural iceberg is hidden below the water and is thus below the level of consciousness. People learn this part of culture through imitating models. Once these behaviors and attitudes are learned, they are automatic and taken for granted.

In short, culture is like an iceberg, it is very beautiful yet dangerous. The majority of culture is below the surface, and only the visible part makes your study of culture difficult. In terms of business culture, the environment, behaviors, ethnic, language, nonverbal symbols, and religion are above the "sea level". They are **norms**（规则）, rules, **perceptions**（知觉）, **stereotypes**（刻板形象）, networks, business philosophy, subcultures and subgroups, and values.

In order to truly understand a culture, you must explore the behaviors below the "sea level". Then how to build successful business relationships when cultural differences exist. The common elements of trust, **sincerity** (真诚), and **integrity** (正直) are necessary.

3.2.2 Culture Is Like an Onion

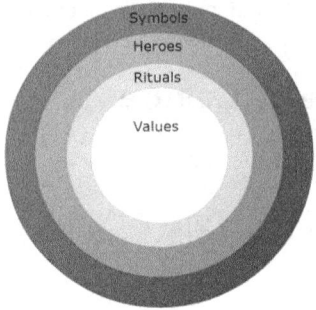

Geert Hofstede describes culture as an onion. He states the following four levels: symbols, heroes, rituals and values, which have been **depicted** (描绘) like the skins of an onion.

Culture is just like an onion; we can peel it layer by layer in order to reveal the content. The outer skin refers to the symbols, such as words, color or other artifacts that carry a special meaning. It indicates that symbols represent the most **superficial** (表面的) and the easiest part to perceive by an outsider and the least important one to an insider. Words, gestures, pictures, dress, hairstyles, flags, status symbols etc. —all belong to this category.

The second layer includes heroes, such as the admired persons who serve as an example for behavior. The third layer is rituals such as the ways of greeting and paying respect. They are collective activities that are considered socially essential within a culture such as sports events. Religious rituals, practical rituals and art performances are emphasized in Japan, Korea and China respectively. For example, the ceremony of serving tea varies from nation to nation. Therefore, tea culture has evolved into diverse styles in the process of spreading throughout the world. And the inner nucleus layer represents values which are the deeper manifestations of culture and the most difficult to understand by an outsider.

3.2.3　Culture is Our Software

According to Geert Hofstede, culture is "the software of the mind". Culture is like DOS or windows. It is a mental set of windows through which all of life is viewed. Humans around the word are physically pretty much the same. We can think of physical selves as the hardware, but we cannot be said to be humans until we programmed and each of us is programmed by our home culture. Culture is the basic operating system that makes us human. An infant is a potential human at birth and become a real human with culture. The computer stops working as a result of its incompatibility with someone else's software.

Individuals embody cultural software: they are literally information made flesh. They spread it to others through communication and social learning. Human minds and institutions provide the ecology in which cultural software grows, thrives, and develops. Human cultural software is created out of the diverse elements of cultural transmission, also known as "**memes**."(文化基因)

3.2.4　Culture Is like the Water a Fish Swims In

A fish takes the water for granted because it is totally surrounded by the water that it really cannot imagine another environment. We usually take culture for granted since everything we see and do takes place in the same culture. Everyone is swimming in the same water. Our culture is so much a part of who we are and what the world is like for us that we do not notice it.

3.2.5　Culture Is the Grammar of Our Behavior

Culture is the grammar of our behavior. Culture is what people need to know in order to behave appropriately in any society. Most people find it difficult to describe the meaning system of their own culture, just as native speakers are unable to describe the grammatical conventions of their native language. Like the grammar of a language, cultural grammars are repetitive. They are made up of basic patterns that occur again and again. This pattern shows up in the language, traditional architecture and in social relationships. For example, in traditional Chinese architecture, rites can be arranged into three levels: etiquette and custom, law and discipline of rite, and sacrifice offering. The first level was **correlated** (有相互关系的) with the distinction between inside and outside; the second level, with priority in rank; and the third level, with the ancestral temple of a ruling house. So Chinese traditional architecture was shown as distinction between inside and outside, priority in rank, and ancestral temple of a raling house must be the first.

3.3 Characteristics of Culture

Warm-up Activities

(1) 老挝谚语："一根柴棍烧不成旺火,一根木棍围不成篱笆。" Can you find any equivalence in Chinese proverbs?

(2) 中国古语："不积跬步,无以至千里。" Can you translate it into English?

(3) 阿拉伯谚语："金字塔是一块块石头垒成的。"欧洲谚语："伟业非一日之功。" Can you translate them into English?

Regardless of how many definitions we could have examined, there would have been a great deal of agreement concerning the seven major characteristics of culture. Examining these characteristics will help you become a better communicator for two reasons. Chairman Xi Jinping set us a good example. He cited these proverbs to talk about the bilateral relations between Laos and China to emphasize the importance of cooperation and trust. As a saying goes in Laos, "One piece of firewood does not make high flames, and a single wood stick does not make a fence." Can you find any equivalence in Chinese proverbs? The Chinese believe that people, if united, are as strong as a fortress, and flame runs high if everyone adds wood to it("众志成城"、"众人拾柴火焰高"). In the opening ceremony for the "Belt and Road Initiative" forum, Chairman Xi Jinping cited the following proverbs to call us for the dedicated efforts and encouraged us to pursue this initiative step by step and deliver outcome one by one in order to bring true benefit to both the world and all people. An ancient Chinese saying goes, "A long journey can be covered only by taking one step at a time."(不积跬步,无以至千里) You will find something in common in the Arabian proverb, which says that the pyramid was built by piling one stone on another. In Europe, there is also the saying that "Rome wasn't built in a day."

As we move through these characteristics, the strong connection between culture and communication will become apparent. You might be exposed to culture—either your own or someone else's. Remember, most of culture is in the taken-for-granted realm and below the conscious level. Learning about culture can therefore be a stimulating awakening as you give meaning to your actions and the actions of others.

3.3.1 Culture Is Learned

Culture is learned. If we can't learn from those who lived before, we would not have culture. Therefore, learning is the most important of all the characteristics of culture. If a baby was cut off from all adult care, training, he can still instinctively eat, drink, defecate, urinate and cry. But what and when he would eat, where he would defecate and urinate, it is most likely that he would do all these things randomly.

But where and how we can learn culture is hard to explain. We learn our culture through interactions with other people. It's hard to name who are the "other people". We receive instructions from our family, friends, and numerous other "teachers" consciously or unconsciously. Without the advantages of knowledge from those who lived before us, we would not have culture. In fact, The idea that "the group's knowledge stored up (in memories, books and objects) for future use, "is at the core of the concept of culture. All of us are born with the basic needs that create and shape behavior—but how we go about meeting those needs and developing behaviors to cope with them is learned. For example, firstly, we need to satisfy our basic needs (food, shelter, physical protection) of the society. Secondly, we should meet our derived needs (organization of work, distribution of food, defense, social control); finally we have our integrative needs such as psychological security, social harmony, and purpose in life.

When we look at the word "learned" as it applies to culture, we find that it has numerous meanings. We learn our culture in many ways and from a variety of sources either consciously or unconsciously. Conscious learning is easier to understand because we are learning at the cognitive level. We are reading about or being told or shown what culture wants us to know. The influence of culture becomes habitual and subconscious for us and makes our life easier, just as breathing, walking and other functions of our body are relegated to subconscious controls, freeing the conscious parts of the brain of this burden and releasing it for other activities.

From these examples we can see that culture is not **innate** (天生的); it is learned. Without learning, we would not have culture. Culture is learned, not inherited. It derives from one's social environment, not from one's genes. We can learn our culture through proverbs, folklore, art, and mass media. We learn our culture through our family, neighborhood, schools, social groups, physical surroundings, etc. Culture is transmitted from generation to generation.

(1) We Learn Our Culture Through Proverbs

In nearly every culture, proverbs, communicated in colorful and vivid language, offer an important set of instructions for members to follow. These "words of wisdom" endure, so each generation learns about what a culture deems important. Proverbs are learned easily and repeated with great regularity; they soon become part of an individual's belief system. Because all people, regardless of their culture, share common experiences, many of the same proverbs appear throughout the world. However, there are also many proverbs that cultures use to teach important lessons that are unique to that particular culture.

(2) We Learn Our Culture from Folk Tales, Legends, and Myths

Legends, folk tales, and myths do more than cultural values: "They confront cosmic questions about the world as a whole." In addition, they can tell us about specific details of life that might be important to a group of people. The stories each culture tells their people, whether in the form of folk tales, legends, or myths, are all intended to transmit the culture from person to person and from generation to generation, whether it is Pinocchio's nose growing larger because of his lying or the boy who cried wolf, in the Western, or folks like **Nvwa** (女娲) patching up the sky, **Houyi** (后羿) shooting down the suns in Chinese folks. Folk tales constantly reinforce our fundamental values.

Every culture has thousands of tales, each stressing a fundamental value. Americans **revere** (崇敬) the tough, independent, fast-shooting cowboy of the Old West, while Chinese like the spirit in Yu Gong moving away the mountains, which tells us the importance of working hard and perseverance. Laziness is regarded a crime. It is said recreation will make you less determined. It is almost like a religion that has deeply impacted Chinese in China and overseas.

The Journey to the West carries a lot of information about traditional Chinese culture. It talks about the real meaning of human life: how to improve oneself and cultivate into Buddha hood etc. *The Journey to the West* has a strong background in Chinese folk religion, Chinese mythology and value systems; the **pantheon** (众神; 名流) of Taoist and Buddhist **deities** (神灵; 神明) reflect the belief that is still current in modern Chinese folk religion.

As we have seen, myths are useful tools for teaching culture because they cover a wide range of cultural concerns. Perhaps their significant contribution is that they deal with the ideas that matter more to a culture—ideas about life, death, relationships, nature, and the like. Although ancient Chinese mythology does not have relatively complete plots and mythological figures who don't have systematic genealogy, they have distinct features of oriental culture, among which the spirit of esteeming virtue is particularly significant. When compared with Western mythology, especially Greek mythology, this spirit of esteeming virtue is even more prominent. In Western mythology, especially Greek mythology, the criteria for judging whether a god is good or not are mostly the god's wisdom and strength, while in ancient Chinese mythology, the criterion lies in morality. This way of thinking is deeply rooted in Chinese culture. For thousands of years, this spirit of esteeming virtue has affected people's comments on historical figures and expectations of real people.

According to ancient Chinese legend, the dragon is a mythical animal which has scales, horns, whiskers, claws, wind, and rain. In traditional Chinese culture, the dragon is regarded as a lucky animal, and the Chinese nation regards itself as the descendant of the dragon. Since ancient times, the dragon is the embodiment of the emperor, and the common people regard the dragon as the pride of traditional culture.

(3) We Learn Our Culture Through Art

As **Nanda** puts it, "Art is a symbolic way of communicating. One of the most important functions of art is to communicate, display, and reinforce important cultural themes and values. The arts thus have an integrative function in society." One of the functions that Nanda is referring to is how the individual, through art, learns about himself or herself. In Eastern cultures, most art depicts objects, animals, and landscapes, and seldom focuses on people. Compared with Western art, Chinese painting is more concerned with water-based techniques, rather than oils or acrylics. In addition, Chinese painting is traditionally more stylized, more abstract and less realistic than Western types. It also emphasizes the importance of white space and may be said to favour landscape painting over portrait art or figure painting.

Western art, however, often emphasizes people. This difference reflects a difference in views. Easterners believe that nature is more powerful and important than a single individual, whereas Americans and Europeans consider people as the center of the universe.

The biggest difference between Eastern and Western architecture is that the East highlights the natural landscape while the West focuses on the building. Sculptures are both the outstanding heritage of human civilization and cultures. Western sculpture originated in ancient Greece which put more emphasis on the human body. The God portrayed as a perfect human being who worship God. In Chinese ancient times, the arts tend to focus on arts and crafts, in ritual, ceremonial vessels on their artistic genius.

In the west, in the Greek temples, the sculptures of various Gods, of the Rome heroes, of the medieval religious sculptures, of the modern Renaissance sculptures. In the process of a series of changes, it reflects the transformation in the culture of the west from the early universe "ontology" to the "epistemology" to the modern "theory of value". As for Chinese sculptures, is can be said to be the history of Buddhist sculpture.

With this idea in mind, Qi Baishi's works feature the natural style, which are based on his life. The subjects of his paintings include almost everything: common animals, scenery, figures, toys, vegetables and so on. Even though Baishi wasn't the first artist to focus on small things in nature, he was acknowledged for his very beautiful and unique way of painting such common images. Some artists praised him for his "freshness and spontaneity that he brought to the familiar genres of birds and flowers, insects and grasses, hermit-scholars and landscapes". One of Baishi's earlier series of works—"The Carp" was praised because of its simple style without any excessive decorations or writings. He is especially good at describing shrimps. The spirit of the shrimp and the way it floats above water are vividly illustrated with a little amount of ink.

(4) We Learn Our Culture Through Mass Media

Mass media are the tools of communication. They allow us to record and pass information rapidly to a large, scattered audience. They extend our ability to each other by helping us overcome limits caused by time and space. Mass media can be divided into two groups: print media and electronic media. By print media, we mean books, newspapers and magazines. Electronic media include television, radio and movie.

In the United States and other Western cultures, the mass media do much more than supply entertainment. Mass media are media intended for a large audience. It may take the form of broadcast media, as in the case of television, radio or print media, like newspapers and magazines. Internet media can also attain mass media status, and many media outlets maintain a Web presence to take advantage of the ready availability of Internet in many regions of the world. Some people also refer to it as the "mainstream media", referencing the fact that it tends to stick to prominent stories which will be of interest to a general audience, sometimes ignoring controversial breaking news. Many people around the world rely on this form of media for news and entertainment, and globally, it is a huge industry.

As former President **Fidel Valdez Ramos** gave the speech in "Kyoto Culture Symposium 2006", in our time, a process of "cultural globalization" has also been gathering force. Cultural globalization is hitting traditional societies even harder than economic globalization has done.

Even in countries where the globalized economy has not yet prevailed, the customs and values of the internationalist culture are fast-spreading, especially among young people through the global mass media. And traditionalist people see this alien culture as threatening ways of life to which they are accustomed.

Traditionalists in Asia complain about the impact of junk food, of sex and violence in the mass media, of "rap" music and "pun" hair-styles, and of the alienating effects these cultural imports from the West can have on impressionable young Asians.

And we all know how difficult it is for parents, schools, communities—and even governments—to protect their societies against intrusive cultures.

As we have said elsewhere, the messages that are strategic for any culture are repeated, reinforced, and come from various sources. Think for a moment of the thousands of ways you have been told the importance of being popular and well like, or the messages you have received concerning competition and winning. Our games, sports, toys, movies, and so on all fortify the need to win.

We conclude our description of the first characteristic of culture by reminding ourselves of how our discussion is related directly to intercultural communication. First, most of the behaviors we label as cultural are not only automatic and invisible, but also engaged in without being a ware of them. Second, common experiences produce common behaviors. The sharing of experience and behavior binds members and makes a culture unique.

3.3.2 Culture Is Dynamic

Culture is subject to change rather than **static** (静止的). It's dynamic, constantly changing and evolving under the impact of events and through contact with other cultures. As ideas and products evolve within a culture, they can produce change through the **mechanisms** (机制) of invention and **diffusion** (传播). Popular culture, which comprises the products of the culture that are widely consumed such as music, food, hairstyles, clothing, recreational activities and their equipment, styles of cars, furnishings—does constantly change.

Usually there are four major aspects accounting for the change of cultures: technological invention, disasters, cultural contact, and environmental factors. History **abounds** (充满) with examples of how cultures have changed because of laws, shifts in values, natural disasters, wars, or other calamities. For example, the COVID-19 has changed the way people greet each other. Technology is called the agent of cultural change. For example, technology has altered the way space and time affecting human communication. Take Gaotie (high-speed rail) in China for example: the emergence of high-speed rail greatly facilitates Chinese people's travel, shortens the time of people's travel, expands the scope of people's travel, and changes people's life.

3.3.3 Culture Is Based on Symbols

Culture combines visible and invisible things around us. Culture is the total sum of human society and its meanings. Culture is pervasive and perpetual. It starts slow but steadily advances like a flywheel to the point where it builds under its own momentum, and is difficult to slow down.

As indicated, the symbols any culture employs take a variety of forms. Culture can use the spoken word as a symbol and tell people about the importance of freedom. They can use the written word as a symbol and let others read about. They can use nonverbal actions, such as shaking hands or bowing as a symbol to greet one another. They can use flags as symbols to claim territory or demonstrate loyalty. They have the means to use automobiles or jewelries as symbols of success and status.

3.3.4 Culture Is Integrated

Culture should be thought of as integrated wholes—cultures are coherent and with logical systems, the parts of which to a degree are interrelated. In order to keep culture functioning, all aspects of the culture must be integrated. As **Edward T. Hall** said, "You touch a culture in one place and everything else is affected." The introduction of a single technological innovation may set off a whole series of related changes.

Values towards materialism will influence family sizes, work ethics, spiritual pursuits and the like. For example, the COVID-19 crisis has caused many of us to question our values and what we stand for as human beings. While the coronavirus crisis has shaken a lot of people's sense of security, it has also helped us to realize which aspects of our lives—both personal and professional—might have been taken for granted. Throughout this crisis, we may have reordered our priorities, realizing that we wish to devote more time to certain things such as family, friends and hobbies. The trauma brought by the pandemic may have also alerted us that how short and precious life is.

3.3.5 Culture Is Adaptive

More and more women work as CEOs in major companies or as officials in government instead of staying at home looking after their children. Both women and men have made adaptation to this cultural change.

To illustrate, the innovation of 5G technology in our material culture has had profound consequences on the nonmaterial aspects of our culture.

5G technology is a product of global innovation and cooperation. Its industrial, supply, and value chains are so widely spread and interlinked that almost everyone has a stake in it.

Drawing an iron curtain would therefore have an impact on all, Chinese, Europeans, Americans, and others alike. "The life history of the individual is first and foremost an accommodation to the patterns and standards traditionally handed down in his community. From the moment of his birth, the customs into which he is born shape his experience and behavior. By the time he can talk, he is the little creature of his culture, and by the culture he is grown and able to take part in its activities, its habits are his habits, its beliefs are his beliefs, its impossibilities are his impossibilities." (Ruth Benedict)

3.4 Classification of Culture

Warm-up Activities

Please match each word from the column: cars, dresses, buildings, food, laws, values, customs, and equality.

Culture identity refers to one's sense of belonging to a particular culture or ethnic group. As we mentioned before, culture can be classified into different types from different perspectives. For example, there is Chinese culture, American culture, Asian culture, European culture, ancient culture, and modern culture.

Take Chinese culture for example: the spirit of **humanism** (人文主义) and morality is the lifeblood of Chinese culture. Old Chinese proverbs, such as "every man alive has a duty toward his country", reflect **patriotism** (爱国主义).

Xi Jinping loves reading books and using **allusions** (成语典故). When making a visit or attending important international meetings, he not only repeatedly quotes Chinese classics, but also does as the Romans do; for example, he more than once cites the visited countries' proverbs, quotes of famous people, speeches of important members of the governments and even skillfully conducts matching of Chinese and favorite foreign quotations through centering on such themes as "friendship, cooperation, peace" and so forth, vividly unfolding Chinese dispositions before the world's eyes, telling Chinese attitude and delivering Chinese voices.

In January, 2016, during the period of making a trip to Egypt, Xi published a signed article. In this article, Xi retrospected the friendly communication history of Chinese and Arabian as well as the profound sentiments of friendship. Xi said, "As the Arabian proverb goes that 'if you want to go fast, walk alone; and if you want to go far, walk together', Chinese people often say ' It is easy to live when we have many friends' , which couldn't be better to describe the Sino-Arab relations. " In general, we can roughly divide culture into three categories.

(1) Material Culture vs. Non-material Culture

The culture of any society is usually thought to be of two kinds: material and non-material. **Material culture** includes the man-made phenomena which have physical properties such as height, breadth, and weight. A boat, a machine, a house—all these objects are part of the material culture. The non-material culture is that portion of the environment which surrounds man and which has an impact on his behavior, but which these material properties: values, beliefs, traditions, and all the other habits and ideas invented and acquired by man as a member of society.

Contemporary sociological theory tends to assign primary importance to the non-material culture in choosing problems for study. It assumes, for example, that boats, planes, automobiles, and so forth, are not nearly so important as the traditions we have developed which make their manufacture possible—indeed, which prescribe how we are to use them. The emphasis of contemporary sociology is to insist that the material culture would not exist. The non-material culture first been available to suggest the ideas which are embodied in the inventions of material culture. There are seven components of non-material culture: gestures, languages, values, norms, sanctions, folkways, and mores.

(选自 http://www.yu100.com/news/1001/370528.html.)

(2) Big Culture vs. Small Culture

Big culture refers to those intellectual and artistic activities, such as education, institution, literature, art, music, etc. Small culture refers to the way of life of the given people who share values, customs, norms, etc.

The "small culture" is sometimes compared to the software of the mind, as it defines people's thinking, action, etc. For example, in terms of their customs, we may want to know how people get married. Parents tell their children about right and wrong; they are actually teaching them values. When we try to observe how people look at each other when they are talking, we make observation about their nonverbal communication.

(3) Dominant Culture vs. Subculture

From the point of influence, culture can be divided into dominant culture and subculture. Dominant culture refers to the culture that is shared by most people and exerts greater influence.

Complex societies are made up of a large number of groups with which people identify and from which distinctive values, norms, and rules for behaviors are derived. These groups have been labeled as subculture.

Can you identify some Chinese ethnic groups? As a large united multi-national state, China is composed of 56 ethnic groups. Among them, Han Chinese account for 91.59% of the overall Chinese population and the other 55 make up the remaining 8.41%.

Sub-culture is a culture that exists within dominant culture, and is often based on economic or social class, ethnicity, race, or geographic region. In China, Han culture can be seen as the dominant culture. We have Northern culture and Southern culture, Tibetan culture, Buddhist culture, youth culture, women culture, etc. However, the prefix "sub" implies that members of the non-dominant group are deficient. Many scholars prefer to use the term "**co-culture**".

We use the word "co-culture" when talking about groups or social communities exhibiting communication characteristics, perceptions, values, beliefs, and practices that are significantly different enough to distinguish them from the other groups, communities, and the dominant culture. It suggests that these groups are equal and co-exist with the dominant culture. When we use culture in discussing the differences, we are applying the term to the dominant culture found in most societies. Finally, we need to know the concept of subgroup. It usually does not involve the same large number of people and is not necessarily thought of as accumulating values and patterns of behavior over generations in the same way as cultures do.

3.5 Language

Language is yet another feature that is common to all cultures. As **Haviland** puts it, "Without our capacity for complex language, human culture as we know, it could not exist." When you communicate with people from other countries, it is unlikely that they will have the exactly same word or meaning in mind. The difference in thought sends shock throughout the communication process. All understanding, therefore, is at the same time a misunderstanding and all agreement of feelings and thoughts is at the same time a means for growing apart.

Language plays an important part in culture learning. Language is a reflection of cultural environment and its values. As **Winston Brembeck** puts it, "to know another's language and not his culture is a very way to make a fluent fool of one's self."

3.5.1 The Relationship Between Language and Culture

Language reflects culture and that language and culture are closely linked. On one hand, language is an expression of a particular culture, which is used as the main medium through which culture is expressed. On the other hand, culture is one of the integral parts of language.

According to Geertz (2000), "culture is a system of inherited conceptions expressed in language, by means of which people communicate, perpetuate and develop their knowledge and attitude towards life." We cannot be competent in the language if we do not understand the culture that has shaped and informed it, and we cannot learn a second language if we do not have the awareness of that culture and do not know how it is related to our own culture.

According to Geert Hofstede, "Knowing a country's language, although clearly helpful, is no guarantee of understanding its cultural mindset, and some of the most difficult problems have been created by individuals who have a high level of fluency but a low level of cultural understanding." "Moreover, members of a culture tend to assume that highly fluent visitors know the customs and rules of behavior, and these visitors are judged severely when violations occur."

3.5.2 The Relationship Between Language and Communication

As Hall points out, "culture is communication and communication is culture." which implies when people look at culture and communication, it is hard to decide which is the voice and which is the echo. Culture and communication are influenced by each other and cannot separate from each other. Culture cannot be what is like today without communication and at the same time communication cannot be what is like today without culture. Communication is influenced by culture and at the same time culture is also influenced by the communication and they are inseparable from each other.

First, the way of the communication and the content in the communication are determined by the culture and help define the culture. As we know all social units develop a culture. Even in two-person relationship, a culture develops over time. Different cultures may cultivate different rules, values and norms. These different rules, values and norms are rooted in people's minds for a long time and unconsciously direct people's behaviors when people communicate with each other.

Second, culture is learned, acted out, transmitted, and preserved through communication. When two people or two groups of people representing two kinds of cultures communicate with each other, it not only means a simple exchange of ideas but also means the exchange of two cultures. In the process of communication, different kinds of cultures are interacted, mingled and learned. So, communication is a medium of cultural exchange and cultural inheritance.

3.5.3 The Relationship Between Culture and Communication

Understanding human communication means knowing about what happens when people communicate, why it happened, and finally what we can do to influence the result of communication. Culture governs and defines the circumstances under which various messages may or may not be sent or interpreted. Communication varies in different cultures. And both the verbal and nonverbal communication reflect the culture of a certain community. The relationship between communication and culture is crucial to the understanding of intercultural communication.

Key Terms

courtesy	礼貌
perceptions	知觉, 觉察
stereotypes	刻板形象
norms	标准, 行为模式
humanism	人文精神
patriotism	爱国主义
allusions	典故

artifacts	物质
material culture	物质文化
nonmaterial culture	非物质文化
dominant culture	主流文化
subculture	亚文化
co-culture	共文化

Notes

1. **Mohandas Karamchand Gandhi** (1869–1948), known as Mahatma Gandhi, the leader of the Indian national liberation movement and the leader of the Indian National Congress Party. Gandhi is the Father of India and the founder of Gandhi Doctrine, a modern political theory advocating non-violent resistance. His spiritual thought led the country to independence and break away from British colonial rule. His philosophy of "Non-Violence" has influenced the Nationalists all over the world and the international movements for peaceful change.

    甘地(1869—1948),被称为"圣雄甘地"和国父,是印度民族解放运动的领导人和印度国民大会党领袖。甘地是印度国父和"甘地主义"的创始人,甘地主义是一种提倡非暴力抵抗的现代政治理论。他的精神思想带领国家走向独立,摆脱了英国的殖民统治。他的"非暴力"哲学思想影响了世界各国的民族主义者和国际和平变革运动。

2. **Clyde K. M. Kluckhohn,** an American anthropologist. He taught at the University of New Mexico and at Harvard University. Kluckhohn is known primarily for his studies of the Navajo and of personality and culture. His other works include *An Introduction to Anthropology, Mirror for Man* (1949) and *Culture: A Critical Review of Concepts and Definitions* (1952).

    克莱德·克拉克洪,美国人类学家。曾在新墨西哥大学和哈佛大学任教。克拉克洪以其对美国最大的印第安部落——纳瓦霍的文化和个性研究而著称。他的其他作品包括《人类学导论》《人类的镜子》(1949)以及《文化:关于概念和定义的探讨》(1952)。

3. **Edward Sapir,** a linguist and an anthropologist. He is noted for his work with the ethnology and linguistics of Native American groups, and sees language as a verbal symbol of human nations. His works include *Language: An Introduction to*

the Study of Speech.

爱德华·萨丕尔，语言学家、人类学家。他以对美国土著的民族学和语言学的研究而著称，他认为语言是人类关系的言语符号。其主要著作为《语言：言语研究入门》。

4. **Ruth Benedict**, a famous contemporary American cultural anthropologist. At the beginning of the 20th century, a few female scholars, influenced by Franz Boas and Edward Sapir, put forward the earliest theory of cultural configuration, believing that culture, like an individual, has different types and characteristics. Benedict studied English literature in his early years, so her works are well written and good at poetry and delicate description. Among her works, *Patterns of Culture* and *The Chrysanthemum and the Sword* are the most famous. Although the importance of her discussion has been replaced by other theories, the problems and concerns raised in her works are still valued and concerned by anthropology, history, and other disciplines.

鲁思·本尼迪克特，美国当代著名文化人类学家。20世纪初，少数女性学者，受到法兰兹·鲍亚士和爱德华·萨皮尔提出最早的文化形貌论的影响，认为文化如同个体，具有不同的类型与特征。本尼迪克特早年学习英国文学，故其作品文笔高妙，并善于写诗和细腻描述。她的作品中，尤以《文化模式》与《菊与刀》最为著名。尽管她论述的重要性已被其他理论取代，但其著作中提出的问题，至今仍受到人类学、历史学及其他学科的重视与关注。

5. **Andre Malraux** (1901–1976), a novelist, a critic, and a politician. In 1933, he won the Goncourt Prize for literature and was the former French Minister of Culture.

安德烈·马尔罗（1901—1976），小说家、评论家、政治家，1933年他获得龚古尔文学奖，曾任法国前文化部部长。

6. **Fei Xiaotong** (1910–2005), born in Wujiang, Jiangsu Province, a famous sociologist, anthropologist, ethnologist, social activist and, one of the founders of Chinese sociology and anthropology. Under the guidance of his tutor Malinowski, Fei Xiaotong completed his doctoral thesis *"Jiangcun Economy"*, which is known as a milestone in the development of anthropological field investigation and theoretical work, and has become a classic work in the international anthropological

field.

费孝通(1910—2005),江苏吴江人,著名社会学家、人类学家、民族学家、社会活动家,中国社会学和人类学的奠基人之一。费孝通在其导师马林诺夫斯基指导下完成了博士论文《江村经济》,被誉为"人类学实地调查和理论工作发展中的一个里程碑",成为国际人类学界的经典之作。

7. *Journey to the West*: a classical Chinese novel which tells the stories between Buddha, Gods, and evil spirits. This novel was written during the mid-Ming Dynasty and reflected the social life of that time. The early circulated editions didn't have the author's name, but now we generally believe that its author is Wu Cheng'en, a man from Huai'an, Jiangsu Province.

《西游记》是一部讲述佛、神、鬼故事的中国古典小说。这部小说写于明朝中期,反映了当时的社会生活。早期流传的版本没有署名,但我们普遍认为作者是吴承恩,江苏淮安人。

8. **Winston Brembeck**, an American educator. "The teaching method without introducing culture of the target and source languages, can only cultivate a big fool who can speak fluently. "The purpose of foreign language teaching is to cultivate intercultural communication ability. Thus, foreign language lessons do not only teach the students to learn foreign language; they should also introduce the culture to the students.

温斯顿·布雷贝克,美国教育家,他说:"没有将目标语和源语的文化引入的教学,只能培养出能够流利说话的大傻瓜。"外语教学的目的是为了培养学生的跨文化交际能力。因此,外语课程不仅要教学生学习语言本身,还应该让学生了解与该语言相关的文化。

Case 1

"Privacy" is translated as "yin si"(隐私) in Chinese. Traditionally, in the Chinese mind, "yin si" is associated with that which is closed or unfair. If someone is said to have "yin si", **meddlers** (冥想者) will be attracted to **pry** (窥探) into his or her affairs. So people always state that they don't have "yin si". On the contrary, Americans often declare their intention to protect their privacy. Their understanding of privacy is that others have no right to pry into things which belong to themselves alone and have nothing to do with others. One who is too noisy and who spreads rumors is said to violate the right to privacy.

In the evening, Sonia and I went to a bar for dinner. In China, when people mention bars, something bad usually comes to mind. But here, the bar was a quiet and tastefully laid out place. People spoke quite softly, afraid of interrupting their neighbors, and sat face to face as they drank, sometimes three or five persons sitting together.

This sort of atmosphere was totally different from my preconception, so I wanted to take a picture. Sonia stopped me, "Don't you see these people pouring out their hearts? Maybe they are colleagues, friends, and secret lovers. They came here looking for a peaceful place free from interruption by others. They wouldn't want to leave any trace of their having come here. So taking their pictures would be a serious violation of their rights to privacy."

Is there a privacy between husband and wife? One of Sonia's friends married a talented Chinese man, but recently she became so angry that she wanted a divorce. The reason was that her husband had opened one of her letters and looked through her purse. The husband didn't realize that this is not tolerated in the U. S. He thought being a couple was like being one person; why couldn't he see the letter or the contents of the purse? Truly, everyone, even those living as a couple, needs room—not only in three-dimensional space, but in the heart.

(选自 http://easylearn.baidu.com/.)

 Questions for Discussion

1. What's the different attitude towards "privacy"?

2. What's the different attitude towards "bar"?

3. How will Americans think about taking pictures in the bar?

4. Is it appropriate that husband open his wife's letters and look through her purse?

5. How do Americans consider the relationship between husband and wife?

Case 2

With traditional Chinese culture spreads cultures around the world and more and more people become interested in Chinese culture, foreign culture and concepts have begun to spread into China too. It is inevitable that with the increasing development of communication and integration, more and more foreigners are studying Chinese and great masses of Chinese people are studying English in order to aid this goal of communication, even popular cultural aspects have begun to spread as well.

Nowadays Chinese are gradually begin to celebrate such Western holidays as Christmas and Valentine's Day. Western food, especially fast food establishments like McDonald's and KFC have become popular. This can be contrasted with the growth of interest in Chinese culture abroad. Chinese food is a phenomenon on its own which can be seen in the growth of such restaurants in North America and Europe. A large part of this expansion into areas outside of Asia is due to the immigration of Chinese that has gone on for centuries. Chinatowns in San Francisco, New York, and London have provided gateways from which Chinese culture has been spread. This had increased as business with China has expanded and international ties are forged. It is through cultural communication and integration that we learn from each other and grow closer.

(选自 www. kekenet. com/Kouyu/200806/42647. shtml.)

 Questions for Discussion

1. What kind of Western holidays do Chinese celebrate and what kind of fast food become popular?

2. Why does Chinese food become so popular in North America and Europe?

Case 3

Chinese Dragon

Dragon is a **deified** (神化) animal worshipped by Chinese from immemorial time. But what is it? No one knows. Some people think that the Yanzi crocodile is the archetype of the dragon. However, most people hold that dragon is a combination of many animals. And the abilities of those animals have been collected to it. Wang Chong, a scholar of Han Dynasty, once pointed that the horn of dragon was like deer's, the head was like camel's, the eyes was like rabbit's, the neck was like snake's, the belly was like clam's, the squama was like carp's, the talon was like eagle's, the palm was like tiger's and the ear was like cattle's .

Among the unearthed cultural relics which have the history of more than five thousand years are there jade pig dragon and jade dragon. They are much simpler than the dragon today. We can imagine people had added more characteristics to it after the jade dragon having been created. Then it turned to the dragon that we know now gradually.

Why ancient Chinese people wanted to create a dragon? Many scholars think that it originated from the worship to animals. In remote **antiquity** (古老) the main activity of human was hunting. So animals were what people most interested in. Ancient people had to survive from hunting animals which were the main food for them and also had to **dodge** (逃避) the attacks which were the threats to their lives from fierce animals. In the process of those activities, worships and fancies to the special abilities of those animals including flying in the sky, swimming in the river, walking without feet and hibernating etc. were originated. They put the special abilities together and created the dragon whose power were beyond all other animals. They made dragon a **deity** (神) and worshiped it thereafter.

Later, dragon became the symbol of power and monarch. Now it is the symbol of whole Chinese.

(选自 http://www.bigear.cn/news-65-26165.html/.)

 Questions for Discussion

1. In Chinese mind, what kind of animal is dragon?
2. According to Wang Chong, what kind of animal is dragon?
3. Why did ancient Chinese people want to create a dragon?
4. How did Chinese make dragon a deity?
5. What did dragon symbolize?

Case 4

The Need to Understand Culture A Designer's Perspective

Imagine this: you buy a new watch and its hands turn **counterclockwise** (逆时针

方向的). Would you return it to the store immediately or would you try to adjust to a whole new way of thinking? What if stop signs all of a sudden were squares instead of octagons; would you immediately recognize them on the road? These two examples, while mildly amusing, start to paint the picture of a world that has been designed without recognizing a user's cultural background. As user experience designers, we must acknowledge not only physical and cognitive differences in people, but cultural ones as well.

Some anthropologists view culture as anything outside of an individual's genetic control that serves to adjust the individual within their ecological communities. Other anthropologists believe culture consists of whatever it is one has to know in order to operate in an acceptable manner with the culture's other members. And still another group of anthropologists view culture as systems of shared symbols and meanings.

Within engineering, questions of culture were also explored by creating a whole new field of study: cultural **ergonomics** (人类工程学). Cultural ergonomics emerged in the mid-1970s when Alphonse Chapanis, the father of ergonomics wrote papers and organized a conference on this topic. He recognized that one of the most challenging problems facing ergonomics today is deciding how to make ergonomics robust enough to cope with national and cultural variables, including anthropometric differences, the babel of tongues, physiological differences, psychological differences, as well as practices and customs.

One approach is for designers to segment cultures in order to inform their designs. Designers have to understand the user's world in order to correctly design for them. So then ask yourself those questions: Is it acceptable for designers to place cultural identities on people? Or do people need to self-assign their culture? Membership of a specific cultural group can be defined in two ways: objectively and subjectively. Theorists define objective sense of culture as when a person has sufficient social attributes in common for members to constitute a distinct social group. Subjective sense of culture, however, requires that some one must be recognized by both themselves and others in one's society as being part of a social category. The subjective sense of culture is also referred to as an "identity sense". This identity sense of culture requires that members of the same culture identify as part of the culture.

Culture is just one dimension in understanding a person's needs, motivations, and desires. While there is no one right way to examine culture, it is clear that designers need to start thinking about the cultural identities of their users. Research shows that a lack of cultural relevance can be a barrier to trust in technology. We need to start a dialog around culturally-informed design and how a focus around culture might impact our methods. How have you incorporated cultural understanding into your UX research and design? What methods have you used with success?

(选自 www.360doc.com/content/15/0107/09/36964_ 438807704.shtml.)

 Questions for Discussion

1. Why did the author mention the two examples at the beginning of the paper?

2. What did anthropologists consider culture?

3. According to Alphonse Chapanis, what's the most difficult problems facing ergonomics today?

4. What do theorists define the objective sense of culture?

5. What is the subjective sense of culture?

Further Reading

Passage 1

Language is part of the culture and also a carrier of the culture. Culture shapes people's behavior. When you observe people's behavior, you can better understand the culture if you understand the words or expressions they are using.

Below are some slogans and sayings that may be confusing people of different cultures. They might interpret the meanings differently from each other. Without fully understanding the culture of the country in which these slogans and saying are used, you may have some misunderstandings in communication. Therefore, it is important to learn the culture of the country whose language you are learning now.

Impossible is nothing. (Adidas's previous slogan) **Anything is possible.** (Li Ning's previous slogan) These two slogans encourage all employees to be innovative and to imagine that everything is possible to accomplish. The values of these two slogans transmit are that these two companies are not content with what they have achieved, instead they strive to be more innovative by doing something different.

Just do it. This slogan is also well known to all. It represents Nike's corporate culture, which can help us see its employee's attitude to work. Meanwhile, it also motivates people to do something, not just talk about something without taking any action.

Don't just stand there, do something! People take pride in quickly taking action in the face of problems or opportunities. To them, doing something, even if it proves to be a mistake, would be better than doing nothing. At least, errors can be mended, or can be a good lesson, but inaction accomplishes nothing.

Tell it like it is! This saying means that frank verbal and written communication is important. Those who are too indirect are likely to be viewed with suspicion, as if they have something to hide, or worse, from an American perspective, have nothing to contribute or lack self-confidence. American people tend to be direct in communication. No "beating around the bush"!

Blow your own horn. If you want a job done right, do it yourself. Speak for yourself. These sayings reflect a strong sense of individualism, which can be seen in an emphasis on individual accountability and singling out a specific person for recognition and reward in the workplace.

In America, you can be both individualistic and also care about other people. Americans often talk about a "win-win" situation in which people, groups or organizations all benefit from a solution.

Questions for Discussion

1. What are the values of Adidas's previous slogan and Li Ning's previous slogan?
2. What does the slogan "Just do it" transmit?
3. What does the expression "No beating around the bush!" mean?
4. What does "Blow your own horn. If you want a job done right, do it yourself." imply?
5. What's the misunderstanding for American individualism in China?

Passage 2

Chinese Culture

China is one of the Four Ancient Civilizations (alongside Babylon, India and Egypt), according to Chinese scholar Liang Qichao (1900). Chinese history began with two legendary figures—Emperor Huang and Emperor Yan, lived together with their tribes, they **inhabited**（居住）the **drainage**（排水）area along the middle reaches of the Yellow River. By the time of Xia Dynasty, after centuries of living side by side, these two tribes had gradually merged into one. Eventually, the Chinese people usually call themselves "the **descendants**（后裔）of Yan and Huang". People at that time believed that the land they lived on was the center of the world, and called their state the "Middle Kingdom", thus giving China as its country name.

Traditional Chinese culture is recorded not only in history books and documents, but also in **archaeological**（考古学的）records, such as ancient city walls, palaces, temples, pagodas, and **grotto**（洞穴）; artifacts, such as bronze objects, weapons, bronze mirrors, coins, jade and pottery objects, and **curios**（小件珍奇物品）; and folk culture, including song and dance, **embroidery**（刺绣）, cuisine, clothing, tea ceremonies, drinking games, lanterns, riddles, martial arts, chess and kites. With a continuous history of 5,000 years, it has undergone frequent transformations to produce a rich and vital cultural heritage.

In the modern days, with the rise of Western economic and military power beginning in the mid-19th century, Western systems of social and political organization have gained **adherents**（支持者）in China. Indeed, within today's globalized environment, modern cultures interact and cooperate increasingly more each other. China's culture of the future will most likely reflect this cross-cultural dimension. Thus, obtaining a solid understanding of China's culture of the past is necessary in order to successfully embrace all that the culture has to offer to the world.

（选自 http://wenku.baidu.com/view/d2693acd9889680203d8ce2f0066f5335b81674b.html.）

 Questions for Discussion

1. According to Chinese scholar Liang Qichao, what was the Four Ancient Civilizations?

2. What is traditional Chinese culture recorded?

3. What is folk culture? Can you name some?

4. In modern days, what have gained adherents in China?

5. In order to successfully embrace all that the culture has to offer to the world, what is essential?

Passage 3

Du Fu

Du Fu (AD 712 – 770), whose courtesy name was Zimei, was born at Gong County, Henan Province. His **ancestral** (祖先的) hometown was located in Xiangyang (now Xiangyang City, Hubei Province).

Revered (可敬的) as the "Poet Historian", he composed poems which extensively and profoundly reflected the social conflicts and historical events of his time. His awareness of the **devastation** (毁坏) of the country and the suffering of the common people is the theme of most of his poems, which reached an **unprecedented** (前所未有的) height in portraying real life and political issues.

The realistic **motif** (主题) of Du Fu's poems is presented by the following aspects: the timely **depiction** (描写) of historical events and major social conflicts and reproach to the ruling class for the calamity they brought to the country and the people; sympathy toward the suffering of the common people; deep concern about the fate of his country which was in constant unrest.

Du Fu was an expert in **epitomizing** (概括) the typical elements of real life and **infusing** (灌输) personal emotions and criticism into the portrayal of realities. His poems are notable for their range and depth, but they do not lack delicateness due to the poet's careful observations. Du Fu was also good at **mingling** (混合) emotions with settings in his poems. "Gloom and density" is the most prominent feature of Du Fu's poetry. This style is attributed to the hard time Du Fu lived in, his drifting experiences, his **melancholy** (忧郁) personality and his worship of the **grandeur** (宏伟) and the grim.

Du Fu inherited the spirit of "**spontaneity** (自发性) over reality" tradition dating back from the folk **lyrics** (歌词) of Han Dynasty and pushed the realistic strain of ancient Chinese poetry to a new height. Du Fu's style is complementary to that of Li Bai's and they are often made comparable in significance in the history of Chinese poetry. Also revered as the "Poet Sage", Du Fu left some 1,400 poems, which have been collected in *The Anthology of Du Gongbu*.

(选自http://www.kekenet.com/read/201601/420557.shtml.)

Questions for Discussion

1. Why was Du Fu remembered as the "Poet Historian"?
2. What's the realistic theme of Du Fu's poem?
3. In what way did people consider Du Fu as an expert?
4. What was Du Fu's poems famous for?
5. What did Du Fu inherit?

Passage 4

Qi Baishi

Qi Baishi (1864–1957) was one of the most well-known contemporary Chinese painters. His original name is Qi Huang and his courtesy name is Weiqing. Baishi ("white stone") is one of his **pseudonyms** (笔名). Some of Qi's major influences include Ming Dynasty artist Xu Wei and early Qing Dynasty painter Zhu Da. The subjects of his paintings include almost everything, commonly animals, scenery, figures, vegetables, and so on. In his later years, many of his works depict mice, shrimps, and birds. Qi Baishi is particularly known for painting shrimps.

Born in a farmer family in Xiangtan, Hunan province, Qi Baishi became a carpenter at fourteen, and it was largely through his own efforts that he became **adept** (擅长) at the arts of poetry, calligraphy, painting, and seal-carving. In his forties, Qi Baishi began traveling and looking for more inspiration. He came upon the Shanghai School, which was very popular at the time, and met Wu Changshuo who then became another mentor to him and inspired a lot of his works. Another influence of Qi Baishi came about fifteen years later, as Qi became close to Chen Shizeng after he settled down in Beijing.

Qi Baishi theorized that "paintings must be something between likeness and unlikeness." His **prodigious** (异常的) output reflects a diversity of interests and experience, generally focusing on the smaller things of the world rather than the large landscape. Shrimps, fish, crabs, frogs, insects, and peaches were his favorite subjects. Using heavy ink, bright colors, and vigorous **strokes** (笔画), he created works of a fresh and lively manner that expressed his love of nature and life. In 1953, Qi Baishi was elected as the president of the Association of Chinese Artists. He was active to the end of his long life and served briefly as the honorary president of Beijing Academy of Chinese Painting, which was founded in May, 1957. He died in Beijing on September 16, 1957.

(选自 http://www.comuseum.com/painting/masters/qi-baishi.)

 Questions for Discussion

1. What was Qi Baishi's courtesy name and pen name?
2. What were the subjects of his paintings?
3. What was Qi Baishi good at?
4. What did Qi Baishi focus on in his paintings?
5. When did Qi Baishi win the honorary president of Beijing Academy of Chinese Painting?

Exercises

I. True or False

Directions: *Decide whether the statements are true (T) or false (F) according to the passage.*

1. Communication is the core of culture. It is a very large, complicated concept.
2. Geert Hofsted's onion theory indicates that symbols represent the most superficial and the easiest to perceive by an outsider and the least important to an insider.
3. The four factors such as technological invention, disasters, cultural contact and environmental factors influence the change of culture.
4. Identity refers to one's sense of belonging to a particular culture or ethnic group.
5. Culture is a system of inherited conceptions expressed in language, by means of which people communicate, perpetuate and develop their knowledge and attitude towards life.
6. Culture is "the arts and other manifestations of human intellectual achievement regarded collectively".
7. Culture is so small and inclusive that it is really easy to define.

8. Rituals are those collective activities that are considered socially essential within a culture such as sports events.
9. Nonverbal symbols are visible and obvious to an outside observer. They are determined by values, which are the deeper manifestations of culture and the most difficult to understand by an outsider.
10. We usually take culture for granted since everything we see and do takes place in different culture.

II. Matching

Directions: *Match the following words and expressions with correct Chinese.*

1. spatial relation   A. 知觉
2. stereotype   B. 空间关系
3. perception   C. 刻板形象
4. allusion   D. 暗喻
5. simile   E. 典故
6. metaphor   F. 明喻
7. symbol   G. 文化适应
8. enculturation   H. 次文化
9. culture identity   I. 符号
10. subculture   J. 文化身份

III. Translation

A. Directions: *Translate the following paragraph into English.*

严寒时节的三位友人，具体指松、竹、梅三种植物。在中国传统文化中，有些植物因其自然属性而被赋予某种人文蕴涵。松、竹四季常青，历冬不凋；梅花凌霜傲雪，美丽绽放。三者都不怕严寒，在严寒中展现自身的生命力和自然美，宛如在严寒中相伴生长的好友，故被世人合称为"岁寒三友"。它们常被用来喻指忠贞不渝的友谊，寄托对孤傲、高洁人格的崇尚和向往。

B. Directions: *Translate the following paragraph into Chinese.*

When the conception of "global village" comes along with the dawn of the 21st century, intercultural communication takes place in more forms than ever before, and it has never been as important as it is today. As used synonymously with cross-cultural communication sometimes, intercultural communication refers to a form of global communication which is used to describe the wide range of communication problems that naturally appear within an organization made up of individuals from different religious, social, ethnic, and educational backgrounds. Intercultural communication research has developed recently through interdisciplinary interaction, namely the behavioral sciences, anthropology, and the language sciences.

Chapter 4

Cultural Patterns

> They should think their (coarse) food sweet; their (plain) clothes beautiful; their (poor) dwellings places of rest; and their common (simple) ways sources of enjoyment.
> ——Tao Te Ching by Lao Tzu
>
> 甘其食，美其服，安其居，乐其俗。
> ——《道德经》老子

本章导读

文化模式是指各民族或国家具有的独特的文化体系。它是由各种文化特质、文化集丛有机结合而构成的一个有特色的文化体系。各民族或国家之间有着不同的文化，即文化模式的不同。文化模式支配着人们的信念、态度和行为，是跨文化交际的核心。西方学者概括了文化模式的内容，包括高语境—低语境文化模式、文化维度、价值取向理论等。

Learning Objectives

In this chapter, students will learn how to understand the definition of cultural patterns, describe the components of cultural patterns, summarize the theory about cultural patterns, and evaluate the importance of cultural patterns.

There does exist such preference for the subject matter in Western and Chinese painting. In classical Western paintings, the portraits of figures take the majority. This is related to the early functions of paintings in Western culture. An important one was to serve religious purposes where religious stories were told with religious figures being the focus. Another function was for political purposes which led to the portraits of governors and nobles. In classical Chinese paintings, however landscape, particularly mountains and water, tend to be one of the most extensive subject matters.

Warm-up Activities

1. What is the subject matter in Western painting?
2. What is the subject matter in Chinese painting?
3. What are the factors that have shaped the cultural patterns?

4.1 Introduction

Warm-up Activities

1. How do you define culture?
2. What are the cultural patterns?

You may encounter a common issue when you first get to your college town. You often compare the regional food and climate of your hometown with those of your college town. What do local people commonly eat for breakfast, lunch, or dinner? Are there any specialty which can only be found in your hometown region? This may tell us the relation between food and geography, which is an inevitable part of culture. Of course it is very abstract and naive to say that a person can learn more than superficial and pop-cultural knowledge about another culture by simply talking to someone else or watching movies from a different culture. To understand how to use language globally, the meaning of culture will be discussed first.

In terms of culture, we tend to make it clear that the simplest definition of culture is a set of values and norms within a group or society and **institutional** (慈善机构的) learned behavior. Culture is also how a person identifies himself, so there is also an individual component to culture that must be understood such as age, gender, class, and any other group identity or **affiliation** (隶属关系).

We focus on how to define cultural patterns. First, an obvious cultural difference lies in the food people eat and tableware they use every day. We identify hamburger with U.S. while we identify chopsticks with China. Second, another obvious difference between cultures is the clothing people wear. We often see men from Middle Eastern cultures with long robes and headdresses. Cultural patterns are the basis for interpreting the symbols used in communication. Moving from communication to culture provides us with a rather seamless transition, for as **Hall** points out "Culture is communication and communication is culture." In a word, culture is a **microscopic** (微小的) integration, so learners are required to realize the existence of cultural norm which refers to a unique cultural rule that people living in a nation or society have long adapted to and adhered to. It is an entire cultural system of value orientation, behavior pattern, and psychological tendency.

Before coming to learn cultural patterns, a group discussion is needed on the following questions. In the future, will you share your home with family members, such as your parents or grandparents? In the future, if young people prefer to live in their own home with only their nuclear family (husband, wife and children), how will this new custom change society? Will children spend time with their grandparents? Will families begin to live far away from one another. For example the grandparents are living in Guangzhou while the parents and children are living in Beijing?

4.2 Definition of Cultural Patterns

Perception is primary in the study of intercultural communication, because our information about and knowledge of our physical and social world are **mediated** (传达) by perceptual processes. Our perceptions give meaning to all those external forces: symbols, things, people, ideas, events, ideologies and faith. "Perception is the process of selecting, organizing, and interpreting sensory data in a way that enables us to make sense of our world." (**Gamble**)

Members of a culture generally have a preferred set of responses to the world. Imagine that for each experience, there is a range of possible responses from which a culture selects its preferred response. In some cultures, for example, it is considered bad luck for the groom to see the bride before the wedding ceremony on their wedding day. It is also customary in some cultures for the bride's family to give a wealthy gift to the groom's family, whereas in othres it is customary for the groom's family to pay for the wedding celebration. In China, it is very traditional for parents to arrange a blind date for their children, although this practice is becoming less popular nowadays. The youth of many Western countries often select their own partner, sometimes without the approval of their parents. They may not accept or understand arranged marriages.

For instance, a Westerner invited a Chinese girl to have lunch and take a tour around the British Parliament. In fact, the girl didn't have lunch but when the Westerner asked her "are you hungry", the girl said "no". Then they didn't have lunch together. The second time, the girl was invited to a restaurant; when the host asked her the same question "are you hungry", she answered, "not really." The host ordered a light meal for her.

In the first situation, the Westerner viewed his question as an invitation. The girl considered it only as a question. According to the Chinese tradition, the man should have invited her to lunch since their appointment was to have lunch first. In the second situation, the Westerner used his question as a question rather than an invitation. According to the Chinese tradition, man should have ordered plenty of food for the girl. The conclusion can be drawn as follows: the same sentence concealed different intentions. People should try to make sense of what it really means.

From the examples above, cultural patterns can be defined as follows: "Shared beliefs, values, norms and social practices are stable over time and can lead to roughly similar behaviors across similar situations." Cultural patterns can be interpreted from two aspects consisting of ways of thinking and ways of acting.

When it comes to ways of thinking, cultural patterns are primarily inside people, in their minds, which provide a way of thinking about the world and the basic set of standards that guide thought and action. Therefore, cultural patterns are shared programs that govern specific behavior choices. These collective mental programs are widely shared only by members of a particular group or culture and understood only by the context of a particular culture.

Concerning ways of acting, cultural patterns are not so much consciously taught as unconsciously experienced as a by-product of day-to-day activities, which are programmed at a very early age and are reinforced continuously.

Perceptions are stored within each human being in the form of beliefs + values = *cultural patterns*.

Belief→Value→Attitude→Behavior

Beliefs form the basis of our values. Attitudes arise from an inner framework of values and beliefs. We assumed attitudes based on observed behaviour.

4.3 Components of Cultural Patterns

Beliefs, values, norms, and social practices together constitute the components of cultural patterns.

4.3.1 Beliefs

As **Samovar** puts it, all cultures possess "A dominant, organized religion with which **salient** (显著的) beliefs and activities like rite, rituals, and ceremonies can be given meaning and **legitimacy** (合法性)." A belief is an idea that people assume to be true about the world. Discussing culturally shared beliefs is difficult because people are usually not conscious of them. In fact, much of what one considers to be reality may, in fact, not be reality to people from other cultures. What one considers to be the important views about the world are based on our culturally shared beliefs.

Beliefs are our convictions in the truth of something—with or without proof. Beliefs are shaped by the individual's culture. Beliefs are important because they are accepted to be truths. One of the most important functions of beliefs is that they form the basis of our values. Beliefs are usually reflected in our actions and communication behavior. For example, a widely shared belief dates back to the time when Europeans believed that the earth was flat. That is, people "knew" that the earth was flat. Most people now "know" that the earth is basically round and will laugh at the suggestion that it is flat.

For another example, in some countries, a good **tan** (棕褐色) is a reflection of a healthy, active lifestyle and makes a person more attractive. People will probably find time to lie out in the sun or even go to a tanning salon. While in other countries, sun-tanned skin reflects a low social status, people will probably make an extra effort to avoid exposing themselves to the sun by wearing hats, long-sleeved shirts, and perhaps gloves, carrying umbrellas on sunny days.

4.3.2 Values

Cultures differ not only in their beliefs but also in what they value. Values involve what a culture regards as good or bad, right or wrong, fair or unfair, just or unjust, beautiful or ugly, clean or dirty, valuable or worthless, appropriate or inappropriate, and kind or cruel. For example, Westerners value youth rather than the elderly. In Eastern Countries, however, respect for the elderly is a positive value.

A value is an enduring belief that a specific mode of conduct or end-state of existence is personally or socially preferable to another. According to Nanda & Warms, values are shared ideas about what is true, right, and beautiful, which underline cultural patterns and guide society in response to the physical and social environment. Values are a learned organization of rules for making choices and for resolving conflicts.

What are the value types proposed by **Schwartz**? Schwartz's value types consist of power, achievement, hedonism, stimulation, self-direction, universalism, security, **benevolence** (仁慈), tradition and **conformity** (遵守). What values do Chinese cultures stress? And what values do Westerners stress? Chinese cultures stress power, conformity, universalism, security, benevolence, and tradition, while Westerners stress achievement, self-direction, hedonism, and stimulation.

According to *Oxford Dictionary*, "Values are one's principles or standards, one's judgment of what is valuable or important in life." **Hofstede** defines value as a broad tendency to prefer certain states of affairs over others. It may include the following elements: evil vs. good, dirty vs. clean, dangerous vs. safe, decent vs. indecent, ugly vs. beautiful, unnatural vs. natural, abnormal vs. normal, paradoxical vs. logical, irrational vs. rational, moral vs. immoral.

Kluckhohn describes value as a concept explicit or implicit, distinctive of an individual or characteristic of a group, of the desirable which influences the selection from available modes, means, and ends of action.

The values of a culture often refer to the learned rules for making choices and for resolving conflicts. Values are broad, abstract concepts which provide guidelines and standards to help determine how people ought to behave in a particular culture. In other words, understanding values is a great help to avoid conflicts, to respect different cultures, and finally to achieve social harmony.

4.3.3 Norms

Norms are the socially shared expectation of appropriate behaviors. Norms can include the folkways, mores, taboos and **rituals** (仪式) in a culture. Norms have great moral significance such as the norms in **folkways** (民俗), which can guide people to behave properly, and societal **taboos** (禁忌), which may persuade people what to do or not to do. Most important norms in a culture apply everywhere and at all times, which move a society smoothly.

When a person's behaviors **violate** (违反) the culture's norm, social sanctions are usually imposed. Like values, norms can vary within a culture in terms of their importance and intensity. Unlike values, however, norms may change over a period of time, whereas beliefs and values tend to be much more enduring. For example, the greeting behaviors of people within a culture are governed by norms.

Similarly, good manners in a variety of situations are based on norms. Norms also exist to guide people's interactions and to indicate how to engage in conversation, what to talk about, and how to end a conversation. Because people are expected to behave according to their cultural norms, they come to see their own norms as constituting the "right" way of communicating. Norms are linked to the beliefs and values of a culture.

4.3.4 Social Practices

Social practices are the predictable behavior patterns that members of a culture typically follow. Thus, social practices are the outward **manifestations** (显示) of beliefs, values, and norms. For example, in the United States, lunch is usually over by 1:30 p.m., but in Italy, lunch doesn't even begin until 1:30 p.m. In Western Countries, gifts brought by dinner guests are usually opened in the presence of the guests, while in China, gifts are never opened in front of the giver because doing so is considered bad manners.

Just like smile, laughing does not always serve the same function in different cultures. Interestingly, for Chinese, laughing often has a special function on some tense social occasions. People may laugh to release the tension or embarrassment, to express their concern about you; their intention is to put you at ease or to help you come out of the embarrassment. In this case, the people there were actually wishing to laugh with the Westerners rather than laugh at her. Their laughing seemed to convey a number of messages: don't take it so seriously; laugh it off; it's nothing; such things can happen to any of us, etc. Unfortunately, the Westerners was unaware of this situation. She thought they were laughing at her, which made her feel more bad and angry, for in her culture laughing on such an occasion would be interpreted as an insult, **humiliating** (羞辱性的), and negative response.

4.4 Edward T. Hall's Context-Culture Theory

Context-Culture Theory is proposed by **Edward T. Hall,** the American anthropologist, who offers us an effective means of examining cultural similarities and differences in both perception and communication. Hall defines context as the information that surrounds an event. It is **inextricably** (不可解脱地) bound up with the meaning of the event.

If the culture of a society was the iceberg, Hall reasoned, then there are some aspects visible, above the water, but there is a larger portion hidden beneath the surface. What does that mean? The external, or conscious, part of culture is what we can see as the tip of the iceberg and includes behaviors and some beliefs. The internal, or subconscious, part of culture is below the surface of a society and includes some beliefs and the values and thought patterns that underline behavior. There are major differences between the conscious and unconscious culture, internal versus external, implicitly learned and explicitly learned, difficult to change and easily changed, subjective knowledge and objective knowledge.

What can we do? Hall suggests that the only way to learn the internal culture of others is to actively participate in their culture. When one first enters a new culture, only the most **overt** (公开的) behaviors are apparent. As one spends more time in that new culture, the underlying beliefs, values, and thought patterns that dictate that behavior will be uncovered. What this model teaches us is that we cannot judge a new culture based only on what we see when we first enter it. We must take time to get to know individuals from that culture and interact with them. Only by doing so can we uncover the values and beliefs that underlie the behavior of that society.

He also categorizes cultures as being either high or low context, depending on the degree to which meaning comes from the settings or from the words being exchanged. The general terms "high context" and "low context" popularized by Hall are used to describe **broad-brush** (粗枝大叶的) cultural differences between societies.

Hall defines these two terms in the following manner: "A high context communication or message is one in which most of the information is already in the person, while very little is in the coded, explicitly transmitted part of the message. A low context communication is just the opposite. The mass of the information is **vested** (既定的) in the explicit code."

4.4.1 High Context

High context refers to societies or groups where people have close connections over a long period of time. Many aspects of cultural behavior are not made explicit because most members know what to do and what to think from years of interaction with each other. Your family is probably an example of a high context environment. A high-context communication or message is one in which most of the information is either in the physical context or in the person, while very little is in the coded, explicit, transmitted part of the message.

High-context cultures don't rely on verbally explicit communication or written/formal information but more internalized understandings of what is communicated. People care about multiple cross-cutting ties and intersections with others and long term relationships with strong boundaries between who is accepted as belonging and who is considered an "outsider". Knowledge is situational and relational. Decisions and activities focus on personal face-to-face relationships, often around a central person who has authority. There are some examples such as small religious **congregations** (教堂会众), a party with friends, family gatherings, expensive **gourmet** (美食家) restaurants and neighborhood restaurants with a regular **clientele** (客人), undergraduate on-campus friendship, regular pick-up games, and hosting a friend in your home overnight.

4.4.2 Low Context

Low context refers to societies where people tend to have many connections but of shorter duration or for some specific reason. In these societies, cultural behavior and beliefs may need to be spelled out explicitly so that those coming into the cultural environment know how to behave. Low-context communication is just the opposite, the mass of the information is vested in the explicit code, and the context or situation plays a minimal role.

In low-context cultures, people play by external rules, which are called rule-orientation. More knowledge is codified, public, external, and accessible and is more often **transferable** (可转让的). They expect sequencing and separation of time, space, activities, and relationships. Different from high-context cultures, they have more interpersonal connections of shorter duration. Since they are task-centered, decisions and activities focus around what needs to be done and division of responsibilities. There are such examples such as large US airports, a chain supermarket, a cafeteria, a convenience store, and sports where rules are clearly laid out.

While these terms are sometimes useful in describing some aspects of a culture, one can never say a culture is "high" or "low" because societies all contain both modes. "High" and "low" are therefore less relevant as a description of a whole people, and more useful to describe and understand particular situations and environments.

Firstly, in the structure of relationships, high context expects dense, intersecting networks and long-term relationships with strong boundaries in which relationship is more important than task. But low context expects loose, wide networks and shorter-term, **compartmentalized** (划分) relationships in which task is more important than relationship.

Secondly, in terms of main type of cultural knowledge, high context shows that more knowledge is below the waterline, called implicit, with patterns that are not fully conscious, hard to explain even if you are a member of that culture. Low context shows that more knowledge is above the waterline, called explicit, which is consciously organized.

Thirdly, it is about entering high and low context situations. High contexts can be difficult to enter if you are an outsider because you don't carry the context information internally, and because you can't instantly create close relationships. Low contexts are relatively easy to enter if you are an outsider because the environment contains much of the information you need to participate, because you can form relationships fairly soon, and because the important thing is accomplishing a task rather than feeling your way into a relationship. Remember that every culture and every situation has its high and low aspects. Often one situation will contain an inner high context core and an outer low context ring for those who are less involved. For instance, a Parent-Teacher Association (PTA) is usually a low-context situation: who can join, when are the dates of the meetings, who is the president, what will be discussed, etc. are all explicitly available information, and it is usually fairly clear how to participate in the meetings. However, if this is a small town, perhaps people who run the PTA all know each other very well and have many overlapping interests. They may "agree" on what should be discussed or what should happen without ever really talking about it, they have unconscious, unexpressed values that influence their decisions. Other parents from outside may not understand how decisions are actually being made. So the PTA is still low context, but it has a high-context subgroup that is in turn a part of a high context small town society.

When you enter a high-context situation, it doesn't immediately become a low-context culture just because you came in the door! It is still a high-context culture and you are just (alas), ignorant. Also, even low-context cultures can be difficult to learn: religious dietary laws, medical training, and written language all take years to understand. The point is that information has been made conscious, systematic, and available to those who have the resources to learn it.

4.5 Kluckhohn and Strodtbeck's Value Orientation

People's attitudes are based on the relatively few, stable values they hold. Kluckhohn and Strodtbeck's (1961) **Values Orientation Theory** proposes that all human societies must answer a limited number of universal problems, that the value-based solutions are limited in number and universally known, but that different cultures have different preferences among them. Suggested questions include human's relations with time, nature and each other, as well as basic human motives and the nature of human nature. Kluckhohn and Strodtbeck suggested **alternate** (交替的) answers to all five developed culture-specific measures of each, and described the value orientation profiles of five cultural groups. Their theory has since been tested in many other cultures and used to help negotiate ethnic groups to understand one another and to examine the inter-generational value changes caused by migration.

Chapter 4 Cultural Patterns

Other theories of universal values (**Rokeach, Hofstede, Schwartz**) have produced value concepts sufficiently similar to suggest that a truly universal set of human values does exist and that cross-cultural psychologists are close to discovering what they are.

Value orientations are complex but definitely patterned principles which give order and direction to the **ever-flowing** (一直在流动的) stream of human acts and thoughts as these relate to the solution of "common human problems". The Theory of Value Orientations is based on the following assumptions: people in all cultures must find solutions to a limited number of common human problems. Kluckhohns and Strodtbeck, after examining hundreds of cultures, reached the conclusion that people turn to their culture for answers to the following questions.

(1) What is the inborn character of human nature?

(2) What is the relation between people and nature?

(3) What is the focus of human life with respect to time?

(4) What is the value placed on activity?

(5) What is the relationship of one person to another?

The answers to these crucial questions serve as the basis for the five value orientations that are at the heart of their approaches. These five orientations might be best visualized as points on a **continuum** (连续体). As you move through these five orientations, you will undoubtedly notice some of the same characteristics discussed by Hofstede. This is very understandable because both approaches are talking about meaningful values found in all cultures. Hence, both sets of researchers were bound to track many of the same patterns.

As indicated above, every culture must find a solution to each of these problems. The solutions available, however, are limited for each of the problems. The range of alternative solutions to a culture's problems is limited, because cultures must select their solutions from a range of available alternatives. Later, when you **elaborate** (说明) on the five problems, you will see the answers to these problems are limited. While one solution tends to be preferred by members of any given culture, all potential solutions are present in every culture. That means within any culture, a preferred set of solution will be chosen by most people. However, not all people from a culture will make exactly the same set of choices, and in fact, some people from each culture will select other alternatives.

Over time, the preferred solutions have shaped the culture's basic assumptions about beliefs, values, norms, and social practices—the cultural patterns. This means people tend to regularly solve one type of problems in the same way. Then little by little, the same behaviors to solve particular problems and the reasons or ideas underlying these behaviors become the preferred beliefs, values, norms, and social practices. Thus, the cultural patterns are formed.

Belief is an idea that people assume to be true about the world. It is about what is and what is not logical and correct. Values involve what a culture regards as good or bad, right or wrong, fair or unfair, just or unjust, beautiful or ugly, clean or dirty, valuable or worthless, appropriate or inappropriate, and kind or cruel. Norms are the socially shared expectations of appropriate behaviors. Social practices are the outward manifestations of beliefs, values, and norms.

4.5.1 Human-Nature Orientation

The human nature orientation deals with the **innate** (天生的) character of human nature. The potential solutions to this problem appear relatively obvious: Humans can be seen as innately good, innately evil, or a mixture of good and evil. It is not quite that simple, however. Humans can be viewed not only as either good or evil but also as either able to change **mutable** (易变的) or not able to change (immutable). In addition, we must recognize that viewing human nature as a mixture of good and evil is not the same as viewing human nature as neutral. If we combine these various aspects, we find that there are six potential solutions to this problem: (1) humans are evil but mutable; (2) humans are evil and immutable; (3) humans are neutral with respect to good and evil; (4) humans are a mixture of good and evil; (5) humans are good but mutable; (6) humans are good and immutable.

When this orientation is applied to the Western Countries, it is not always easy to decide which solution predominates. Most people in the Western Countries inherited a view of human nature as evil but mutable from their Puritan **predecessors** (前辈). Puritans were convinced that human beings were **predestined** (注定的) by God before they were born. Some were God's chosen people while others were predestined to be damned to hell. In order to be God's select, people must work hard, spend little, and invest for more business to become very successful in his calling. In this view, discipline and self-control are seen as necessary if humans are to change. Some subcultures within the Western Countries definitely adopt this solution, but **predominant** (占支配地位的) view in the middle-class subculture is probably the view of human nature as a mixture of good and evil.

4.5.2 Man-Nature Orientation

Three potential types of relations exist between humans and nature: subjugation (屈服) to nature, harmony with nature and mastery over nature.

(1) subjugation to nature

The most powerful forces of life are beyond their control. Whether the force be a god, fate, or magic, a person cannot overcome it and must therefore learn to accept it. This orientation is found in India and parts of South America. For the Hindu, because everything is a part of a unified force. This "oneness" with the world helps create a vision of a world operating in harmony. For example, some Hindu sects such as the bishops do not allow the cutting down of any trees or the slaughter of animals. This is extreme reverence (尊敬) for Nature, which has precedence (优先权) over human activities. In Mexico or among Mexican Americans, there is a strong tie to Catholicism (天主教) and the role of fate in controlling life and nature.

(2) harmony with nature

The harmony view is widespread and is associated with East Asians. Chinese people believe the balance and harmony between man and the natural world. This belief permeates (遍布) in every aspect of Chinese culture. Chinese medicine, for example, is mainly to adjust the unbalanced human body. In Japan and Thailand, there is a perception that nature is a part of life and not a hostile force waiting to be subdued. This orientation affirms that people should, in every way possible, live in harmony with nature. The desire to be part of nature and not control it has always been strong among American Indians.

(3) mastery over nature

Western people believe they are the masters of nature. This value orientation is characteristic of the Western approach, which has a long tradition of valuing technology, change, and science. People with this orientation see a clear separation between humans and nature. Americans have historically believed that nature was something that could and had to be mastered. Early West European immigrants to North America encountered a vast, unforgiving wilderness that they set about to "tame," and modern astronauts are working to "conquer" space.

4.5.3 Time Orientation

The **temporal** (世俗的) focus of human life can be directed on the past, the present, or the future. Some cultures choose to describe the future as most important, others emphasize the present, and still others emphasize the past. The past orientation predominates in cultures placing a high value on tradition, worshipping ancestors or, emphasizing strong family ties. Also included here are cultures where there is some degree of traditionalism and aristocracy (e.g., England). In Japanese and Chinese cultures, the anniversary of the death of a loved one is observed, illustrating the value these cultures place on the past. The present orientation predominates where people pay relatively little attention to what has gone on in the past and what might happen in the future. In this orientation, the past is seen as unimportant, and the future is seen as vague and unpredictable. The Navajo Indians of northern Arizona, for example, have this orientation. To them, only the here and now is real; the future and the past have little reality. The future orientation predominates where change is valued highly. In this orientation, the future generally is viewed as "bigger and better", while being "old-fashioned" (the past) is scorned. Both Kluckhohn and Strodtbeck and Hall see this orientation predominating in the Western Countries.

4.5.4 Activity Orientation

Human activity can be handled in three ways: being, being-in-becoming, and doing.

(1) Being

The being orientation is a non-developmental model. It is a belief that all events are determined by fate and are therefore inevitable. People in being-orientated cultures accept people, events, and ideas as flowing spontaneously. They stress release, indulgence of existing desires, and working for the moment." Most Latino cultures have the view that the current activity is the one that matters the most. In Mexico, for example, people take great delight in the simple act of conversation with family and friends. Mexicans will talk for hours with their companions, for they believe that the act of "being" is one of the main goals and joys of life. African American and Greek cultures are also regarded as "being" cultures.

(2) Being-in-becoming

This orientation sees humans as evolving and changing; people with this orientation, including Native Americans and most South Americans, tend to think of ways to change themselves as a means of changing the world. The being-in-becoming orientation stresses the idea of development and growth. It emphasizes the kind of activity that contributes to the development of all aspects of the self as an integral whole. It usually correlates with cultures that value a spiritual life more than a material one. For example, in both Hinduism and Buddhism, people spend a portion of their lives in meditation and contemplation in an attempt to purify and fully advance themselves. Many of the New Age religious movements in the United States also stress the need to develop the being-in-becoming approach to daily life.

(3) Doing

A "doing" orientation involves a focus upon those types of activities that have outcomes external to the individual, which can be measured by someone else. Activities must be tangible. People in the U. S. often ask, "what do you do?" when they first meet someone, a common greeting is "Hi! How are you doing?" Monday morning conversations between coworkers often center on what each person "did" over the weekend. Similarly, young children are asked about what they want to do when they grow up. According to this orientation, if you are sitting at your desk thinking, you are not doing anything because your thoughts cannot be externally measured.

4.5.5 Relational Orientation

This value orientation is consistent with the broad **dimension** (维度) of cultural variability, individualism-collectivism, but there are sufficient differences that it needs to be discussed here.

Kluckhohn and Strodtbeck isolate three potential ways in which humans can define their relationships to other humans: individualism, **linearity** (直线性), and **collaterality** (旁系). As we might expect, individualism is the predominant orientation in the US. This orientation is characterized by the autonomy of the individual; in other words, individuals are seen as unique, separate entities. In this orientation, individual goals and objectives take priority over group goals and objectives. The linearity orientation, on the other hand, focuses on the group, with group goals taking **precedence** (优先权) over individual goals. The crucial issue in the linearity orientation, according to Kluckhohn and Strodtbeck, is the continuity of the group through time. Specific individuals are important only for their group memberships. One example of this orientation is the **aristocracy** (贵族阶层) of many European countries. Collaterality, the third orientation, also focuses on group, but not the group extended through time. Rather, the focus is on the laterally extended group (an individual's most immediate group memberships in time and space, i. e. , one's nuclear and extended families, neighbors, work groups, and social organizations). The goals of the group take precedence over those of the individual. In fact, in this orientation, people are not considered except **vis-à-vis** (相关) their group memberships. One example of this orientation is the identification of the Japanese with the company for which they work or the university from which they graduated.

4.6 Hofstede's Dimensions of Cultural Variability

The **Theory of Cultural Dimensions** put forward by Hofstede is the most influential intercultural theory in the world. Here are Hofstede's dimensions of culture values, including **individualism** (个人主义) versus **collectivism** (集体主义), uncertainty avoidance, **power distance** (权力差距), **masculinity** (男性气质) versus **femininity** (女性气质), long-term orientation versus short-term orientation, and **indulgence** (放纵) versus restraint.

4.6.1 Individualism and Collectivism

Individualism looks at how much a culture emphasizes the rights of the individual versus those of the group (whether it be family, tribe, company, etc.). In individualistic cultures, values of individual achievement, freedom, and competition are stressed. People give priority to the task and are supposed to look after their own self-interests. While in collectivistic cultures, values of group harmony, **cohesiveness** (粘结性), and consensus are very important. And priority is given to relationship with people and group interest. For example, Westerners advocate individualism. When they speak, they emphasize more on "I", while Chinese advocate collectivism, they emphasize more on "we".

What is the main difference between individualism and collectivism? The individual is the single most important unit in any social setting, regardless of the size of that unit, and the uniqueness of each individual is of great value, emphasizing individual's needs when they do things such as setting goals. For example in most of the Western Countries, personal achievements are emphasized. Collectivism is characterized by a rigid social framework that distinguishes between in-groups and out-groups. People count on their in-group to look after them, and in exchange for that they believe they owe absolute loyalty to the group. In collectivist cultures such as in China, Korea, and Japan, they emphasize the group such as the family and at work, this manifests in a strong work group mentality.

According to Hofstede, uncertainty avoidance refers to the lack of tolerance for **ambiguity** (歧义) and the need for formal rules and high-level organizational structure. Uncertainty avoidance measures a country or culture's preference for strict laws and regulations over ambiguity and risk. Uncertainty avoidance is the tendency to behave so as to arrange things in a way that minimizes unforeseen consequences.

Hofstede's uncertainty-avoidance measure indicates the extent to which a culture conditions its members to feel either comfortable or uncomfortable in unstructured, ambiguous, and unpredictable situations.

In strong uncertainty avoidance cultures, people tend to be rigid and intolerant. In weak uncertainty avoidance cultures, people are more easygoing. In Japan, people emphasize formal communication, planning, regulations, rituals, and ceremonies. They have strong need for rules. In Singapore, they value diversity and are able to tolerate differences in belief and behavior. What are the main features in the cultures of low uncertainty avoidance and high uncertainty avoidance?

A high uncertainty avoidance ranking indicates the country has a low tolerance for uncertainty and ambiguity. This creates a rule-oriented society that **institutes** (制定) laws, rules, regulations, and controls in order to reduce the amount of uncertainty. Cultures characterized by high uncertainty avoidance feel especially anxious about the uncertainty in life and try to limit and control it as much as possible. They have more laws, regulations, policies, and procedures and a greater emphasis on obeying them. They also have a strong tendency toward conformity and hence predictability. People take comfort in structure, systems, and expertise—anything that can blunt or even **neutralize** (使中立化) the impact of the unexpected. The unknown is frightening.

In cultures of low uncertainty avoidance, it is likely to have lower stress levels, accept different ideas and take risks more than cultures of high uncertainty avoidance. New Zealand, USA, and India are good examples. In cultures of high uncertainty avoidance, it is likely to have a lower tolerance for uncertainty and ambiguity, which expresses itself in higher levels of anxiety, great need for formal rules and absolute truth, and less tolerance for people or groups with different ideas, behavior, or emotions, such as Peru, Japan, Belgium, and Greece.

4.6.2 Power Distance

Power distance is "the extent to which the less powerful members of institutions and organizations accept that power is distributed unequally". Power distance looks at how much a culture does or does not value **hierarchical** (等级制度的) relationships and respect for authority. The degree to which a country accepts the differences in its citizens' physical and intellectual capabilities give rise to inequalities in their well-being. In high power distance cultures, inequalities is allowed to persist or increase organizations tend to be hierarchical and inequality is accepted. Countries like Arabic speaking countries, Russia, India, and China all belong to this category. The relationship between boss and subordinate is rarely personal. Subordinates are not given important work and expect clear guidance from above. Subordinates are expected to take the blame for things going wrong.

In low power distance cultures, people dislike the development of large inequalities in rights and opportunity in the workplace. What's more, government uses taxation or social welfare programs to reduce inequalities. Japan, Australia, and Canada are typical examples. In those countries, superiors treat subordinates with respect and do not pull rank. Subordinates are entrusted with important assignments. To take the Blame is either shared or very often accepted by the superior due to their responsibility to manage. Managers may often socialize with subordinates. Liberal democracies are the norm. Societies lean more towards **egalitarianism** (平等主义).

What are the main features in the cultures of low power distance and high power distance? In cultures of low power distance people believe power should be used only when it is **legitimate** (合法的) and prefer expert or legitimate power, such as Australia, Norway, New Zealand, and Austria. In cultures of high power distance such as Philippines, Mexico, and Brazil, people tend to accept power as part of society. As a result, superiors consider their subordinates to be different from themselves and vice versa.

4.6.3 Masculinity versus Femininity

Cultures high in the masculinity dimension focus on achievement, assertiveness, heroism, and material success, regarding work as more central to one's life. (Performance society). Japan, Austria, Venezuela, Italy, Switzerland, Mexico, Ireland, the Philippines, Greece are among the countries where you can find many of the masculine values described by Hofstede.

Cultures high in the femininity dimension value interpersonal relationships, nurturance, modesty, compassion, caring for the weak and quality of life. (Welfare society). Nations such as Sweden, Norway, the Netherlands, Finland, Denmark tend toward a feminine worldview.

What are the main differences between masculine and feminine cultures? The major differentiation between masculine and feminine cultures is how gender roles are distributed in cultures. In masculine cultures, both men and women are relatively tough, and in these cultures social gender roles are clearly distinct. Men are supposed to be assertive, tough, and focus on material success, whereas women are supposed to be more modest, tender, and concerned with the quality of life in some countries such as Japan, Austria, Switzerland, and Italy. In feminine cultures, social gender roles overlap. In these cultures, no one should fight and no one should be too ambitious. Everyone should be concerned with maintaining good relationships with others. Both men and women are supposed to be modest, tender, and concerned with the quality of life in some countries such as Sweden, Spain, and Norway.

4.6.4 Long-Term Orientation versus Short-Term Orientation

In long-term orientation countries, people value towards the future, like thrift (saving) and persistence. For example in Japan, the country with a long-term vision to investment, annual profit is not important, but the progress year after year to achieve a long-term goal. In short-term orientation countries, people value the past and present, maintaining personal stability or happiness and living for the present; they are concerned with short-term results. For example, in the Western Countries, the company pays more attention to the quarterly and annual profit results, managers in the year or quarter by quarter on staff performance assessment in profit.

4.6.5 Indulgence versus Restraint

Indulgence stands for a society that allows relatively free **gratification** (满足) of basic and natural human drives related to enjoying life and having fun. Restraint stands for a society that suppresses gratification of needs and regulates it by means of strict social norms. Australia is a typical country for indulgence. On the contrary, Pakistan is a typical country for restraint.

Hofstede's theory of cultural values provides us with an operational theoretical framework, and in his monograph "The Influence of Culture" (2001) cited a large number of survey data. The reason why the influence of the results has continued to this day is that it is widely used in management, social learning, psychology, intercultural communication, and even finance and telecommunications. However, its limitations cannot be ignored.

First of all, this theory can only be used to explain the general value orientation of members of a culture rather than individual members. In addition, the value level of the theory has the trend of "averaging" the cultural value of a country. In other words, his theory presupposes that every cultural group should have typical members, but in fact, it is difficult to find typical members in any cultural group.

Second, although Hofstede's theory has been used by many scholars to study the impact of cultural differences between the East and the West on behavior. Most of data are collected from Hong Kong, Taiwan and Singapore, not from Chinese mainland. This defect makes his theory have great limitations in explaining the cultural and social phenomena in Chinese mainland. Many overseas scholars did not seriously consider the cognitive deviation caused by this deficiency when making cross-cultural comparisons between China and foreign countries. Taking individualism and collectivism as an example, how many Chinese people today, especially young people, have collectivist values? Is Chinese collectivism the same as his collectivist cultural value? How will Chinese solve the problems when there are contradictions between people, do you always think that avoiding positive conflict is the best way? In addition, does the explanation of Hofstede's power distance apply to our superior subordinate relationship and family members relationship?

Thirdly, Hofstede's research design did not take into account the values of cultural groups outside the west at the beginning. In this way, when we apply and extend the theory to Chinese culture or general collectivist cultural groups, it has become a controversial issue whether it still has theoretical explanatory power.

Key Terms

subgroup	亚群体
high context	高语境
context	情境
low context	低语境
interpersonal communication	人际交际
norm	规范
message	信息
religion	宗教
taboo	禁忌语
action	行为
cultural pattern	文化模式
culture identity	文化身份
integration	融合
cultural shock	文化冲击
intention	目的
subculture	亚文化
individualism	个人主义
rule	规则
anxiety	焦虑
power distance	权力距离

uncertainty avoidance　　　　　　对不确定因素的回避态度

 **Notes**

1. **Hedonism** is a theory of motivation that emerged in the 18th century. It is an important source for the formation of dynamic psychology. It is believed that human behavior is caused by the desire to seek pleasure and avoid suffering.

   享乐主义是18世纪出现的一种动机理论。它是动态心理学形成的重要源泉。该理论认为，人类的行为是由寻求快乐和避免痛苦的欲望引起的。

2. **Edward T. Hall** (1914-2009), an American anthropologist, is credited with being the first person to systematically study cross-cultural communication.

   爱德华·T. 霍尔（1914—2009）：美国人类学家，被誉为系统研究跨文化交际的第一人。

3. **Kluckhohn and Stodtbeck,** also known as K-S Framework, is a reference framework for cross-cultural research. This framework proposes six dimensions to evaluate the basic culture, namely, the relationship between people and the environment, time orientation, conception of humanity, activity orientation, responsibility orientation and space orientation.

   Kluckhohn 和 Stodtbeck 框架，也称为K-S框架，是跨文化研究的参考框架。该框架提出了评估基本文化的六个维度，即人与环境的关系、时间取向、人的本质、活动取向、责任取向和空间取向。

4. **Puritan,** a member of a 16th and 17th century Protestant group in England and New England opposing as unscriptural the ceremonial worship and the prelacy of the Church of England or one who practices or preaches a more rigorous or professedly purer moral code than that which prevails.

   清教徒，16—17世纪英国和新英格兰的新教团体的成员，反对英国国教的宗教仪式和礼拜仪式，实践或宣扬比当时更严格或更纯粹的道德准则。

5. **Navajo,** also known as Navaho. The largest of the American Indian groups, numbering about 170,000 in the late 20th century. They are scattered throughout northwestern New Mexico, northeastern Arizona and southeastern Utah. The Navajo speak an Apache language, which is a member of the Athabascan family. It is not known exactly when the Navajo and Apaches migrated from Canada into southwestern North America; other Athabascan-speaking Indians still settled in

Canada; other scholars, however, place the migration between A. D. 900 and 1200.

纳瓦霍人，美洲印第安人团体中最大的团体，在 20 世纪后期大约有 170 000。他们散布在新墨西哥州西北部，亚利桑那州东北部和犹他州东南部。他们说一种阿帕奇语，属于阿萨巴坎语。纳瓦霍人和阿帕奇人何时从加拿大迁移到北美西南地区尚不清楚。其他说阿萨巴坎语的印第安人仍定居加拿大。但是，也有其他学者认为迁移发生在公元 900 年至 1200 年之间。

6. **Geert Hofstede,** a professor of the social humanities, PhD, has been director of IBM branch personnel investigation of Europe, the Dutch town, Maastricht university emeritus professor of international Management, many universities in Europe, and served as honorary professor at the University of Hong Kong is engaged in the Organization of Anthropology and international Management (Organizational Anthropology and International Management). After his retirement in 1993, he continued to be a visiting professor at several universities in Hong Kong, Hawaii, and Australia.

吉尔特·霍夫斯塔德，人文社会科学教授，博士学位。曾担任位于荷兰小镇的 IBM 欧洲分支机构人事调查主任，马斯特里赫特大学国际管理名誉教授，以及欧洲许多大学的教授，并担任香港大学的名誉教授，从事人类学和国际管理（组织人类学和国际管理）组织的研究。1993 年退休后，他继续在中国香港、夏威夷和澳大利亚的几所大学担任客座教授。

Case 1

Wang Bin, a Chinese student studying in Britain, was once invited by her British classmate Brain to his house to cook a Chinese meal. Her two Chinese friends were also invited. They busied themselves in the kitchen, making dumping while Brain did something in the garden and his wife sat on the sofa reading. Wang Bin felt a little upset for she thought that both the host and the hostess should offer to help with the kitchen work. The meal was great and everyone enjoyed themselves. The couple kept complimenting them on their cooking skills and asked for the recipe. But then after the meal, the couple just put down their chopsticks and started minding their own business, leaving the Chinese guests to clear the table and do the dishes. Wang Bin felt absolutely confused or even angry. She concluded that guests to a Chinese family will never be allowed to do any housework. This is one of the ways the host and hostess show their hospitality. Even if the guests offer to cook a dish, the host or the hostess should stay around them and offer help whenever they can. It is even harder to imagine that they would let their guests clear the table and do the dishes, though the guests should always volunteer to help. Wang Bin's meal at a British family sets a great contrast to her Chinese experience. This is why Wang Bin got angry. What she should do is to avoid a hasty conclusion. She should first observe the situation without making judgment. And then analyze the situation using what she knows about the differences between Chinese and British culture.

(选自 http://wenku.baidu.com/view/b496090413661ed9a51f01dc281e53a580251a1.html.)

 Questions for Discussion

1. Why did Wang Bin feel a little upset while preparing the meal?
2. Why did Wang Bin feel absolutely confused or even angry after dinner?
3. What should she do to avoid this misunderstanding?

Case 2

In the university, Li Fang, a Chinese student, met an Western exchange student named Sally who has also recently come to China to study. One day, they went out for dinner in a little restaurant nearby and each of them had a bowl of noodles. After dinner, Li Fang felt that since Sally was new in China, she should treat her to dinner and gave the waiter money for both of their dinners. When Sally realized what Li Fang had done, she seemed surprised and not very happy and said that she wanted to pay for her own dinner. She said that they should "go Dutch". Li Fang kept refusing to take Sally's money and finally she gave in. Li Fang found the experience a little awkward and unpleasant, because she didn't have the good feeling that she had when she treated her Chinese friends to a meal. Let's consider why Westerns always pay for their own meals. Firstly, Westerners don't emphasize relationships between people as much as Chinese do. Westerners are often more distant in their social relationships than Chinese are and keep you from being obligated to other people, while Chinese people tend to value the obligations that bind people together. Secondly, another Westerners value reflected by the custom of paying for yourself is fairness. Each person will pay for exactly what they ordered so that no one is taking advantage of anyone else while Chinese don't care about who will pay more than others. Thirdly, paying for themselves may even reflect the Westerners passion for efficiency. They think there is no need to spend time arguing over the bill while Chinese seem to enjoy fighting over the bill at the end of meal, which is seen as unnecessary fuss by Westerners.

 Questions for Discussion

1. Why did Sally want to pay for her own dinner?
2. Why did Li Fang feel a little awkward and unpleasant with refusal?
3. What are the differences in paying the bill after dinner between East and West?

Case 3

Peter is the general manager of an American company in China. Recently, Jun Chen, one of the Chinese managers made a mistake at work that caused some difficulties that required a lot of effort to fix. Jun Chen was very upset about what had happened, and came to Peter's office to make a formal apology.

Jun Chen went into Peter's office after being told to, smiling before he spoke, "Peter, I've been feeling very upset about the trouble I've caused for the company. I'm here to apologize for my mistake. I'm terribly sorry about it and I want you to know that it will never happen again." Jun Chen said, looking at Peter with the smile he had been wearing since he walked into the office.

Peter found it hard to accept the apology. He looked at Jun Chen, and asked, "are you sure?" "Yes, I'm very sorry and I promise this won't happen again," Jun Chen said, with a smile even broader than before. "I'm sorry I just can't take your apology. You don't look sorry at all!" Peter said angrily.

Jun Chen's face turned very red. He did not in the least expect Peter to take it negatively. He was desperate to make himself understood. "Peter," he managed to smile again, "trust me, no one can feel any sorrier than I do about it." Peter was almost furious by now, "if you're that sorry, how can you still smile?"

Questions for Discussion

1. Why did Peter find it hard to accept Jun Chen's apology?
2. Why did Jun Chen keep smiling all the time?

Case 4

Lisa was invited to a Chinese friend's home to have dinner. The hostess was very kind and busied herself in the kitchen making tasty dishes, and the host served the dishes on the table one by one. Lisa kept finishing all the food on her plate because she wished to be polite. That was a big mistake because she found her plate refilled and many more dishes following. In the West, even if it was a formal dinner, it would be usually just three courses: soup, main dish, and dessert. But in China, an informal dinner would have four dishes and a soup; a formal dinner would have at least eight dishes and a soup. In Britain, hospitality is not measured by how many dishes are provided as in China. It is shown by giving you freedom to choose whatever you really want. They never press you. They never put food on your plate but just ask you to help yourself. If you, as a guest, are shy or modest, waiting for the food to be put on your plate, you will remain half-starved.

 Questions for Discussion

1. Why did Lisa finish all the food on her plate?
2. Why did the hostess refill the plate and offer more dishes?
3. What are the differences in expressing hospitality at table between the East and the West?

Further Reading

Passage 1

Intercultural Communication

Intercultural communication is an interdisciplinary field of study which incorporates research from disciplines such as social psychology, sociology, cultural anthropology, sociolinguistics, and, of course, communication. One of the most important areas of research addressed by intercultural scholars is how misunderstandings can be minimized when people communicate with others from different cultures.

First, context is very important to understanding intercultural communication. There are two ways individuals use context in communication: one is low-context and the other is high-context.

Low-context communication is like a computer program; everything must be specified in the coded message or the computer program will not run. In a low-context culture, individuals must express themselves as explicitly as possible for effective communication to occur. High-context communication, in contrast, is like communication between twins who were raised together. Twins intuitively understand each other and use shortened sentences and words when they talk.

If Chinese do not understand the low-context system used in the Western Countries and they do not understand the high-context system used in China, misunderstandings will occur.

Understanding cultural norms and rules such as the way we are expected to greet others, the way we are expected to dress, the way we are expected to eat, and the way we are expected to answer questions are also important in improving communication with people from other cultures. For example, if you greet a westerner by asking him or her "Where are you going?" or "Have you eaten yet?" he or she might feel very uncomfortable because asking these questions could be interpreted as an invasion of privacy. But in the Chinese culture, these are appropriate greetings which do not invade the other person's privacy.

These examples do illustrate the importance of studying the influence of culture on communication if we are to overcome culture barriers to effective communication.

(选自 http://www.geto.com/article-4286.)

Questions for Discussion

1. What are the most important areas of research addressed by intercultural scholars?

2. What's the difference between low-context communication and high-context communication?

3. How do you improve communication with people from other cultures?

Passage 2

Mountains and Water in Chinese Art
Karin Albert

Mountains and water play prominent roles in Chinese art. Over the centuries, Western painters have boldly explored new themes and media, continuously striving to transcend the familiar and challenge the unknown, while their Chinese counterparts have relished the creation of timeless natural sceneries. Painting scrolls feature towering mountain peaks and pouring waterfalls, slopes receding far into the distance and gently rolling streams. No classical Chinese garden would be complete without mountains and water.

To some extent, China's geography offers an explanation. Mountainous terrain makes up most of the country, water is abundant in the central and southern regions, and two of the world's greatest streams, the Yellow River and the Yangtze River, define much of the land. Her natural environment has shaped China's culture and traditions and molded the minds of her people.

Ancient Chinese mythology abounds with tales of mountain **mysticism** (神秘主义). Outstanding peaks were believed to be the dwelling places of immortals, spurring man's imagination and fueling his desire to command the **elixir** (长生不老药) conferring eternal life. Emperor Wudi of the Han Dynasty sent an expedition to the Three Blessed Isles of the Eastern Sea, a group of island mountains off the coast said to be a favorite **haunt** (鬼魂出没的地方) of immortals, in the hope of partaking in their secret. His envoys never returned, but Emperor Wudi, in an effort to **entice** (诱惑) those **elusive** (难以捉摸的) immortals to take up residence with him **commemorated** (纪念) the magic islands by having three peaks set up in the lake of his luxurious garden Shang Lin (Great Grove). Although different in purpose and aesthetic appeal, Wudi's garden and similar imperial parks built during the Han Dynasty may be viewed as an early form from which the garden of the scholar-official, the mainstream of the classical Chinese garden as we know it today, evolved.

A profound faith in nature's powers to uplift and nourish the spirit and to purify the soul has been shared by the two great philosophies indigenous to China, Confucianism and Daoism. Although Confucius was mostly concerned with the ordering of social and governmental affairs rather than metaphysics, moral integrity, and the continuous perfection of man, through learning are cornerstones of his ideal of family and state. Confucius coined the phrase that "the wise take pleasure in rivers and lakes, the virtuous in mountains (*Analects*)."

Mountains and water are central to the Daoist conception of the world. This school of thought views man as an inseparable part of the universe. Harmony is attained if each individual's energy is attuned to the energy of the cosmos at large. Intimate encounters with natural phenomena are the path leading to this goal. Tranquility induces a relaxed condition in which the workings of the universe may be understood. In a state of heightened spiritual awareness, man's ability to adjust his rhythm to the pulse of the cosmos and to eventually merge with it will prevail.

Mountains not only offer a life in seclusion, devoid of restraints. A wealth of stimulating shapes, a multitude of colors, and the ever changing moods so typical of mountainous surroundings—impressions of this kind are apt to reveal the all-pervading spirit of the universe to the perceptive mind. Nature's sheer power and grandeur is more easily comprehended in a setting with rugged peaks capped by misty clouds.

The Daoist notion of water is yet more essential. In their efforts to describe the Dao, the Way of the Universe, Laozi and Zhuangzi, the major personages of early Daoism, employed water as their chief metaphor. Water is omnipresent embracing all living things with no trace of partiality or hidden motives. It is the great mediator between contrasts, forever seeking balance.

Continuously dissolving and solidifying, water attains an infinite number of fresh manifestations of unity by way of perpetual transformation. The superior qualities of water are to be emulated by man: It follows its own course and always fills the bottom level, equivalent to the wise man being true to himself and maintaining a low profile. Water is the emblem of the unassertive. Taking the path of least resistance, always yielding, its effectiveness is unsurpassed.

The third great philosophy which has formed the traditional Chinese mind, Buddhism, was introduced to China by monks from India, in the declining years of the Han Dynasty. With an unerring sense for scenic grandeur, Buddhist monks set up monasteries in the pristine mountain wilderness. These sites became gathering grounds for those seeking spiritual enlightenment and islands of hope for the deprived and the disheartened. The narratives of pilgrims spread the word of the magic spell cast by China's great mountains and of the healing powers of nature on the soul.

Buddhism began to find widespread acceptance in China at a time of political and social upheaval known as the Six Dynasties. During this period, the Confucian scholars, greatly esteemed and entrusted with high government posts in the preceding Han Dynasty, found themselves at odds with a political situation abundant with intrigue, nepotism, and corruption. For some high-minded literati, seeking refuge in the mountains became the only alternative to compromising their ideals. Individuals who were willing to sacrifice careers and luxuries in an immoral world for a frugal, pure existence in the mountains became models and were immortalized in poetry and painting for centuries to come.

The Six Dynasties period, then, was a time when a large number of people came to view nature as a refuge, in a spiritual or political sense. It was also the time when nature as a theme entered the arts. Landscape painting as a genre was born and would soon outstrip all other forms. Poetry began to extol the thoughtful life to be found in beautiful natural surroundings. The poem "A reply" by the great Tang poet Li Bai exemplifies the prevailing mood of the time. Country estates Tastefully laid out which were…the forerunners of the urban gardens of the scholar-officials we associate with garden art today, proliferated. Nature had captured the artistic spirit.

Though creating landscape painting, gardens, or penjing, Chinese artists have not sought to recreate nature in a realistic manner. Never has outward resemblance been a major objective. A superior piece of art possesses the quality to transmit life, to convey the very spirit inherent in nature. In pursuit of this goal, the artist concentrates on the essential, leaves out all superfluous detail, and eliminates anything that would distract the viewer's attention.

In the arts dealing with nature, mountains and water are fundamental compositional elements. Mountains and water are viewed as the very representative of nature. Drawing an analogy between the Earth and the human body, the Chinese have referred to mountains as the "bones" to water as the "blood" of the Earth.

Creating mountains and water as essential manifestations of nature, Chinese artists have made generalized philosophical statements. They have translated a deeply felt fundamental truth into visual images.

（选自：王守仁，陈向京. 新一代大学英语综合教程［M］. 2 版. 北京：外语教学与研究出版社，2019.）

Questions for Discussion

1. What are the factors that have shaped Chinese perception of mountains and water?

2. What are the spirits of nature in mountains and water according to the Chinese philosophical thinking?

3. What is the goal of art according to traditional Chinese artists?

Exercises

I. Multiple Choices

1. The simplest definition of culture is a set of ____ within a group or society and institutional learned behavior.

    A. beliefs and behaviors   B. values and norms

    C. rules and regulations   D. customs and concepts

2. Guests to a Chinese family will never be allowed to do any housework to show the ____ of the host and hostess.

    A. hospitality   B. friendliness   C. generosity   D. intimacy

3. Cultural patterns can be interpreted from two aspects consisting of ways of ____.

    A. thinking and learning   B. speaking and gesturing

    C. speaking and living   D. thinking and acting

4. The phrase "go Dutch" means ____.

    A. visiting a country   B. having dinner individually

    C. splitting the cost   D. treating someone to dinner

5. ____ together constitutes the components of cultural patterns.

    A. Beliefs, values, norms and social practices

    B. Behaviors, religions, norms and social practices

    C. Beliefs, values, norms and customs

D. Beliefs, values, concepts and social practices

6. What one considers to be the important views about the world are based on ____.

A. laws and regulations   B. commonly recognized customs

C. culturally shared beliefs   D. traditions and religions

7. Hall suggests that the only way to learn the internal culture of others is to actively ____ their culture.

A. research   B. participate in   C. care for   D. accept

8. ____ deals with the innate character of human nature.

A. Person-nature orientation   B. Time orientation

C. Activity orientation   D. The human nature orientation

9. Uncertainty avoidance is the tendency to behave to arrange things in a way that ____.

A. maximizes unforeseen consequences   B. minimizes unforeseen consequences

C. ignoring unforeseen consequences   D. minimizes foreseen consequences

10. In ____ both men and women are relatively tough, and in these cultures social gender roles are clearly distinct.

A. femininity cultures   B. individualistic cultures

C. masculine cultures   D. collectivistic cultures

II. Matching

Directions: *Match the following words and expressions with the correct Chinese.*

1. hedonism   A. 文化冲击
2. puritan   B. 仁爱
3. individualism   C. 普世主义
4. collectivism   D. 女性气质
5. egalitarianism   E. 享乐主义
6. masculinity   F. 男性气质
7. femininity   G. 集体主义
8. universalism   H. 个人主义
9. benevolence   I. 清教徒
10. culture shock   J. 平等主义

III. Translation

A. **Directions:** *Translate the following paragraph into English.*

反映在艺术和文学中的乡村生活理想是中华文明的重要特征。这在很大程度上归功于道家对自然的感情。传统中国画有两个最受青睐的主题，一个是家庭生活的各种幸福场景，画中往往有老人在下棋或饮茶，男人在耕耘或收割，妇女在织布或缝衣，小孩在户外玩耍。另一个则是乡村生活的种种乐趣，画有渔夫在湖上打渔，农夫在山上砍柴采药，或是书生坐在松树下吟诗作画。这两个主题可以分别代表儒家和道家的生活理想。

B. **Directions:** *Translate the following paragraph into Chinese.*

Plain line drawing is one of the traditional Chinese styles of artistic presentation. It features the contours of images sketched in black ink lines. This style of painting is mostly used in planting human figures and flowers. Although not much ink is applied, this technique can achieve a very lively effect. Plain line drawing originated from the plain drawing of earlier times; through variations in length, thickness, pressure, and changes in trajectory, the artist can portray the texture and motion of images. Plain drawing is also very important style of expression in narrative literature. In this context it refers to a simple and concise style of writing, without embellishment, so as to produce fresh, lively images.

Chapter 5

Verbal Communication

> The mouth is the passage of the heart, through which wisdom pass.
>
> ——Guiguzi (the Warring States period)
>
> 口者，心之门户，智谋皆从之出。
>
> ——鬼谷子（战国）
>
> If we spoke a different language, we would perceive a somewhat different world.
>
> ——Ludwig Wittgenstein
>
> 如果我们说另一种语言，我们将感知一个些许不同的世界。
>
> ——路德维希·维特根斯坦

本章导读

语言是人类使用的一个相对稳定的交际符号系统。在全球化背景下，跨文化交际中的言语交际离不开语言和文化两个要素，而语言和文化也互相影响。本章通过介绍言语交际的定义、基本要素和意义，梳理了语言与文化之间的关系，介绍了不同文化对言语交际风格的影响以及语言的多样性，有助于学习者更全面、更深刻地了解语言与文化之间不可分割的关系，意识到文化及语言差异，从而能够在跨文化交际中更好地理解和尊重他人，并调整自己的语言以达成顺畅交流的目的。

Learning Objectives

In this chapter, students will learn how to understand the definition of verbal communication, describe the relationship between language and culture, summarize the verbal communication styles, and understand the phenomenon of language diversity.

The plateau area of New Mexico is rich in apple, which is popular because of its good quality. A farmer's annual advertisement for his apple is "If you are dissatisfied with the apples you received, please write to me. There is no need to return the apples, but the payment will be refunded to you. One year, there was a huge hailstorm on the plateau, which made all the apples scarred. The farmer thought the apples would be unsalable this time. But he didn't want to waste a year of hard work, so he took an apple and bit it. As a result, he smelled a strong fragrance and the taste was very good. He still sent the apples to different places according to the original order requirements and attached a piece of paper in each box, which said "all apples have scars, but please take a closer look at them. This is the scar caused by hail, and it is the unique mark of apples produced in plateau area. This kind of apple is very crisp and juicy with a super-sweet flavor and a unique fructose taste. "As a result, all the "scarred" apples were sold out, and none of them returned.

 Questions for Discussion

1. Why does the farmer always put a written note in the apples he sells?
2. Can you guess why the customers didn't return the scarred apples?

While-class Learning

5.1 Significance of Verbal Communication

Warm-up Activities

(1) Does verbal communication only refer to the language spoken by people in communication?

(2) Use some examples to list the differences between Chinese and English.

Verbal means "consisting of words". Therefore, verbal codes refer to spoken or written languages. A verbal code comprises a set of rules governing the use of words in creating a message, along with the words themselves. We acquire or learn the rules and contents of our native language as we grow up; thus, we can express our thoughts, emotions, and needs easily in our first language. The study of language begins with identifying its components and how they are put together. Now let's look at the four interrelated components. They are: **phonology** (音韵), **morphology** (词法), **semantics** (语义) and **syntax** (句法).

Phonology explores how sounds are organized in a language. The smallest sound unit of a language is called a phoneme. The phonological rules of a language determine how sounds are combined to form words. For example, the phonemes [s] and [i:] can be used to form the word "see" [si:] in English. Mastery of a language requires the speaker to be able to identify and pronounce different sounds accurately. This may prove difficult for second language speakers, particularly those whose native language does not have a similar sound system to the new language.

Morphology refers to the combination of basic units of meaning, morphemes, to create words. For example, the word "like" consists of one morpheme, meaning "to be similar to sb./sth". The word "unlike" contains two morphemes "like" and the prefix "un-" meaning "not". Used together, they refer to being different from a particular person or thing. Morphemes, and the ways in which they are combined, differ across cultures.

Semantics refers to the study of the meanings of words, and the relationships between words and the things to which they refer. In any language, mastery of vocabulary is an important part of language proficiency. When we learn a second language, we spend much time memorizing words and their meanings. However, it's not enough to just memorize their dictionary meaning for successful intercultural communication because meaning often resides in a culture and words are different in different languages.

Syntax concerns the grammatical and structural rules of language. We combine words into sentences according to grammatical rules in order to communicate. In Chinese, prepositions are often placed after nouns, whereas in English they are placed before nouns or noun phrases. For example "桌子上有一本书", "The book is <u>on the desk</u>". Every language has a set of grammatical rules that govern the sequencing of words. Mastery of another language means knowing those grammatical rules in addition to building a stock of vocabulary.

Language is extremely important to human interaction because it is the way we interact with our surroundings. If we were to survey a normal day, we would soon discover that we use words for a wide variety of purposes. We may use "Good morning!" to greet others at the beginning of a day. We may use language to share a pleasant experience and to instruct others, like "My interview yesterday was very successful. Let me tell you my experience. This may be helpful to you." We use language to persuade, exchange ideas, express opinions, seek information, and express feelings.

In summary, language is a very complex phenomenon and is an integral part of human lives and thus has a powerful influence on people's ability to communicate interculturally. It is not enough to memorize or understand the form, syntax, and meaning of a language because language is not isolated, but exists in culture and must be influenced and restricted by culture.

In China mainland, the east wind generally occurs in spring, which is a symbol of the arrival of spring, while the west wind and northwest wind are the symbols of autumn and winter. In ancient Chinese poetry, there's such sentence like "The wind blows from the east, and spring is everywhere!" However, Britain is located in the Western Hemisphere and has an oceanic climate. The west wind represents the arrival of spring in English. Shelley's *Ode to the West Wind* is an **eulogy** (颂词) to spring.

 Questions for Discussion

1. What do the different attitudes toward the west wind and the east wind in Chinese and English indicate?

2. Can you give other similar examples?

3. Can you think about what other factors affect language?

5.2 Language and Thought

The relationship between language and thought is well captured in the **Sapir-Whorf Hypothesis,** which was developed by the American linguist and anthropologist **Benjamin L. Whorf and Edward Sapir**.

Sapir: Human beings...are very much at the mercy of the particular language which has become the medium of expression for their society...the "real world" is a large extent unconsciously built upon the language habits of the group. (1929)

Whorf: We dissect nature along lines laid down by our native language. The categories and types that we isolate from the world of phenomena we do not find there because they stare every observer in the face; on the contrary, the world is presented in a kaleidoscopic flux of impressions which has to be organized by our minds—and this means largely by the linguistic systems in our minds. [Benjamin Lee Whorf (1956: 213)]

Whorf proposed first that all higher levels of thinking are dependent on language. Or put it more **bluntly** (率直地): language determines thought, hence the strong notion of **linguistic determinism** (语言决定论). Because languages differ in many ways, Whorf also believed that speakers of different languages perceive and experience the world differently, that is, relative to their linguistic background, hence the notion of **linguistic relativism** (语言相对论). The hypothesis holds that a culture is embodied in the language of the people who speak the language. This cultural framework shapes the thoughts of the language's speakers.

Linguistic determinism believes that language structure controls thoughts and cultural norms. Therefore, the world is largely predetermined by language. The differences between languages reflect the basic differences between diverse cultural worldviews.

Linguistic relativism believes that culture is controlled by and controls language. Language provides a conceptual category that affects how the speaker's perception is encoded and stored.

Consider some examples of how language categorizes our world. In Chinese language, there is no single words equivalent to the English word "cousin". Instead, Chinese has different words for one's elder or younger brother or sister-in-law. Chinese even has different words for mother's elder brother and younger brother, father's elder brother and younger brother and so forth. This diversity of vocabulary may indicate that in China, the interpersonal relationship between an individual and his or her extended family is more complex and perhaps more important than that of an English-speaking country.

We create meaning for our world by highlighting certain qualities and characteristics, and by organizing seemingly random events into meaningful categories. For example, we divide different modes of travel into the fastest(plane), faster(train), slower(car/bus), or most comfortable(taxi), most crowded(subway/bus), etc.

Some examples show that culture indeed influences language. In Arabic, the camel plays significant roles in people's life, and so there are more than 40 words for "camel".

In English, we have the word "corner" as in "street corner", "corner of the room" and "corner of the desk". In Japanese, there really is no single word that has the same comprehensive semantic range as the English word. In Japanese, there is the word "kado", which refers to a projecting corner, an actual object, like the "corner" of a table. Then there is the word "sumi", which designates the contained inner space between converging walls, such as the "corner" of a room or inside a box.

Language categorizes our experiences without our full awareness. Only when one learns a second language and moves back and forth between the first language and the second language does he realize the influence of language on perception. The Sapir-Whorf Hypothesis shows that language, thought, and culture are closely connected. As a part of culture, language influences our perception of the world and thus the meaning conveyed by the words. Correspondingly, the language also reflects its culture and environment.

5.3 Language and Culture

5.3.1 Language as a Reflection of the Environment

Language reflects the environment in which we live. We label the things that are around us. In the tropics, snow is not a part of the environment, and therefore, people in that region do not have a word for snow. But in countries and regions where it snows occasionally, the word for snow might be one word without any differentiation. That's the extent of most people's snow vocabulary. But people living in snowy environments may have various terms for snow. Most Canadians, for example, use terms such as snow, powder snow, sleet, slush, blizzard, and ice. The Eskimo's complex classification of types of snow is a classic example of the close connection between language and culture. There is one word for falling snow, another word for fallen snow, still another word for snow packed into ice. The Eskimos view snow as categorically different substances because their very survival requires a precise knowledge of snow conditions. English doesn't have the equivalent of flaky snow or crusty snow. For example, when the needs become more specific, however, longer phrases can be made up to meet these needs, such as corn snow, fine powder snow and drifting snow etc.

It can be said that the environment plays a decisive role in the development of a person's language. Generally speaking, children who grow up in bilingual families are more likely to master two different languages than children in monolingual families.

The environment affects the development of technology, products, and the appropriate vocabulary. For example, the culture in mountain areas does not develop the ship industry, so there are no accompanying words, just as people in the desert do not need to master vocabulary of flood. Cultures in tropical climates will not develop heating systems and, as a result, will not have any of the accompanying words, just as people in cold climates have no need for air conditioning.

5.3.2 Language as a Reflection of Values

Culture of an area is aptly reflected in the language spoken there. In Japanese culture, there's a word かろうし for "death from overwork". At first, this word is not present in other languages, even in countries close to Japan, like China. However, "karoshi" is more than a simple word. It reflects Japanese culture and how committed Japanese people are to their work. In recent years, the corresponding vocabulary has appeared respectively in China and other countries, which might reflect a tendency or current situation of people's work.

For another example, the concept of "privacy" is different in Chinese culture and Western culture. In China, there is no equal word like "privacy" in traditional culture and even no term "privacy" in Chinese Ci Hai (1997 edition) until 1983 the term "privacy" was collected in Modern Chinese Dictionary (2nd edition). Typically, "private" right of individuals was considered as self-interest and was paid little attention to. Even now in the most casual social interactions, friends or neighbors ask about each other's family, marriage, and so on and it is always considered as a courtesy and a means of maintaining intimacy. However, the word "privacy" has positive connotation for people in English-speaking countries. They think of the privacy of their homes and their personal information as human rights, which cannot be easily invaded.

"Good fences make good neighbors" is taken from Robert Frost's poem *Mending Walls;* literally this proverb means that neighbours can get along well when the fence between their individual homes are strong enough to avoid unwanted interference from each other. The proverb now generally implies that in order to maintain a good relationship with others, people need to mind their own business and respect others' privacy.

There are great differences between Chinese and western culture, which leads to their different views on privacy. For thousands of years, most of Chinese people living in the country and people often live in the village from generation to generation, so they are very familiar with and care about each other. It is common for them to talk about family or personal problems. In addition, Chinese people always don't agree with "private" and regard individual rights as private interests. However, medieval agriculture of Western Europe was developed by the form of manor. The circumstance of closed and non-interference in each other makes westerners gradually produced a relatively independent character. So, westerners advocate independence and are not willing to others to interfere in their life. They think that privacy can't be violated.

A close, intimate connection exists between language and culture. They mirror each other obviously, but the connection actually runs deeper. Culture enriches as well as develops the language. According to experts, culture started with the beginning of speech only. Many experts are in the view that it is impossible to completely understand a culture unless people understand the language.

5.4 Language and Identity

Warm-up Activities

Can you give an example to illustrate that the language or regional language we speak influences what others think of us?

The language people speak defines their world, and their social, national, and ethnic identities.

5.4.1 Social identity

Language variations within cultures have an effect on how people communicate and how they categorize themselves. For example, people may use local or regional language to signify their identities as people from that region. The language or regional language they speak also influences what others think of them. The fact that someone speaks another language or speaks our language with a foreign or regional accent influences our social attitudes toward that speaker. People's language attitudes are also influenced by the situations in which the language is used. Many people speak two or more languages and may use these languages in different contexts and for different purposes (e. g. one language in public and another at home).

The concept of social identity is a crucial element in the cognitive approach to prejudice. It is the part of the self-concept derived from membership in one or more social groups, along with the evaluation associated with it. When it comes to prejudice, however, people's concern is not merely with the groups they belong to, but with other groups as well, with which their own group maybe in conflict. If we can assign people to a category, then that tells us things about those people. We couldn't function in a normal manner without using these categories. Similarly, we find out things about ourselves by knowing what categories we belong to. People define appropriate behavior by reference to the norms of groups they belong to, but one can only do this if he or she can tell who belongs to his or her group.

An individual can belong to many different groups. If one has categorized himself or herself as a student, the chances are that he/she will adopt the identity of a student and begin to act in the ways he or she believes students act (and conform to the norms of the group). There will be an emotional significance to one's identification with a group, and his or her self-esteem will become bound up with group membership.

5.4.2 National identity

The sense of national unity is concerned with the integrity of the national language, territory, and religion. The 18th century German philosopher **Johann G. Herder** claims that language expresses the inner consciousness of the nation. When factors like language, national colors, national symbols, the history of the nation, blood connections, culture, cuisine, music, and other factors all play a part. If one views national identity positively, it is typically called "patriotism", but if one views this negatively, it is sometimes known as "chauvinism" asserted its own distinct national language. When the head of state visits abroad, he or she must speak his or her own language, even if he or she can speak the language of the country he or she visits. This is a manifestation of national identity and dignity, representing the exchange of one country and another.

One's national identity refers to the sense of belonging—one has to a state or a nation—or a sense of solidarity one feels with a particular group without regard to one's actual citizenship status. This is not a trait with which people are born; rather, experiences from the common situation of people's lives build their sense of national identity.

5.4.3 Ethnic identity

Language is a vital aspect of any ethnic group's identity. Often, immigrant groups maintain their cultural heritage and identities by using their native languages in their new cultures. Many immigrants in English-speaking countries tend to use English in formal, public settings and their native languages in informal, private environments. Many Chinese immigrants in America ask their children to study Chinese after class. Here is an example.

The author's aunt and her two sons have already got the U.S. green card. After studying in the United States for three years, she returned to China with two sons. When I asked her about their future plans, she said that her two sons planned to apply for colleges in United States in the future. I then asked her why she came back, and she said that the younger son rarely spoke Chinese and they came back for his Chinese learning. In addition, she was not good at English, which hindered her communication with others in the U.S.. She found it hard to be accepted in the circle of natives and her loneliness deepened.

The real case fully demonstrates that the relationship between language and ethnic identity is inextricably linked. Different languages represent different ethnic and social groups. It's hard to communicate smoothly with people in different groups without understanding their languages and cultures.

5.5 Verbal Communication Styles

Warm-up Activities

What are the differences in communication behaviors in the following cases?

(1) When an American girl's new hairstyle is praised by her boss, she directly thanked him.

(2) Scholars observed that Chinese students seldom raise their hands to answer questions in class, and generally do not directly ask questions or question what the teacher said.

(3) In South Korea, new and young actors use **honorifics** (敬语) when communicating with actors who have been in the acting business for a long time.

(4) In class, several American students and teachers had a heated debate on a certain topic.

Language is an important way of communication, so it is assumed that we can communicate successfully if we master the language. However, it is not the case. Successful communication not only depends on what is said but also on how the message is communicated. Culture influences the style of communication at a great level.

Theorists have described five communication styles: direct and indirect styles, self-enhancement and self-effacement styles, elaborate, exacting and succinct styles, personal and contextual styles, instrumental and affective styles, and Recognizing the differences in communication styles can help us understand the cultural differences underpinning the verbal communication process so as to avoid intercultural communication failure.

5.5.1 Direct vs. Indirect Communication Styles

A direct communication style is one in which the speaker's needs, wants, desires, and intentions are explicitly communicated. Conversely, an indirect communication style is one in which the speaker's true intentions or needs are only implied or hinted during the conversation.

Although both styles are, to some extent, universally used in communication, research indicates that indirect styles are more likely to be used in or Asian cultures, such as in Japan, China, and South Korea, where harmony is considered important for maintaining good interpersonal relationships.

Let's look at the talk between an American student and his Nigerian roommate. An American student said, "Hey, buddy. I'm invited to attend a party this evening. But it's a little bit far from here. Would you like to give me a lift?" This American student may think if his roommate has no time, he will say no. To this request, the Nigerian student's reaction is like this, "Oh! I have promised my sister to babysit my niece so that she could go to work. What should I do!" And then the Nigerian student asked, "En...do you still remember my sister?"

The American student answered, "Sure, last time she made a good dinner for me, I appreciate that!" "And?" He actually is wondering, "Why does my roommate talk about his sister?" the Nigerian roommate continued, "Yeah! I told her you are my best friend. She likes you very much. Do you remember her little daughter?" The American student answered, "Of course! She is an angel! ... but do you have time this evening?" Apparently, the American student doesn't know what his roommate means. Then the Nigerian student proceeded, "Em... my sister has got a new job recently. She has to go out to work at night occasionally. But most of time she is at home. Tonight is her working night. ...so..."

Here, the Nigerian student assumes that his American roommate realizes that he has to babysit his niece when his sister goes out. But the American student is puzzled, "So what?" So the Nigerian student has to say, "Er... I have to babysit my niece tonight."

The American student finally realized, "Oh! You mean you cannot give me a lift! That's all right!"

In this case, instead of saying "Sorry, I'm afraid I cannot", the Nigerian student replied by talking about his sister and her daughter. The American student felt confused as to what his Nigerian roommate was trying to say. In American culture, if such a request for a lift is inconvenient, one would simply respond by saying "Sorry, I can't do it". However, in collectivist cultures like Nigeria, it is not considered polite to say "no" to a friend—but it is the responsibility of the person who made the request to figure out it is not appropriate to ask for the favour. Differences in expectations for appropriate communication styles can lead to misunderstandings between speakers.

5.5.2 Self-enhancement and Self-effacement

Self-enhancement verbal style emphasizes the importance of boasting about one's accomplishments and abilities. The self-effacement verbal style, on the other hand, emphasizes the importance of humbling oneself through verbal restraints, hesitations and modest conversation.

For example, in many Asian cultures, self-effacement talk is expected to signal modesty or humility. Japanese, when serving tea, tend to say, "So-cha desuga ..." which means "This is not very delicious, but..." In China, when someone praises one's child for his or her achievement, verbal self-deprecation is expected. There are set expressions for verbal humility such as "That's not worth mentioning", "Don't praise him, he is nothing special" and "It's far from success." When a hostess offers her guest the meal that she has prepared, she apologizes to her guest saying "there is nothing special" even though she probably spent two days planning for the meed. Of course the guest should protest such "disclaimer" and reemphasize her gratitude. Self-effacement is a necessary part of politeness of rituals in some Asian cultures.

In the U. S. culture, people encourage individuals to "sell and boast about themselves." Mothers tell their children they are special and unique in the world. However, the notion of merchandising oneself does not set well with the Japanese. In Japan, one does not like to stand out or be singled out, even by others; it is far worse to promote oneself. For example, there are Japanese "personals" in the classified ads in magazines that are similar to those in the United States. However, an American ad might begin with "A handsome, athletic male with a good sense of humor seeks a fun-loving partner...", while the comparable Japanese ad might read, "Although I am not very good-looking, I'm willing to try my best."

5.5.3 Elaborate, Exacting and Succinct styles

This dimension is concerned with the quantity of talking about a culture values, and reflects a culture's attitudes toward talk and silence. The elaborate style involves the use of rich, expressive, and embellished language in everyday communication. For example, rather than simply saying that someone is thin, a comment such as "she is so thin that she can walk between rain drops without getting wet" embellishes and colours the statement. Arab, Middle Eastern, and African-American cultures tend to use metaphorical expressions in everyday conversation.

An exacting style that focuses on precision and use of right number of words to convey message is used by Americans. They tend to prefer an exacting style of interaction consistent with a "just the facts" mentality.

In the succinct communication style, simple assertions and even silence are valued. The use of the three styles is closely related to Hall's high-context and low-context cultures. Elaborate style tends to characterize low-context cultures. Conversely, in high-context culture, silence rather than talk can be used to maintain control in a social situation. For example, in Europe, the Finns place a high value on silence, and it is not unusual to pass a companiable evening in Helsinki with virtually no words exchanged at all.

5.5.4 Personal and Contextual Styles

This dimension is concerned with the extent to which the speaker emphasizes the self as opposed to his or her role. Gudykunst and Ting-Toomey define personal style as one that amplified the individual identity of the speaker. This style is often used in individualistic cultures, which emphasize individual goals over those of the group. Person-centred communication tends to be informal and is reflected by the use of the pronoun "I". On the other hand, contextual communication style is oriented by status and role. Formality and power distance are often emphasized. Contextual style is often seen in collectivistic cultures where one's role, identity and status are highlighted. For example, instead of using "you" for all persons, as is the case in English, Chinese use an elaborated system of linguistic forms to show respect to people of different ranks or social statue, like "你" and "您".

5.5.5 Instrumental Styles and Affective Styles

People in some cultures may be more direct and goal-oriented, preferring efficient linguistic forms, while other cultures may have a preference for more emotional and expressive communication. We see this in the way that offers are made in America and China. In Northern American countries, the correct sequence is "offer→request/decline". For example, "Would you like some iced tea?" "No, thanks." or "Okay." But in Some Eastern Asian Countries, one should offer food or hospitality even if one is not willing or able to give it at that time, just to be polite; the other person, even if hungry or tired, should decline the request, just to be polite. The function of such offers in these cultures, then, is to make someone feel welcome. The correct sequence becomes "offer→decline→insist→[resist→double insist→] accept/decline". A larger offer may require multiple resistance and insistence turns.

5.6 Language Diversity

Warm-up Activities

1. Do you agree that accent is an important marker of sociolects? Please use some examples to explain that.

2. How do people differ in their attitudes toward the word "old" in Chinese and Western cultures? Please give an example.

People who use the same language in a sense all speak differently. Which language each of them chooses to use depends, to a certain extent, on their cultural background. Language diversity includes several aspects. They are dialects and sociolects, taboo and euphemism, Pidgin and Lingua Franca and idioms.

5.6.1 Dialects and Sociolects

Dialects are versions of a language with distinctive vocabulary, grammar, and pronunciation that are spoken by particular groups of people or within particular regions. Dialects are geographically different and nationally, regionally, or locally different. For example, Australia English and British English are different, English used in London and Manchester are different. The most common dialect categories of German are High, Middle, and Low, but there are numerous sub-dialects of these classifications that are often unintelligible to someone speaking Standard German. Chinese is usually considered to have seven distinct, major dialects (Cantonese, Mandarin, **Hakka** (客家语), etc.), which are bound by a common writing system but are mutually unintelligible when spoken. In different dialect areas, people's awareness of dialect is also different. Usually these linguistic differences include pronunciation and intonation, so they are often referred to as accent differences; however, if they also include vocabulary and grammar, they involve dialect differentiation.

Dialects can play an important role in intercultural communication because people who speak the same dialect often regard each other as fellows and share an intimate relation. Examples of different dialects can be seen all around the world, China is no exception. Each province in China has its own dialect. Most of the time, dialects are material of cross talk and sketches, which are very popular among the youth.

Sociolect is a variety of speech associated with a particular social class, occupational group, and other factors or the community communication habits formed by these factors. They are also known as social dialect, group idiolect, and class dialect. We have known that one's social identity is reflected by his/her linguistic forms and language. In this aspect, accent is an important marker of sociolect. For example, the so-called "**Received Pronunciation**" (英语的标准发音) in British English has become characteristic of upper class speech in Britain in the 19th century. And in America, speakers who speak African-American Vernacular English (AAVE, Black Standard English) are sometimes unfairly assumed to be less reliable, less intelligent, and of lower status than those who speak Standard American English. Accent will influence people's attitude when they communicate. In addition to accent, vocabulary, syntax, and discourse are reflected differently in social dialects.

Linguistic research has shown that sociolects refer not only to one's social condition but also to one's style according to the communicative situation. In a formal situation, one could say "How do you do, Mr. Johnson", and in an informal situation, one could say "Hi buddy!" **Martin Joos,** a well-known American linguist, identified five levels of social variation: frozen, formal, consultative, casual, intimate. The five varieties correspond to five degrees or levels of formality. An example of the difference can be considered in the following:

In real communication event, appropriate choice of vocabulary, syntax, and phonological variants is equally important. If any awkward vocabulary is used in an utterance, it may make the hearer(s) laugh, frown, and even show great anger. For instance, in a class, when a junior speaks to his senior, "I know your father is a policeman" certainly reveals a higher degree of deference to the interlocutor than "I hear your old man is a cop."

There are many forms of social dialects, such as **argot, slang, jargon,** and of course, network language, such as **Leetspeak,** is definitely regarded as a kind of sociolect. It is limited and informal but popular in the network, especially. among young netizens; however, it's uneasy to integrate into the real social languages.

A big challenge to communicative effect is presented by these dialects or sociolects which also play an important role in intercultural communication because people speaking the same dialects or sociolects often regard each other as fellows and share an intimate relation. If both parties use the same dialect or sociolect, it will increase the trust and intimacy between them and the communicative effect will be in line with the satisfaction of both parties.

5.6.2 Taboo and Euphemism

Taboo is one way in which a society expresses its disapproval of certain kinds of behavior. In fact, taboo is culture specific. Cultural taboo is a unique phenomenon, representing the characteristics of a certain culture and protecting a culture from being offended. Different people from different cultures have their own taboo terms. Those words, phrases, and topics that imply something bad or unrefined cannot be used in intercultural communication. If the participants do not have knowledge of taboos in other cultures, conflicts in intercultural communication can easily arise.

Conversation taboos are topics inappropriate for conversation with people in certain cultures or groups. Divine & Braganti (1992) summarize some appropriate and inappropriate topics of conversation in selected countries.

In respect of women, for example, it is impolite to ask about their ages. Age is considered a taboo for Westerners, especially for ladies. Their cultural background makes them treat "old" as "useless" and "outdated".

(1) Naming Taboo

Naming taboo is a cultural taboo against speaking or writing the given names of noble persons in China and neighboring nations in the ancient Chinese cultural sphere.

There are several kinds of naming taboos. One of them is the naming taboo of the "state", which discouraged the use of the emperor's given name and those of his ancestors. For example, during the Qin Dynasty, Qin Shihuang's given name *Zheng* (政) was avoided, and the first month of the year *Zhengyue*(政月) was rewritten into *Zhengyue* (正月: the upright month), and furthermore renamed as *Duanyue* (端月: the proper/upright month). The character 正 was also pronounced *Zeng* instead of *Zheng* to avoid similarity.

In English, taboos on the names of gods include taboos on the name of God, of Jesus Christ, of Saint Mary, of Satan and of some other gods, such as fairies and **goblins** (小妖精) and so on. Taboos on the names of gods are very strict. For the people who believe in Christianity, God exists everywhere, and the name of God and other words connected with the religion can only be used in the religious situations.

(2) Death and Illness

Death and illness are main disasters for human being, while health is a great bliss that people hope to achieve all the time. Taboos on death and illness are universal. But there is something special in Chinese taboo on death. Because death is everyone's destiny, Chinese people just hope for longevity, and death that follows longevity is also a blessing. For example, people will say *Jiahe* (驾鹤), *Xianshi* (仙逝), *Yuanji* (圆寂) for the Buddhist monks and so on instead of si(死).

Chinese taboo on illness has much to do with Chinese tradition. The Chinese people seldom speak of illness directly. They do this because illness itself is unpleasant, and because they think mentioning their own illness would appear self-centered by paying too much attention to themselves and by giving burden to the hearer. They don't mention other's illness because they do not intend to increase other's worries and because they want to express their wish for the patient to recover soon.

Western people rarely talk openly about death. Even in hospital, if somebody's death is announced directly to him or her, hospitals will receive complaints for doing so. It seems that people still prefer the traditional practice of telling the truth mildly, because it seems to show more human concern and consideration.

Euphemism is the avoidance of words that may be seen as offensive or disturbing to the addressee. Taboo and euphemism are actually interconnected. Death is an inevitable stage at the end of one's life's journey. People use euphemisms to respect the dead, to memorize them, to praise them, or sometimes only to avoid direct mention of death. There are hundreds of euphemisms relating to "death" in both Chinese and

English. Here are just a few examples meaning "to die" in English: "to pass away", "to go west", "to go to heaven," "to fall asleep in the Lord", "to be in Abraham's bosom", "to leave this world", "to join the silent majority", "to go to one's eternal reward", "to cross to the other side", and so on.

To get along with people from other cultures, we need to understand that people from different cultural backgrounds will have a unique way of doing things, analyzing situations, and reacting to circumstances.

Euphemism is widely and frequently used figure of speech. It literally means "to speak with good word". The general characteristics of euphemism—the use of pleasant, polite, or harmless-sounding terms in the place of those considered unpleasant, rude, or offensive. Since euphemism is culturally relevant, namely, different cultures show different attitudes toward the same taboo, which is deep-rooted in a country's cultural environment. Having an inherent association with the country's history, customs, values, national character, etc. suggests the basic characteristics of a culture in a comprehensive manner. Euphemism is products of social language and **embodiments** (体现) of culture as well.

(1) Positive Euphemisms vs. Negative Euphemisms

Hugh Rawson divides euphemisms into two general types—positive and negative. Positive euphemisms can also be called stylistic euphemisms or exaggerating euphemisms. "The positive ones inflate and magnify, making the euphemized items seem altogether grander and more important than they really are." (Rawson 1981: 1) In order to avoid thrill, to be polite or to achieve cooperation, British and American people, especially contemporary Americans, prefer using the technique of exaggeration to euphemize something unpleasant and embarrassing.

The positive euphemisms include many fancy occupational titles, which save the egos of workers by elevating their job status. For example, "exterminating engineers" for rat catchers, "beautician" for "hairdressers". In ancient China, there did exist occupational titles, for example, eunuch was called "gonggong" or "zhishi" (both were respectful forms of address, the former meaning "grandpa", and the latter, "executive"). "Xizi" (**derogatory** (贬义的) term for actors or actresses in days of gone) was called "lingren" (a beautified address). Since the founding of the P. R. C, especially the carrying out of the reform and opening-up, many new euphemisms have been created. People's ideology, values, and their way of thinking have undergone a great change, especially in showing respect for others. For example, "清洁工" (sanitary worker/street cleaner), "护士" (hospital nurse) and "邮递员" (postman/mailman) are often called euphemistically "环境美容师" (environmental beautician), "白衣天使" (angle in white) and "绿衣使者" (messenger in green). Hence, it might be said that quite a few positive euphemisms are words with good-will. They usually appear in the political, military and commercial context.

The negative euphemisms can be called traditional euphemisms or narrowing euphemism. They are extremely ancient, and closely connected with the taboos. A euphemism and its corresponding taboo are in fact two faces of the same coin. They refer to the same thing though they have different looks, the euphemism having a much more pleasant face than the taboo. In many cultures, it is forbidden to pronounce the name of God. So there are euphemisms such as "Jeeze", "Jeepers Creepers", or "Gee" for "Jesus", "Jesus Christ" or "Christ", "goodness" for "God" or "My Gum" for "My God". The names of the tabooed subjects as the dead, and the animals that are hunted or feared, may also be euphemized this way. In Northeast China, the bear is called "老爷子" (grandfather) by people and the tiger is alluded to as the "猫" (cat) or "山神爷" (god of the mountain). Some Chinese call "黄鼠狼" (weasel) and "狐狸" (fox) as "黄仙" (weasel fairy) and "狐仙" (fox fairy) respectively.

(2) Conscious Euphemism vs. Unconscious Euphemism

Euphemisms, whether positive or negative, can be divided into unconscious and conscious euphemisms. The criterion is whether the euphemistic meaning is correlative with the original meaning or not.

Unconscious euphemisms are used unconsciously, without any intent to deceive or evade. For example, now the standard term as "cemetery" has been a replacement for the more deathly "graveyard" since the 14th century. "**Indisposition**" (小病) has been a substitute for "disease" for a long period; people seldom realize that its original meaning is incapacity for dealing with something. Take "dieter" for another example: the original meaning, taking food by a rule or regulation, has been substituted by the euphemistic meaning "the one moderate in eating and dining for losing weight". From the above, we can conclude that unconscious euphemisms were developed so long ago that few can remember their original motivations.

Conscious euphemisms are widely employed, which involves more complex categories. When people communicate with each other, speakers are conscious to say tactfully, and the listeners understand their implied meanings. For example, when a lady stands up and says that she wants to "powder her nose" or "make a phone call" at a dinner party, the people present realize that is means "something else", that is, "going to the ladies' room".

(3) Vague Words or Expressions

Vague words and expressions can **blur** (模糊) the undesirable yet explicit associations that taboo words arouse and are therefore euphemistic. So in both English and Chinese, people use abstract, general, and vague words and expressions to euphemize the oral taboos.

To avoid using the word "fat", such words as "round", "plump", "stout", "well-fed", "full", "full-bodied", "king-sized" and so on are employed in English. Similarly, Chinese use "发福" (put on weight), "富态" (portly) to replace "胖" (fat). Chinese terms such as "有外遇" (carry on with some other woman), "婚外恋" (extramarital affair), which refer to having sexual relations outside marriage, are euphemistic expressions of "有姘头" (having a paramour), "通奸" (commit adultery). In English, this kind of relation is used vaguely as "to have an affair with someone", "to work late at the office", etc.. Still there are other examples: "The needy" and "the disadvantaged" stand for "the poor"; "gay" and "queer" for "homosexual"; "a lady of the street" for "prostitute"; "a growth" for "cancer"; "有困难" (have difficulty) vaguely means "穷" (be hard up); "腿脚不方便" (to have difficulty walking) means "腿脚有残疾" (to have a deformed leg).

5.6.3 Pidgin and Lingua Franca

Pidgins are formed and used when two communities that do not share a common language come into contact and need to communicate. This is very common, especially in trade or other business activities. Common pidgins are based on English, French, Spanish, and Portuguese. A pidgin has a simplified grammatical structure and reduced lexicon and refers mainly to a small set of contexts—it is about situational use.

A pidgin is a restricted language which arises for the purposes of communication between two social groups of which one is in a more dominant position than the other. The less dominant group is the one which develops the pidgin. Historically, pidgins arose in colonial situations where the representatives of the particular colonial power, officials, tradesmen, sailors, etc. came in contact with natives. The latter developed a jargon when communicating with the former. This resulted in a language on the basis of the colonial language in question and the language of the natives. Such a language was restricted in its range as it served a definite purpose, namely basic communication with the colonists. In the course of several generations such a reduced form of language can become more complex, especially if it develops into the mother tongue of a group of speakers. This latter stage is that of creolization. **Creoles** (克里奥尔语) are much expanded versions of pidgins and have arisen in situations in which there was a break in the natural linguistic continuity of a community, like on slave plantations in their early years.

The interest of linguists in these languages has increased greatly in the last few decades. The main reason for this is that Pidgins and Creoles are young languages. In retracing their developments it may be possible to see how new languages can arise. Furthermore, the large number of shared features among widely dispersed pidgins and creoles leads to the conclusion that Creoles at least show characteristics which are typical of language in the most general sense, the features of older languages, such as complex morphology or intricate phonology, arising due to the action of various forces over a long period of time after the birth of these languages. In type, Creoles are all analytic and generally lack complexity in their sound systems.

Pidgin languages possess two characteristics. First, they have no native speakers. Second, the linguistic and grammatical structure of pidgin language is always simple and based on one or two other languages. For example, some pidgin language is still spoken in Hong Kong. It is the mixture of Cantonese—the native language in Hong Kong—and British English. The meaning of "how much dollar" is expressed as "How muchee dollar" in pidgin. "Long time no see" is a typical example of a pidgin used by early Chinese immigrants in the U. S. and has been used by many people now.

Compared with the relatively low status of pidgin, a lingua franca is of higher value. A **lingua franca** is also used for communication between different groups of people, each speaking a different language. However, it is seen as a means of international communication and enjoys prestige among different groups of people. Today, English is considered a lingua franca because it has become the most widely used language spoken by non-native speakers. It is often called a global language that sustains communication in the world.

A lingua franca is a language or way of communicating between people who do not speak one another's native language. Bridge language, link language, and common language are alternative names for lingua franca. For example, imagine a conference for which experts all over the world attend. Since there are attendees with various native languages, the conference will be conducted by a language (or few languages) that is understood or known by most of them.

Furthermore, it is important to note that lingua franca refers to any language that serves as a common language between people who do not share a native language. Therefore, a pidgin can also serve as a lingua franca. A lingua franca can also be a **vernacular language** (白话); for example, English is the vernacular language in the United Kingdom, but it is also used as a lingua franca in South Asian countries. Languages like English, French, Spanish, Arabic, and Mandarin Chinese are the main languages that serve as a lingua franca in the modern world. Latin, however, was one of the most widespread of the early lingua francas.

5.6.4 Idioms

Idiom is a group of words established by usage as having a meaning not deducible from those of the individual words. For example, "rain cats and dogs". Indeed, idiomatic expressions convey a unique aspect of culture. They offer cultural understandings into societal standards, principles, and beliefs. Idioms give us insight into the thoughts, emotions, and views of the speaker's cultural values. Sometimes we see that various cultures use a different version of the same phrase. For example, "to live in an ivory tower" can be found in more than 35 languages. Most of time, we see cultural difference from the idioms. For example, in China, "龙" is the symbol of royalty, good fortune, power and even used as the symbol of China. There are more than three hundred idioms and most of them convey positive meanings, such as "龙凤呈祥", "望子成龙", "龙腾虎跃", "龙马精神" etc., while "dragon" in English refers to a very fierce, terrible, mythological beast and is seen as the embodiment of a monster in Western countries. Chinese are proud of calling themselves the descendants of "龙". However, *Collins Cobuilt English Language Dictionary* explains it in this way: "If you call a woman a dragon, you mean that she is fierce and unpleasant." The different cultural values decide the different meanings of the word. As a reflection of the cultural values, idioms provide a useful approach to gain insight into different cultural values and their roots. Understanding the cultural meaning of idioms contributes to the intercultural communication.

So far, we have mainly talked about the definition of language code and the composition of language, the importance of verbal communication, the relationship between language and culture, the influence of culture on communication styles, and the diversity of language. Language is a relatively stable communication symbol system used by humans. In the context of globalization, language communication is inseparable from culture in intercultural communication. The various components that make up the language also receive cultural influence. What we have discussed in this chapter may be helpful to get to know verbal communication more comprehensively and deeply understand the inextricable relationship between language and culture. Realizing how to adjust our language to others will contribute to the awareness of our own communication behavior when interacting with others.

Key Terms

verbal communication	言语交际
verbal code	语言代码
phonology	音韵
morphology	词法
syntax	句法
semantics	语义
sapir-whorf hypothesis	萨丕尔—沃尔夫假说
social identity	社会认同
national identity	国家认同
ethnic identity	族群认同
direct communication styles	直接沟通风格
indirect communication styles	间接沟通风格

self-enhancement styles	自我夸耀型交际风格
self-effacement styles	自我谦逊型交际风格
elaborate, exacting and succinct styles	详尽、确切和简洁的交际风格
personal and contextual styles	强调个人和强调语境的交际风格
instrumental and affective styles	工具型和情感型交际风格
accent	口音
dialect	方言
sociolects	社会方言
conversational taboo	会话禁忌
euphemism	委婉语
idiom	习语
pidgin	洋泾浜语
lingua franca	族际通用语

Notes

1. **Edward Sapir** (1884–1939), one of the foremost American linguists and anthropologists of his time, most widely known for his contributions to the study of North American Indian languages. A founder of ethnolinguistics, which considers the relationship of culture to language, he was also a principal developer of the American (descriptive) school of structural linguistics. His publications include *Language* (1921), which was most influential, and a collection of essays, *Selected Writings of Edward Sapir in Language, Culture, and Personality* (1949). Sapir and his student Whorf put forward Sapir-Whorf Hypothesis.

   爱德华·萨丕尔(1884—1939)，重要的美国语言学家和人类学家之一，以对北美印第安语言研究的贡献而闻名。是人类文化语言学的创始人，重视文化与语言的关系，还是美国（描述）结构语言学学派的主要发展者。其代表作为《语言论》，还著有《萨丕尔选集》。他与学生沃尔夫提出了萨丕尔—沃尔夫假说。

2. **William B. Gudykunst** (1977—), one of the most famous writers and scholars in the field of intercultural communication and human communication theory, he is a professor of Speech Communication at the College of Communications, California State University, Fullerton. Bill has written and edited many books, inclu-

ding *Handbook of Intercultural And International Communication*, *Bridging Differences: Effective Intergroup Communication*, *Cross-Cultural and Intercultural Communication*, *Theorizing About Intercultural Communication* etc.

威廉 B. 古迪昆斯特（1977—）是跨文化交际和人类交际理论领域著名的作家、学者之一，也是美国加州州立大学富勒顿传播学院的言语交际学教授。撰写和编辑了许多书籍，包括《跨文化和国际交流手册》《弥合差异：有效的群体间交流》《跨文化交际理论建构》等。

3. **Martin Joos** (1907-1978), a distinguished linguist and a professor of German at the University of Wisconsin-Madison. Holding broad interests in several fields of linguistics. Among Joos's books on linguistics, the most famous is *The Five Clocks*, in which introduced influential discussions of style, register, and style-shifting.

   马丁·朱斯（1907—1978）是一位杰出的语言学家和德语教授，对语言学的多个领域均有涉猎，就职于威斯康星大学麦迪逊分校。朱斯在其语言学著作《五个时钟》一书中提出的对文体、语域和文体转换的讨论颇具影响力。

4. **Argot** is a language used by various groups to prevent outsiders from understanding their conversations. The term argot is also used to refer to the informal specialized vocabulary from a particular field of study, occupation, or hobby, in a sense, it overlaps with jargon.

   暗语是一种不同群体用来防止外人理解他们谈话的语言。这个词也可以用来指某一特定研究、职业或爱好领域中的非正式专业词汇，在某种意义上，它与行话的意义有所重叠。

5. **Slang** is vocabulary that is used between people who belong to the same social group and who know each other well. Slang is a very informal language. It can offend people if it is used about other people or outside a group of people who know each other well. We usually use slang in speaking rather than writing. Slang normally refers to particular words and meanings but can include longer expressions and idioms. Slang changes quickly, and slang words and expressions can disappear from the language.

   俚语是指那些属于同一个社会群体、互相很了解的人之间使用的语言。俚语是一种非常不正式的语言。如果它用于其他人或一群彼此熟稔的群体之外，可能会冒犯别人。俚语通常用于口语中而非书面语，通常指特定的单词和含义，但也可以包括较长的表达和习语。俚语变化很快，有时其词汇和表达会不再被人们使用。

6. **Jargon** is the specialized terminology associated with a particular field. Jargon is normally employed in a particular communicative context and may not be well understood outside that context. It is sometimes understood as a form of technical slang and then distinguished from the official terminology used in a particular field of activity. For example, law enforcement officers and professionals have their own set of police jargon as well, "10-4"-radio jargon meaning is "Okay" or "I understand".

行话是与特定活动领域相关的专业术语。行话通常在特定的交流环境中使用，在该环境之外可能无法很好地被理解。有时行话被看作一种技术术语，区别于特定活动领域中使用的官方用语。例如执法人员和专业人士也有自己的警察行话，"10-4"在他们的无线电通话中意为"好的"或"我明白"。

7. **Leetspeak** is an informal language or code used on the Internet, in which standard letters are often replaced by numerals or special characters that resemble the letters in appearance. For example: noob(newbie) 和 haxor(hacker)

火星文是人们在因特网上使用的一种非正式的语言或代码，通常用数字或外观上与字母相似的特殊字符代替标准字母。例如：noob 表示 newbie；haxor 表示 hacker。

8. **David Crystal** (1941—), a British linguist, academic, and author. He is an honorary professor of linguistics at the University of Bangor, and works as a writer, editor, lecturer, and broadcaster. He received an OBE for services to the English language in 1995. His research covers many aspects of linguistics, such as English language, children language, Internet language, language death and diversity, etc. His publications include *Cambridge Encyclopedia of English, Making Sense: The Glamorous Story of English, A Little Book of Language*, etc.

大卫·克里斯托(1941—)，英国语言学家、学者和作家。班戈大学语言学荣誉教授，也是作家、编辑、讲师和播音员。1995年，克里斯托因对英语的贡献而被授予大英帝国勋章。他的研究涵盖了英语语言、儿童语言、网络语言、语言的死亡和多样性等多个与语言相关的领域。著有《剑桥英语百科全书》《理解：英语语法的故事》《语言小书》等著作。

Case 1

In an attempt to locate an outlet for its products in Europe, a large U. S. manufacturer sent one of its promising young executives to Frankfurt to make a presentation to a reputable German distributor. The U. S. company had considerable confidence in the choice of this particular junior executive because the man not only spoke fluent German but also knew a good deal of German culture.

When the American entered the conference room where he would be making his presentation, he did all the right things. He shook hands firmly, greeted everyone with a friendly guten tag, and bowed his head slightly as is customary in Germany. Drawing on his experience as a past president of the Toastmasters Club in his hometown, the U. S. executive started his presentation with a few humorous anecdotes to set a relaxed mood. At the end of his presentation, however, he sensed that his talk had not gone well. In fact, the presentation was not well received, for the German company chose not to distribute the U. S. company's products.

（选自：许立生，吴丽萍. 新编跨文化交际英语教程［M］. 上海：上海外语教育出版社，2009.）

 Questions for Discussion

1. What may have been the factors contributing to the failure of the presentation?

2. What can we learn from the story?

Case 2

A: We're going to Surrey this weekend.

B: What fun! I wish we were going with you. How long are you going to be there?

A: Three days. (I hope she'll offer me a ride to the airport)

B: (If she wants a ride, she will ask.) Have a great time!

A: (If she had wanted to give me a ride she would have offered it. I'd better ask somebody else.) Thanks. I'll see you when I get back.

Questions for Discussion

1. Is this an effective communication?
2. If yes, how did it achieve its outcome? If not, what's wrong with it?

Case 3

When meeting someone you know, English people often say, " Hi" or "Hello", "How are you? " " Good morning! " " How have you been? " " How are things getting on? " " How are you going?" "How is everything? " "Nice to meet you here!" "What a surprise!"... However, Chinese people would say: "Have you had your meal?" "Where are you going? " If we say " Have you had your meal?" to an English person, he would probably think that you are inviting him to dinner, he may feel very happy! If we say " Where are you going ? " to a foreigner, he would think, "Wow, it's none of your business!"

When picking up someone at the airport, we Chinese often say, " Welcome, welcome! You must be tired all the way!" In English, we'd better say, " Did you have a long flight? " That would be much better and polite.

When inviting some friends at dinner, we Chinese often say, "The dishes are not good, Please forgive me." In fact, it is a Chinese way of being modest, what he or she really means is that all the dishes here are really wonderful ! What he or she really hopes is compliment from the guests! But the English would not understand it at all! Now that it is not good, why should you present the dishes before us?! The English would say to their guests: "Enjoy yourselves" when eating and " Hope you've enjoyed yourself!" after eating.

 Questions for Discussion

1. What's the common way of greeting in China? How would Western people interpret it?

2. When inviting some friends at dinner, what would Chinese host expect his friends to say?

Further Reading

Passage 1

Xi: Improve telling of China story to world

President Xi Jinping called on the China Foreign Languages Publishing Administration to further enhance its communication capacities and better tell China's stories to the outside world.

Xi, also General Secretary of the Communist Party of China Central Committee and chairman of the Central Military Commission, made the remark in a congratulatory letter on Wednesday to honor the administration's 70th anniversary.

Xi said the Administration has played an important role in introducing China's development and changes to the world. He also praised its efforts to facilitate international exchanges and tell China's stories and convey its voices to the world.

Xi called on the administration to build itself into a world-class international communication institution with comprehensive strength to better introduce China in the new era and present a true, multidimensional and panoramic view of China.

Xi's letter was read at a symposium in Beijing by Huang Kunming, a member of the Political Bureau of the CPC Central Committee and head of the Publicity Department of the CPC Central Committee. Huang said it shows the expectations and high value that the central leadership places on publicity work. Huang encouraged the administration to better shoulder its responsibility and further spread Xi Jinping Thought on Socialism with Chinese Characteristics for a new era to the world.

"It should also make new achievements on telling stories of China and better promoting communications and mutual learning between the country and the world," he said.

The Administration, also known as China International Publishing Group, was founded in 1949 to introduce New China to foreign countries through books, magazines and other media.

In seven decades, it has produced some 80,000 types of publications with a total volume of nearly 1.9 billion issues. It now has 34 subsidiaries in 13 foreign languages and publishes over 4,000 kinds of books in 40 languages every year.

"We are proud to take the responsibility of introducing China to the world, which is also our mission," said Du Zhanyuan, head of the administration. "To do so, it will continue developing talent, strengthening research and promoting integrative development," he said.

(选自 http://www.Chinadaily.com.cn/a/201909/05/ws5dbff998a310cf3e35569c2a.html.)

 Questions for Discussion

1. Why did Xi Jinping call for better storytelling of China?
2. What achievements has the government made in introducing China to the world?
3. In your opinion, what kind of China story should we tell the world?

Passage 2

National Identity and Cultural Confidence

We will remain committed to the policy for the Hong Kong people to govern Hong Kong and the Macao people to govern Macao, with patriots playing the principal role. We will develop and strengthen the ranks of patriots who love both our country and their regions, and foster greater patriotism and a stronger sense of national identity among the people in Hong Kong and Macao. With this, our compatriots in Hong Kong and Macao will share both the historic responsibility of national rejuvenation and the pride of a strong and prosperous China…

The culture of socialism with Chinese characteristics is a powerful source of strength that inspires all members of the Party and the people of all ethnic groups in China. Our whole Party must strengthen our confidence in the path, theory, system, and culture of socialism with Chinese characteristics. We must neither retrace our steps to the rigidity and isolation of the past, nor take the wrong turn by changing our nature and abandoning our system. We must maintain our political orientation, do the good solid work that sees our country thrive, and continue to uphold and develop socialism with Chinese characteristics…

(选自 http://www.Chinadaily.com.cn/a/201711/06ws5d034782a3103dbf1432840b

_ 7. html/.)

 Questions for Discussion

1. What is a powerful source of strength that inspires all members of the Party and the people of all ethnic groups in China?

2. Do you have some good ideas on strengthening the patriotism and national identity of people of Hong Kong and Macao?

Passage 3

Chinese Taboo Words

In ancient China, the Chinese regarded the names of their emperors and elders as taboos. It was forbidden to write the name of an emperor when quoting anything old or composing anything new. To avoid such problems, later emperors were given names with characters invented for them—characters that were utterly useless for any other purpose.

To illustrate the principles involved here, let us take up the case of the man who founded the Ming Dynasty (1368–1644). As an individual, he was a man of the Zhu family named Yuanzhang, so according to the usual manner he would be called Zhu Yuanzhang. However, once he ascended the throne, his personal name became taboo; thenceforth, he would be referred to by his dynastic name or Miaohao (temple name) Great Ancestor of the Ming, or Ming Taizu. According to the conventions of English usage, we would refer to him as Emperor Taizu.

Since a Chinese character has different elements, or morphemes, and most Chinese names mean something, there were some ways to avoid taboo words for ordinary people. For instance, a person can use any word element morpheme of a taboo word as his or her name; replace the taboo word with its synonyms or para-synonyms; use homophones or words with similar pronunciation as substitutes of the taboo word; change the pronunciation of the tattoo word when using it; use characters in similar shapes; add components to the taboo character to create a new one and so on.

(选自 http://wenku.baidu.com/view/d92e064502f69e3143323968011ca3 00abc3f60f.html.)

Questions for Discussion

1. Why it was forbidden to write the name of an emperor when quoting anything old or composing anything new in ancient China?

2. How to avoid taboo words in ancient China?

3. What are the cultural differences between China and the West in naming their children?

Exercises

I. True or False

Directions: *Decide whether the statements are true (T) or false (F) according to the passage.*

1. The language one speaks is totally independent of his or her culture. (　)
2. Chinese hospitality toward the Westerners is always greatly appreciated. (　)
3. Speaking dialect in the hometown gives people a sense of belonging. (　)
4. English is the only lingua franca in the world. (　)
5. Often, immigrant groups maintain their cultural heritage and identity by using their native language in their new cultures and teaching them to their children. (　)
6. The self-enhancement verbal style is usually used by people in high context cultures. (　)
7. One's accent may sometimes affect the attitude of others towards him or her. (　)
8. Americans tends to be self-effacing in their compliments responses. (　)
9. The meaning of the Western dragon is different from that of the Chinese "龙". (　)
10. Euphemisms are only used by Asian people. (　)

II. Matching

Directions: *Match the following words and expressions with the correct Chinese.*

1. ethnic identity　　　　　　　　A. 方言
2. self-enhancement styles　　　　B. 语言代码

3. dialect   C. 语言相对性
4. pidgin   D. 族群认同
5. verbal code   E. 行话, 术语
6. euphemism   F. 语境
7. linguistic relativity G. 自我谦逊型交际风格
8. syntax   H. 洋泾浜语
9. context   I. 句法学
10. jargon   J. 委婉语

III. Translation

A. Directions: *Translate the following paragraph into Chinese.*

Intercultural communication is an interdisciplinary field of study which incorporates research from disciplines such as social psychology, sociology, cultural anthropology, sociolinguistics, and, of course, communication. One of the most important areas of research addressed by intercultural scholars is how misunderstandings can be minimized when people communicate with others from different cultures. Low-context communication is like a computer program; everything must be specified in the coded message or the computer program will not run. In a low-context culture like the United States, individuals must express themselves as explicitly as possible for effective communication to occur. High-context communication, in contrast, is like communication between twins who were raised together. Twins intuitively understand each other and use shortened sentences and words when they talk.

B. Directions: *Translate the following paragraph into English.*

社会科学家告诉我们，不同的文化是各不相同的，每种文化都是独一无二的。因为文化具有多样性，所以语言也是多样的。很自然，由于文化和语言的差异，不同文化之间和跨文化之间的交流往往会出现困难，而理解并非易事。学好一门外语不仅仅意味着掌握这门语言的发音、语法、单词和习语，还意味着学着从以这门外语为母语的人的角度来看待世界，了解他们的语言所反映的其社会的思想、习俗和行为的方式，学着理解他们思维的语言。其实，学习一门语言，与学习它的文化是密不可分的。

Chapter 6

Nonverbal Communication

> There is language in her eyes, her cheeks, her lip, nay, her foot speaks.
> ——Shakespeare *Troilus and Cressida*
> 她的眼睛、她的脸颊、她的嘴唇在说话，不仅如此，她的脚也在说话！
> ——莎士比亚《特洛伊罗斯与克瑞西达》

本章导读

人们在传递信息、表达语意时，除了使用言语交际，还会使用内容极为丰富的非言语交际。非言语交际在人类交际活动中运用广泛，占有重要地位，人们利用面部表情、触摸、姿势、眼神、气味等非言语符号传递信息、增进了解。本章首先介绍非言语交际的概念、在日常交际中的重要性和发挥的作用，然后具体介绍非言语交际的不同种类以及在不同文化中的差异。由于文化背景各不相同，交流中非言语交际的方式和含义也会有所差异，本章将帮助学习者了解非言语交际的不同方面，提高文化差异的意识，在国际交往中正确使用非言语交际。

Learning Objectives

In this chapter, students will learn how to define nonverbal communication, understand the significance of nonverbal communication, describe the functions of nonverbal communication, and categorize nonverbal intercultural communication.

Warm-up Activities

(1) What is the relationship between verbal communication and nonverbal com-

munication?

(2) Can you think of some examples of nonverbal communication?

6.1　Definition of Nonverbal Communication

Nonverbal communication is the kind of communication as opposed to verbal communication. The term "nonverbal communication" was introduced in 1956 by psychiatrist **Jurgen Ruesch** and author **Weldon Kees** in the book *Nonverbal Communication: Notes on the Visual Perception of Human Relations*.

There are many definitions concerning nonverbal communication. In the field of intercultural communication, Edward T. Hall was the first scholar to carry out systematic **empirical** (实验的) studies of nonverbal communication. Hall defined nonverbal communication as communication that does not involve the exchange of words.

Another classic definition is given by **Larry Samovar, Richard Porter, and Lisa Stefani**: Nonverbal communication involves all those nonverbal stimuli in a communication setting that are generated by both the source and his or her use of the environment and that have potential message value for the source or receiver. To put it simply, nonverbal communication is the process of sending and receiving messages without using words in either spoken or written context. Instead, it uses nonverbal stimuli like voices, behaviors, or settings, including time and space, to convey meaning. It may be intentional; it may be based on societal cues; or it may be completely unconscious.

To further define nonverbal communication, we need to make a distinction between vocal and verbal, nonvocal and nonverbal aspects of communication.

A vocal element of verbal communication is spoken words—for example, "Come back here." A vocal element of nonverbal communication is **paralanguage** (副语言), which is the **vocalized** (发声) but not verbal part of a spoken message, such as speaking rate, volume, and pitch. Nonvocal elements of verbal communication include the use of unspoken symbols to convey meaning. Writing and American Sign Language (ASL) are nonvocal examples of verbal communication and are not considered nonverbal communication. Nonvocal elements of nonverbal communication include body language such as gestures, facial expressions, and eye contact. Gestures are nonvocal and nonverbal since most of them do not refer to a specific word as a written or signed symbol does.

It is important to note that nonverbal communication is really about a lack of words, rather than a lack of vocalization. Therefore, most writing would not be considered a nonverbal means of communication, although elements like handwriting styles could be considered nonverbal signifiers. By the same token, sounds like **grunts**(咕哝声) are still considered nonverbal, even though they are oral sounds.

Verbal and nonverbal communications are part of the complete interaction process and, in practice, are inseparable. Rather than thinking of nonverbal communication as the opposite of or as separate from verbal communication, it's more accurate to view them as operating side by side—as part of the same system. Verbal and nonverbal communications are not contradictory to each other, but they are complementary as somebody has rightly said, "Actions are louder than words. " In short, verbal and nonverbal communications go side by side and help a human being to interact with and respond to other human beings.

6.2 Significance of Nonverbal Communication

Nonverbal messages have been recognized for centuries as a critical aspect of communication. For instance, in *The Advancement of Learning* (1605), Francis Bacon observed that "the **lineaments**(典型特征) of the body do disclose the **disposition** (性情) and **inclination**(意愿) of the mind in general, but the motions of the **countenance**(面容) and parts do not only so, but do further disclose the present **humour** (情绪) and state of the mind and will. "

The importance of nonverbal communication can be perceived from the following four aspects. Firstly, nonverbal communication is important because nonverbal messages constitute much of the meaning we get from an interaction. "Many, and sometimes most of the critical meanings generated in human encounters are **elicited**(引出) by touch, glance, vocal **nuance**(细微差别), gestures, or facial expression with or without the aid of words. "

As a whole, about 93% of the meaning in a conversation is communicated nonverbally—38% through the voice and 55% through the face. People's emotions and attitudes are reflected in their postures, faces, and eyes. Even silence or no expression in the face communicates something.

Secondly, nonverbal communication is important because it spontaneously reflects the sub-consciousness. Nonverbal communication is more **involuntary** (无意识的) than verbal. That is to say, many of our nonverbal behaviors are not easily controlled or faked consciously. Thus, they are more reliable and trustworthy. When what someone says is contradictory to what he does nonverbally, we tend to believe the nonverbal message.

Thirdly, nonverbal communication is important in that it affects relationships. To successfully relate to other people, we must possess some skills at encoding and decoding nonverbal communication. The nonverbal messages we send and receive influence our relationships in positive or negative ways and can work to bring people together or push them apart.

And finally nonverbal communication can be open to many interpretations. This makes it more important in intercultural communication. Although some nonverbal behaviors speak a universal language, like smiling and crying, others can be interpreted differently in different cultures, resulting in misunderstanding. Thus, proper use of nonverbal messages in intercultural communication is very important, if we don't want to be involved in a communicative failure or disaster.

6.3 Functions of Nonverbal Communication

Nonverbal communication evolved earlier than verbal communication and served an early and important survival function that helped humans later develop verbal communication. There are some important ways in which nonverbal communication directly affects our verbal discourse. Generally speaking, there are five functions of nonverbal communication: repeating, complementing, substituting, regulating and contradicting.

6.3.1 Repeating

People often use nonverbal messages to repeat a point they are trying to make. Nonverbal communication is used together with verbal one to repeat or emphasize what the speaker is saying. All good speakers know how to do this with forceful gestures, changes in vocal volume or speech rate, deliberate pauses, and so forth. In daily life, when you say "yes", you will nod your head. If you are telling someone that what he is proposing is a bad idea, you might move your head from side to side while you are uttering the word "no". When you are giving someone directions: "turn left and then go straight ahead", you will at the same time use gestures to show directions; and when you say "quiet", you may put your index finger to your lips. In these examples, nonverbal behaviors are used to repeat or emphasize the verbal message, although they could have been used alone to convey the same meaning.

6.3.2 Complementing

This function is closely related to repeating, but not the same. For example, you may smile and say, "Hi, how are you?" while you may bow and say, "I'm sorry." You may also pat one's shoulder and say "good job". Smiling, bowing, and patting may have different meanings when used in different situations. However, when they are used together with "Hi, how are you?", "I'm sorry." and "good job", they are given the specific meaning, that is, to complement the verbal message. In this way, nonverbal signals help to clarify the words we use and reveal the true nature of our feelings.

6.3.3 Substituting

We use nonverbal messages to replace verbal messages. If it is noisy at a big meeting, the speaker may stop for a few seconds as an alternative to say "please calm down so that I can speak." Instead of raising your voice and shouting "bravo" after a great performance of the orchestra, you may silently sit there with an awed expression. Your expression automatically indicates that the performance is excellent and that you are moved by the experience.

Often, there isn't much need to put things in words. A simple gesture can **suffice** (足够) (e. g. , shaking your head to say no, using the thumbs-up sign to say "nice job," etc.). Moreover, sometimes verbal communication is impossible or inappropriate, and then nonverbal messages may substitute for verbal ones. For example, in a quiet situation where verbal communication would be disturbing or in crowded or loud places, we may use gestures to substitute for words. There are also occasions when we know it's better not to say something aloud. For instance, if you want to signal to a friend that you think his or her date is a loser, you're more likely to do so nonverbally.

6.3.4 Regulating

People can regulate their conversations through nonverbal signals. This is mostly concerned with turn-taking. For example, when you raise your hand, you indicate that you have something to say. Other turn-taking signals include the rising or falling intonation of your voice. A rising intonation usually indicates a question, and a falling one indicates the conversation is coming to an end. We may also stop making hand gestures and shift our eye contact to the person who we think will speak next. These gestures and vocalizations, called turn-taking signals, make it possible for us to alternate the conversational roles of speaking and listening.

6.3.5 Contradicting

On some occasions, nonverbal actions send signals opposite from the literal meanings contained in our verbal messages. For example, a person may say, "You can't do anything right!" in a mean tone, but follow that up with a wink, which could indicate the person is teasing or joking. When someone misses the bus and is going to be late for work and he says, "That's great" with an angry face and a downcast tone, we know the person is frustrated instead of feeling great. A friend tells us she had a great time at the beach, but we're not sure because her voice is flat and her face lacks emotion. All these examples show nonverbal messages sometimes contradict what we say.

Nonverbal communication may serve different purposes. According to **Peter A. Andersen,** while verbal communication is our primary tool for solving problems and providing detailed instructions, nonverbal communication is our primary tool for communicating emotions or attitudes.

6.4 Categories of Nonverbal Communication

A substantial portion of our communication is nonverbal. Every day we respond to thousands of nonverbal cues and behaviors, including postures, facial expressions, eye contact, gestures, and tone of voice. From our handshakes to our hairstyles, nonverbal details reveal who we are and impact how we relate to other people. There are different forms of nonverbal communication. We will focus on the vocal, that is, **paralanguage,** and nonvocal aspects of nonverbal communication: **body language, time** or **chronemics** (时间行为), and space or **proxemics** (空间行为). Other categories like **chromatics** (色彩学) and **attire** (服饰) will be dealt with very briefly.

6.4.1 Paralanguage

All of us are aware that the meaning of what we say is contained, in part, in the words, and that how we say things also contains powerful messages. Paralanguage is related to oral communication. It refers to the rate, pitch, and volume qualities of the voice, which interrupt or temporarily take the place of speech and affect the meaning of a message.

"Every time we speak, we speak in a certain tone of voice, a certain pitch, at a certain pace, etc. depending on the type of emotion we wish to convey to the other person. This is known as paralanguage." It refers to the set of audible sounds that accompany oral language to **augment** (加强) its meaning. To put it simply, paralanguage studies the voice and the use of vocal signs in communication.

We may understand the importance of paralanguage from two aspects. First, paralanguage plays a role in determining whether we like a certain speaker, or whether we find a speech appealing or boring. Since we were babies, we have learned to tell a pleasing voice from a gruff one, long before we learn what the words mean. In real life, we often find that the same words said by different speakers may have different effect. For example, we all have the experience that we are especially drawn to a certain radio host or a storyteller. Baract H. Obama, former US President, is known for his wonderful speeches. Besides his language, the way he delivers his speech, that is his vocal qualities including volume, pitch, rhythm, and tone, adds to the charm of his language. Thus, if we want to be a good speaker, we have to pay attention to our paralanguage, which also reveals, to a certain extent, what kind of person we are.

Another aspect about paralanguage is that for the same sentence, the change in paralanguage such as tone, intonation, and stress may convey us different meanings. Consider Hamlet's famous **soliloquy** (独白): "To be or not to be, that is the question. " How can you read the sentence with different intonation and stress to express different meanings?

Tone of voice can have powerful effect on the meaning of a sentence. When words are said in a strong tone of voice, listeners might interpret approval and enthusiasm. The same words said in a hesitant tone of voice might convey disapproval and a lack of interest. Simply changing your tone of voice might change the meaning of a sentence, and your vocal qualities may reveal your feelings and emotions to others. A friend might ask you how you are doing, and you might respond with the standard "I'm fine", but how you actually say those words might reveal a tremendous amount of how you are really feeling. A cold tone of voice might suggest that you are actually not fine, but you don't wish to discuss it. A bright, happy tone of voice will reveal that you are actually doing quite well. A somber, **downcast** (情绪低落的) tone would indicate that you are the opposite of fine and that perhaps your friend should inquire further.

From these examples, you can see paralanguage is concerned with how something is said instead of the actual meaning of the spoken words. What matters is not what you say, but the way you say it.

This may bring a problem in intercultural communication, as people from different culture have different use of and response to paralanguage. For example, Arabs speak very loudly because loudness for them connotes strength and sincerity, and softness stands for weakness, while in Japan, raising one's voice often implies a lack of self-control and a gentle and soft voice reflects good manners. In China and Japan, people nod or say "mmmh", "uhuh", "是", "hai" when they are talking with someone to show their attentiveness, but native English speakers often misinterpret this as agreement.

Silence as a form of paralanguage may result in great misunderstanding in intercultural communication too. The Eastern culture usually attaches more meanings to silence, while most Western cultures consider silence to be absence of communication and rude communicative behavior. In a study of the differences between Japanese and Australian students in the seminars of an Australian university, the researcher finds that the Japanese students are considered quiet and shy due to their lack of participation and unwillingness to speak out in class. In Japanese teaching situations, the students are often expected to remain silent and unquestioning while the teacher talks. Unfortunately, the Australian lecturers often misunderstand this silence as either denoting a lack of knowledge or unwillingness to participate.

Paralanguage also conveys emotions. It is easier for us to distinguish negative emotions such as impatience, fear, and anger than to distinguish positive emotions like satisfaction and admiration. An increased rate of speech could indicate anger or impatience; a decrease in rate could suggest lack of interest or a reflective attitude. Learning the nuances in speech will help to identify the real meaning of people from other cultures.

6.4.2 Body Language

Body language is one of the most studied forms of nonverbal communication. There are different understandings and different classifications concerning body language. We use body language to refer to various forms of nonverbal communication through physical behaviors, just as the name implies. We will cover five aspects of body language: facial expressions, posture, gestures, eye contact or **oculesics** (目光语) **and touch or haptics** (触觉行为).

(1) Facial Expressions

Facial expressions play a big role in expressing a person's emotion. When we are talking with someone, we will look at his or her face to see the response. A look on one's face will tell us a lot about the person's emotional state, whether he is happy, sad, frustrated or angry. And we will thereby continue our talk or change the subject. When we talk online, for example on WeChat, we use a lot of emoji so as to convey to others our feelings or emotions at the moment. Moreover, you can use emoji alone without saying anything. This use of emoji is intentional, while in real life our facial expressions can be conscious or unconscious, or mostly unconscious. Compared with what we say, our facial expressions may reveal our true feelings.

Paul Ekman, an American psychologist, is a pioneer in the study of facial expressions and emotions and an expert in deception detection. In 1967, Dr. Ekman worked with clinical cases in which patients lied about their emotional state. He studied patients who claimed they were not depressed and later committed suicide. Upon examining films of the patients in slow motion, Dr. Ekman and Dr. Friesen spotted micro facial expressions, which revealed strong negative feelings the patient was trying to hide. Micro expressions are facial expressions that occur within a fraction of a second. This involuntary emotional **leakage** (泄露) exposes a person's true emotions.

Between 1967 and 1968, Dr. Ekman travelled to Papua New Guinea to study the nonverbal behavior of the Fore people. He chose these people as they were an isolated, Stone Age culture located in the South East Highlands. Ekman's research provided the strongest evidence to date that facial expressions are universal. According to him, combinations of eyes, eyebrows, lips and cheek movements help form different moods of an individual. For example, for surprise, eyebrows are raised. Eyes are wide open and mouth is open and relaxed.

There are seven universal emotions based primarily on facial expressions. They are happiness, surprise, contempt, sadness, fear, disgust, and anger.

Besides this universality, "cultural norms often dictate how, when, and to whom facial expressions are displayed." In some cultures, such as those in the Mediterranean, people are more likely to express their emotions in public while in some other cultures, like the Chinese and the Japanese, people tend to conceal rather than reveal their real emotions in public or to strangers.

Even for the smile, "the amount of smiling, the stimulus that produces the smile, and even what the smile is communicating often shift from culture to culture." In America, a smile can be a sign of happiness or friendliness while in some Asian countries, like China, Japan and Thailand, the smile is far more complicated. A smile can also be used to avoid answering a question or express shyness, embarrassment, discomfort, apology or even sadness and hatred.

(2) Posture

The term "posture" refers to how we hold our bodies as well as the overall physical form of an individual, such as the way we stand, sit, or walk. Posture can convey a wealth of information about how a person is feeling as well as hints about personality characteristics, such as whether a person is confident, open, or submissive.

Sitting up straight, for example, may indicate that a person is focused and paying attention to what's going on. Sitting with the body hunched forward, on the other hand, can imply that the person is bored or indifferent.

When you are trying to read body language, try to notice some of the signals that a person's posture can send. Open posture involves keeping the trunk of the body open and exposed. This type of posture indicates friendliness, openness, and willingness. Closed posture involves hiding the trunk of the body often by hunching forward and keeping the arms and legs crossed. This type of posture can be an indicator of hostility, unfriendliness, and anxiety.

Posture is an important element of nonverbal communication, because it can affect how we are perceived by others. In her speech "Your Body Language May Shape Who You Are", social psychologist Amy Cuddy says our posture can be an expression of our power. When people feel powerful they will assume a high-power pose. When people feel powerless, they tend to hide themselves through a low-power pose. What Amy wants to argue in this speech is that we can actually "fake it until we become it". That is, if we try "high-power poses"—standing or sitting in a posture of confidence, even when we don't feel confident—just for two minutes, we can boost our feelings of confidence, and it might have an impact on our chances for success. Our posture can not only affect how we are perceived by others, but also to a large extent, affect how we feel about ourselves.

Posture and sitting habits offer insight into a culture's deep structure. Every culture has its rules concerning good behaviors and good manners. Posture can send positive or negative nonverbal messages in different cultures, which may cause problems in intercultural communication. For example, Chinese people often say, "站如松, 坐如钟, 行如风。" These rules indicate how a person should stand, sit, and walk. If a person doesn't behave properly, he may encounter problems or failures in interactions with others.

In the United States, being informal and friendly is valued. People often fall into chairs or **slouch** (低头垂肩地站) when they stand. This may cause a problem in Germany and Sweden, because people there tend to be more formal, and slouching is considered a sign of rudeness and poor manners. Also if you sit with your legs crossed, you may offend people from Ghana and Turkey, as this kind of sitting is extremely offensive.

In some cultures, people believe that feet are the lowest part of the body and thus the bottoms of the feet should never be pointed in the direction of another person. In Middle Eastern cultures, it's insulting to cross an ankle over a knee and display the sole of the shoe to the person you are talcing with.

(3) Gestures

Gestures also act as a form of nonverbal communication, although this should be differentiated from hand gestures used as a form of verbal communication, like sign language. Gesture refers to the way we use our hands to convey messages. It is a convenient and effective way of communication. A wide range of hand gestures can be found in most cultures, and in the West there are almost some universal gestures, such as a wave goodbye, a thumbs-up to demonstrate everything is okay, or hands outspread to signify offerings. Other gestures are arbitrary and related to culture.

For example, the Chinese often rub or pat their stomachs to show they have had enough food, but if one does this to the American host and hostess, they may be confused, for Americans usually put a hand on the throat to show they are good, while this gesture may indicate a threat like "I will kill you" in Chinese culture.

Another example is counting numbers on fingers. People in different parts of the world use different ways to count numbers on their fingers. The Chinese can easily count from one to ten on only one hand. The American and the British count one to five the same way as the Chinese, while other Europeans like the French and the Germans start counting on their thumbs and end with five on their pinky fingers. And then they repeat this with the other hand to get to ten.

So the same gesture may mean differently in different cultures. The "OK" gesture for an American means zero to the French, money to the Japanese, while it is insulting to make this gesture in Turkey, Brazil, and Greece.

Besides meaning "one" in mainland Europe, the "thumbs-up" gesture may also be a signal for hitchhiking in Britain, or used to show "good", "good job" in many other cultures. However, it is an insult offensive gesture in countries such as Greece and Iran.

Similarly, the "two" or "victory" gesture, and the "ten" or "I surrender" gesture in many countries can also have different meanings in other countries and some meanings can be very offensive. So, we should be very careful when using these familiar gestures in a foreign country.

(4) Eye Contact

Eye contact or oculesics involves communicating through the eyes. Eyes play an

177

important role in nonverbal communication and such things as looking, staring and blinking are important nonverbal behaviors. When people encounter people or things they like, the rate of blinking increases and pupils dilate. Looking at another person can indicate a range of emotions including hostility, interest, and attraction.

People also utilize eye contact as a means to determine if someone is being honest. Normally, steady eye contact is often taken as a sign that a person is telling the truth and is trustworthy. Shifty eyes and an inability to maintain eye contact, on the other hand, is frequently seen as an indicator that someone is lying or being deceptive.

Again, there are cultural differences as to whether to look at your partner in the eye in a conversation and how long you maintain your eye contact. People in the West often expect the person they are talking with to look at them in the eye. In fact, they will suspect the person's honesty if he fails to do so, as is said above. However, people from Latin American and Caribbean cultures are taught to avoid eye contact with elders, teachers, and other people with status as a sign of respect. Japanese children are taught in school to direct their gaze at the region of their teacher's Adam's apple or necktie. As adults, the Japanese lower their eyes when speaking to a superior as a gesture of respect. And when a Japanese is listening to a lecture, he may even close his eyes instead of looking at the speaker to show attentiveness. In Japanese culture, prolonged eye contact is rude and disrespectful. Arabs, on the other hand, tend to look directly into the eyes of their partners, and they do so for a long period of time.

With different practice in eye contact, it is advisable to mirror the native speakers' eye contact. Notice how they look at people and do likewise.

(5) Touch

Haptics, communicating through touch, is another important nonverbal behavior. There has been a substantial amount of research on the importance of touch in infancy and early childhood.

Harry Harlow's classic monkey study demonstrated how deprived touch and contact **impede** (阻碍) development. Baby monkeys raised by wire mothers experienced permanent **deficits** (不足) in behavior and social interaction. Touch can be used to communicate affection, familiarity, sympathy, and other emotions.

Touch can be very different in different cultures. Since childhood, our culture has taught us how to communicate through touch. We have learned who to touch and where they may be touched. For example, there are different ways of greeting in different cultures. People may shake hands, hug each other, kiss each other on the cheek, or touch nose to nose. Even for the same kind of greeting, people in different cultures do it differently. For example, American colleagues usually shake hands when seeing each other for the first time and then to shake again when departing company, while many European colleagues shake hands each time they see each other. The number of "**pumps**" (摇动), that is, the squeezes and up-and-down shakes in a handshake also varies among cultures. The Germans and French typically only give one or two pumps and then hold the shake for a few seconds. The British tend to give three to five pumps, while Americans tend to give five to seven pumps. Besides hand-shaking, Americans also hug a lot, either to greet someone or to say goodbye.

Another example of cultural differences in touching behaviors is patting someone on the head. In some countries like the U. S. A, Korea, or China, people like to pat someone, especially a child on the head to convey affection, but in the Middle East or part of Asia, like Thailand, India, and Indonesia, it is forbidden to pat someone, including a child, on the head because in their beliefs, the head is the most sacred part of the body.

In conclusion, the use of touch is governed by the culture. Different cultures can be generalized into high-touch or low-touch cultures. Americans, the English, Germans, Northern Europeans, and many Asians are said to belong to low-touch cultures, exhibiting very limited touching in public. Hispanics, Italians, the French, Arabs, and Jews are all said to belong to high-touch cultures. These cultures encourage outward expression of affection, so they do more touching.

Besides cultural differences, touching behavior can also be influenced by gender and social status. In her book *Interpersonal Communication: Everyday Encounters*, author Julia Wood writes that touch is also often used as a way to communicate both status and power. Researchers have found that high-status individuals tend to invade other people's personal space with greater frequency and intensity than lower-status individuals. Sex differences also play a role in how people utilize touch to communicate meaning. Women tend to use touch to convey care, concern, and **nurturance** (关

怀). Men, on the other hand, are more likely to use touch to assert power or control over others.

6.4.3 Time

Chronemics is the study of the use of time, and the way that time is perceived and valued by individuals and cultures, particularly as regards nonverbal communication. These time perceptions include things like punctuality, willingness to wait, approaches to face-to-face interactions, and reactions to time pressure.

Attitudes to time may differ between different cultures in often quite significant ways. For example, being late for an appointment, or taking a long time to get down to business, is the accepted norm in most Mediterranean and Arab countries, as well as in much of less-developed Asia. Such habits, though, would be **anathema** (可恶的事) in punctuality-conscious USA, Japan, England, Switzerland, etc. In the Japanese train system, for example, "on time" refers to expected delays of less than one minute, while in many other countries, up to fifteen minutes **leeway** (回旋余地) is still considered "on-time".

6.4.4 Space

Space, or proxemics, refers to the study of spatial relations. The study of proxemics includes three aspects of space: **fixed features of space** (固定空间), **semifixed features of space** (半固定空间), and personal space.

Fixed features of space usually refer to public places such as parks, streets, and buildings whose structures and functions are all fixed. Semifixed features of space refer to spatial arrangements of movable objects within a room, such as furniture arrangement and seating. These features reflect the general attitude of people towards space, and thus are a mirror of culture.

Personal space refers to the invisible boundary surrounding us. Most people are very aware of others in "their space", and many require the area to remain relatively clear in order to feel at ease. The idea of personal space is rooted in psychology, and there are many theories about how the space develops and how people react to violations. Some of this is based on genetics and brain chemistry, but a lot is also cultural.

The complexity of personal space comes from the fact that its size is affected by many factors; some of them are very varied from person to person. These factors actually cause a social "accident", when different people have a different concept about the "right distance" to stand from each other. Some of these factors are:

a. The social situation

b. The personal relation with that person

c. The status of the people involved

d. Our personal liking or disliking towards that specific person

e. The gender

f. Culture—perhaps the most major factor.

Personal space, like a bubble, changes in shape and size depending on what situations we are in. Edward T. Hall reports that psychologists have identified four zones within which Americans interact: the intimate zone, the personal zone, the social zone, and the public zone.

Intimate zone ranges from 15 to 45 centimeters. It's the space reserved only for the most trusted and loved in our social circles. Parents, siblings, and romantic partners can usually enter this area at will without causing alarm or anxiety.

Personal zone ranges from 46 cm to 1.22 meters. This area is reserved for friends and family members or for encounters like hand-shaking, gesturing, standing near others at cocktail parties or other social gatherings.

Social zone is between 1.22 and 3.6 meters. It's the most neutral and comfortable zone to start a conversation with strangers or between people who don't know each other well.

Public zone is the most outer "bubble" and is usually larger than 3.6 meters. This zone is reserved for public speaking or talking to a large group.

Personal space is different from culture to culture. Americans like standing two to four feet away from people when they talk or wait in line. Asians stand much closer and not doing so makes them uncomfortable. In fact, in many places in Asia, people are often attractive toward one another. In India, if you are sitting in a nearly empty theater, an Indian will be likely to sit right next to you. In Indonesia, if you are standing by yourself on an escalator, an Indonesian will come and stand on the same step with you. Latin Americans and Asians require less personal space because they're used to crowded conditions. Large populations share small areas of space.

People standing on a bus or a subway are likely to be pressed against someone else's sweaty body. This close contact makes Americans and Northern Europeans embarrassed. Growing up, they've been taught not to touch strangers. On a bus or a subway, they go out of their way not to touch another person. If there are plenty of empty seats, no one will sit directly beside another passenger. An Arab's idea of personal space may even make an Asian uncomfortable. Arabs like to stand close enough to breathe on others and smell their breath as they talk and not doing so is disrespectful. On the other hand, people from the Netherlands feel that standing four feet apart is too close.

Generally speaking, in cultures that stress individualism and privacy, such as England, the United States, Germany, and Australia, people generally demand more space. By contrast, people in South Europe, the Middle East, and South America are considered to be "warm" by nature: close proximity is more welcome and socially accepted.

In conclusion, the personal space is not only culturally determined but also varied from person to person. Much of how a person defines his or her own personal space is shaped by upbringing. Some cultures are naturally much closer than others, and how comfortable a person is with others nearby is often a factor of the country or region where he or she grew up. Family of origin also plays a part in this. A person reared up in a family that hugs a lot or prizes physical contact often has less of a problem with strangers being in the intimate or expected contact zones than does a person who grew up with a lot more distance.

6.4.5 Chromatics

Chromatics refers to the study of color use in affecting people's perceptions, emotions, and impression of others. Colors carry deep meanings with them in every culture. Some colors may be connected with coldness in one culture but with warmth in another; some colors stand for life in one culture but death in another. The symbolism of colors often stems from religious, spiritual, social, or historical events.

In China, red represents luck and fertility. For example, during the Chinese New Year's celebration, small red envelopes are distributed to symbolize good fortune. Women often wear red on their wedding days to symbolize fertility and a marked change in their lives. In Thailand, red symbolizes Sun God Surya. Red also marks Sunday, as every day of the week in Thailand is represented by a certain color. Red in African cultures symbolizes death and grief. In Nigeria and South Africa, red symbolizes violence and sacrifice. The flag of South Africa has red in it to symbolize the violence that occurred during its fight for freedom. In ancient Greece, green represented victory. In England, people wear green as a mark of honor. In Mexico, green represents freedom and independence. This color is an integral part of its national flag. In India, yellow is for a businessman or a farmer. Yellow is a predominant color in Chinese culture and is the color representing the imperial court in traditional China. In the United States, white means purity and happiness and it is typically worn by brides at weddings. In China and Japan, people wear white clothes at funerals. Thus, it is advisable to determine cultural meanings associated with various colors to make sure the use of colors will not be misunderstood or misinterpreted in different countries.

6.4.6 Attire

Dress culture is made up of varieties of factors including clothing, accessories, and the way people dress. Dress culture is the materialization of the quality of certain culture, the national inner spirit, and the social outlook for a nation and a country.

The way you dress can affect how people perceive you in any situation. However, different cultures have different opinions on what constitutes professional attire. In some countries, women are expected to cover their heads and most of their bodies. Some societies consider wearing bold colors disrespectful. Take note of how your clients and partners dress and model your clothing after theirs. You can also ask your guide if your attire is appropriate when travelling. Make sure you're not wearing attire that has religious symbolism to avoid giving offense accidentally.

 Key Terms

nonverbal communication	非言语交际
paralanguage	副语言
body language	身体语言
facial expression	面部表情
posture	姿势

gesture	手势
eye contact/oculesics	目光语
touch/haptics	触觉行为
time/chronemics	时间行为
space/proxemics	空间行为
personal space	个人空间
chromatics	色彩学
attire	服饰

Notes

1. **Jurgen Ruesch** (1909–1995), M. D., Professor of Psychiatry, University of California School of Medicine, was a distinguished psychiatrist, communications expert and psychotherapist.

   约尔根·鲁伊奇（1909—1995），医学博士，加利福尼亚大学医学院精神病学教授，一位有名的精神病医生、沟通专家和心理治疗师。

2. **Weldon Kees** was born in Beatrice, Nebraska. Interested in art and music as well as poetry, Kees began publishing poems and short stories during college. In 1951, Kees moved to San Francisco, where he studied jazz piano and took photographs for the book *Nonverbal Communication* (1956), which he wrote in collaboration with the psychologist Dr. Jurgen Ruesch.

   韦尔登·凯斯出生于内布拉斯加州的比阿特丽斯，他对艺术、音乐和诗歌感兴趣，大学时开始发表诗歌和短篇小说。1951年凯斯搬到旧金山，在那里他学习爵士乐钢琴，并为《非言语交际》(1956) 一书拍摄照片，这本书是他与心理学家约尔根·鲁伊奇博士合作撰写的。

3. **Francis Bacon** (1561–1626), one of the most important philosophers of England, was born in London and educated at Cambridge University. His ideas about how scientists should study things in nature help to bring the modern way of thinking, called the scientific method. Bacon wrote on questions of law, state and religion, as well as on contemporary politics; but he also published texts in which he speculated on possible conceptions of society, and he pondered questions of ethics (*Essays*) even in his works on natural philosophy (*The Advancement of Learning*).

弗朗西斯·培根(1561—1626)，英国最重要的哲学家之一，生于伦敦，在剑桥大学接受教育。他是近代实验科学的创始人，著作涉及法律、国家、宗教，以及当代政治等问题；也发表了一些文章，思考对社会的一些构想，他思索社会伦理问题（《论说文集》），甚至在他关于自然哲学的著作（《学术的进步》）中也有所体现。

4. **Paul Ekman,** an American psychologist and expert in the fields of emotions, nonverbal communication, and deception detection. His research on facial expression and body movement began in 1954, as the subject of his Master's thesis in 1955.

   保罗·埃克曼是美国心理学家，情绪、非言语交际和欺骗检测领域的专家。他对面部表情和身体动作的研究始于1954年，1955年他将此作为硕士论文的主题。

5. **Amy Cuddy** was born in 1972. She is an American social psychologist, assistant professor in Harvard Business School. She is well-known in the field for a series of studies on human prejudice and discrimination, emotion, competence, nonverbal behavior, and the impact of social environment on people.

   艾米·卡蒂生于1972年，哈佛商学院工商管理学院副教授，美国社会心理学家，以对人类的成见和歧视、情感、能力、非语言行为和社会环境对人影响的一系列研究闻名业界内外。

6. **Harry Harlow,** an American psychologist who is best-remembered for his series of controversial and often outrageously cruel experiments with rhesus monkeys. During the first half of the 20th century, many psychologists believed that showing affection towards children was merely a sentimental gesture that served no good. In order to study the effects of maternal separation and social isolation, Harlow placed infant monkeys in isolated chambers. Harlow's experiments offered irrefutable proof that love is vital for normal childhood development. Additional experiments by Harlow revealed that long-term devastation caused by deprivation will lead to profound psychological and emotional distress and even death. Harlow's research contributed a great deal to our understanding of the importance of caregiving, affection, and social relationships early in life.

   哈利·哈洛是美国心理学家，他对恒河猴进行了一系列有争议的、常常是残酷得离谱的实验。20世纪上半叶，很多心理学家认为，喂养婴儿的时候，母亲不应该和孩子有过多的拥抱和肢体接触，以免养成孩子娇惯的性格。

为了研究母爱剥夺和社会隔离的影响，哈洛把幼猴放在隔离的房间里。哈洛的实验提供了无可辩驳的证据，证明母爱对正常的儿童发育至关重要。哈洛的其他实验揭示了母爱剥夺会造成长期危害，会导致严重的心理和情感压抑，甚至死亡。哈洛的研究有助于我们理解幼儿期关爱、情感和社会关系的重要性。

7. **Julia Wood** joined the faculty at the University of North Carolina at Chapel Hill when she was 24. During her 37 years on the faculty, she taught classes and conducted research on personal relationships as well as gender, communication, and culture.

茱莉亚·伍德 24岁时成为北卡罗来纳大学教堂山分校的一员。在37年的教师生涯中，她教授课程，并对性别、沟通和文化以及人际关系开展研究。

Case 1

Obama's Bow

US President Barack Obama was greeted by Emperor Akihito upon arriving at the Imperial Palace in Tokyo November 14, 2009. Obama greeted Emperor Akihito, whose father ruled when Japan bombed a US naval base at Pearl Harbor in 1941, with a simultaneous handshake and nearly 90-degree bow, sparking furious online commentary, much of it negative.

（选自 http://www. chinadaily. com. cn/world/2009 - 11/18/content _ 8990726. htm.)

 Questions for Discussion

1. What is your reaction to this news?
2. Why did Obama's bow spark criticism?

Case 2

Left in the Cold

Katherine came to Beijing in 1998 and found a job as an English teacher in a foreign language institute. Soon after her classes began she found that her students showed no interest in her teaching style. Quite a few of them avoided attending her class. She was feeling quite upset and discouraged, so she decided to ask the Director, Prof Wang for help. Prof Wang reviewed his timetable and suggested they meet at ten o'clock on Thursday morning. When Thursday came, Katherine arrived at Prof Wang's office at exactly ten o'clock finding him talking with another teacher in Chinese. Seeing that she had come, Prof Wang smiled and gestured her to sit down. Katherine sat down and the professor excused himself and continued to talk with the other teacher. After five minutes, he finished his conversation and apologized to Katherine, and began to focus his attention on her situation. Prof Wang showed great concern and asked her what the problem was. Just as she was discussing her problem, another Chinese teacher interrupted, with a form that required the Director's signature. The Director smiled, apologized to Katherine again, and turned to talk with the Chinese teacher in Chinese. Katherine became impatient, and wondered why their discussion should be interrupted since she had made an appointment. Also, she was upset and frustrated that they continued to speak Chinese in front of her. Although their talk continued, she was apparently unhappy about what had happened.

(选自 https://wenku. baidu. com/view/7d2e3232541252d380eb6294dd88d0d232d43c71. html.)

 Questions for Discussion

1. How would you explain the Director's behavior toward Katherine?

2. How would you make the Director understand why Katherine felt frustrated and angry?

Case 3

Personal Space

Mark had recently moved from Denmark to Sydney to work as a salesperson for a large Australian company. After three weeks, he was invited to join a local club. During the first few weeks at the club, Mark would either stand in the corner talking with someone or sit on a sofa, listening to other people talk and chat. As time went by, he came to know most of the club members, and seemed to enjoy talking with them. One day, at an evening party one of the female members approached him. Mark immediately showed his interest by talking about the atmosphere of the party. At first, the conversation between them seemed to go quite smoothly, but as it progressed the lady seemed to step further and further away from Mark as he had been gradually moving closer to her. The lady obviously seemed uncomfortable. As Mark was about to ask her questions regarding Australian social customs, another man standing nearby directed a glance toward the lady. She excused herself and went to talk with that man, leaving Mark standing alone and wondering why the conversation had come to such a sudden stop.

(选自 https://wenku.baidu.com/view/7d2e3232541252d380eb6294dd88d0d232d43c71.html.)

 Questions for Discussion

Why did the lady suddenly stop talking with Mark and turned to another man?

Further Reading

Passage 1

Nonverbal Communication

If anyone asked you what were the main means of communication between people, what would you say? That isn't a catch question. The answer is simple and obvious. It would almost certainly refer to means of communication that involve the use of words between speakers and listeners—oral communication, and writers and readers—written communication. And you'd be quite right. There is, however, another form of communication which we all use most of the time, usually without knowing it. This is sometimes called body language. Its more technical name is nonverbal communication, because it does not involve the use of words. NVC is the abbreviation.

When someone is saying something with which he agrees, the average European will smile and nod approval. On the other hand, if you disagree with what they are saying, you may frown and shake your head. In this way, you signal your reactions and communicate them to the speaker without saying a word. I referred a moment ago to "the average European", because body language is very much tied to culture, and

Chapter 6 Nonverbal Communication

in order not to misunderstand, or not to be misunderstood, you must realize this. A smiling Chinese, for instance, may not be approving but somewhat embarrassed.

Quite a lot of work is now being done on the subject of NVC, which is obviously important, for instance, to managers, who have to deal every day with their staff, and have to understand what other people are feeling if they are to create good working conditions. Body language, or NVC signals, are sometimes categorized into five kinds: body and facial gestures; eye contact; body contact or "proximity"; clothing and physical appearance; and the quality of speech. I expect you understand all those, except perhaps "proximity". This simply means "closeness". In some cultures—I am sure this is a cultural feature and not an individual one—it is quite normal for people to stand close together, or to more or less thrust their face into yours when they are talking to you. In other cultures, this is disliked; Americans, for instance, talk about invasion of their space.

Some signals are probably common to all of us. If a public speaker (like a professor, for example) is all the time fiddling with a pencil, or with his glasses, while he is talking to you, he is telling you quite clearly that he is nervous. A person who holds a hand over his mouth when he is talking is signaling that he is lacking in confidence. If you start wriggling in your chairs, looking secretly at your watch or yawning behind your hands, I shall soon get the message that I'm boring you. I'm sure you could make a whole list of such signals—and it might be fun if you did.

All the signals I have mentioned so far can be controlled. If you are aware that you are doing these things, you can stop. You can even learn to give false signals. Most public speakers are in fact nervous, but a good speaker learns to hide this by giving off signals of confidence. Other kinds of NVC are not so easy to control, eye contact, for instance, is hand to control lake eye contact. Unless you are confessing intense love, you hardly ever look into someone else's eyes for very long. If you try it, you'll find they will soon look away, probably in embarrassment.

I've already mentioned proximity, so just a brief word now about our last two categories, which concern the way people dress and the way they speak. These are both pretty obvious signals. People may dress casually and speak casually, which signals that they are relaxed. Or they can dress formally and speak formally, showing their tenseness. In fact, nonverbal communication can, as the saying goes, speak volumes.

(选自 http://www.bigear.cn/news-514-64265.html.)

Questions for Discussion

1. What does NVC stand for?

2. How many kinds of NVC signals are mentioned in this passage? What are they?

3. Do you think nonverbal signals can be controlled? Why?

Passage 2

What Is Emotional Intelligence?

Emotional intelligence (EI) refers to the ability to perceive, control, and evaluate emotions. Some researchers suggest that emotional intelligence can be learned and strengthened, while others claim it's an inborn characteristic.

The ability to express and control emotions is essential, but so is the ability to understand, interpret, and respond to the emotions of others. Imagine a world in which you could not understand when a friend was feeling sad or when a co-worker was angry. Psychologists refer to this ability as emotional intelligence, and some experts even suggest that it can be more important than IQ in your overall success in life.

Components

Researchers suggest that there are four different levels of emotional intelligence, including the ability to perceive emothions, the ability to reason using emotions, the ability to understand emotions, and the ability to manage emotions.

Perceiving emotions: The first step in understanding emotions is to perceive them accurately. In many cases, this might involve understanding nonverbal signals such as body language and facial expressions.

Reasoning with emotions: The next step involves using emotions to promote thinking and cognitive activity. Emotions help prioritize what we pay attention to and react to; we respond emotionally to things that garner our attention.

Understanding emotions: The emotions that we perceive can carry a wide variety of meanings. If someone is expressing angry emotions, the observer must interpret the cause of the person's anger and what it could mean. For example, if your boss is acting angrily, it might mean that they are dissatisfied with your work, or it could be because they got a speeding ticket on their way to work that morning or that they've been fighting with their partner.

Managing emotions: The ability to manage emotions effectively is a crucial part of emotional intelligence and the highest level. Regulating emotions and responding appropriately as well as responding to the emotions of others are all important aspects of emotional management.

The four branches of this model are arranged by complexity with the more basic processes at the lower levels and the more advanced processes at the higher levels. For example, the lowest levels involve perceiving and expressing emotion, while higher levels require greater conscious involvement and involve regulating emotions.

Tips for Improving EI

Being emotionally intelligent is important, but what steps can you take to improve your own social and emotional skills? Here are some tips.

(1) Listen

If you want to understand what other people are feeling, the first step is to pay attention. Take the time to listen to what people are trying to tell you, both verbally and nonverbally. Body language can carry a great deal of meaning. When you sense that someone is feeling a certain way, consider the different factors that might be contributing to that emotion.

(2) Empathize

Picking up on emotions is critical, but you also need to be able to put yourself into someone else's shoes in order to truly understand their point of view. Practise empathizing with other people. Imagine how you would feel in their situation. Such activities can help you build an emotional understanding of a specific situation as well as develop stronger emotional skills in the long term.

(3) Reflect

The ability to reason with emotions is an important part of emotional intelligence. Consider how your own emotions influence your decisions and behaviors. When you are thinking about how other people respond, assess the role that their emotions play.

Why is this person feeling this way? Are there any unseen factors that might be contributing to these feelings? How do your emotions differ from theirs? As you explore such questions, you may find that it becomes easier to understand the role that emotions play in how people think and behave.

(选自 https://www.verywellmind.com/types-of-nonverbal-communication-2795397.)

Questions for Discussion

1. What is EI?
2. What are the four levels of EI?
3. How can we improve our EI?

Passage 3

Our Personal Space

Our personal space, that piece of the universe we occupy and call our own, is contained within an invisible boundary surrounding our body. As the owners of this area, we usually decide who may enter and who may not. When our space is invaded, we react in a variety of ways. We back up and retreat, stand our ground as our hands become moist from nervousness, or sometimes even react violently. Our response shows not only our unique personality, but also our cultural background.

For example, cultures that stress individualism such as England, the United States, Germany, and Australia, generally demand more space than collective cultures do, and tend to be aggressive when their space is invaded. The idea of space is quite different from the one found in the Mexican and Arab cultures. In Mexico, the physical distance between people when engaged in conversation is closer than what is usual north of the border. And for Middle Easterners, typical Arab conversations are at close range. Closeness cannot be avoided.

As is the case with most of our behavior, our use of space is directly linked to the value system of our culture. In some Asian cultures, for example, employees do not stand near their bosses; the extended distance demonstrates respect. Extra interpersonal distance is also part of the cultural experience of people in Scotland and

Sweden, for whom it reflects privacy. And in Germany, private space is sacred.

(选自 https://wenku.baidu.com/view/22964c6fa300a6c30d229f74.html.)

 Questions for Discussion

1. How would a person react when he felt his personal space invaded?

2. Why do employees in parts of Asia stand at a certain distance from their bosses?

Exercises

I. Multiple Choices

Directions: *Choose the best answer from the four choices.*

1. The message sent without using words are called ____ communication.

A. nonvocal   B. vocal   C. nonverbal   D. verbal

2. The functions of nonverbal communication don't include ____.

A. repeating   B. complementing   C. substituting   D. monitoring

3. Which of the following doesn't belong to the category of paralanguage?

A. stress   B. intonation   C. smile   D. pitch

4. The social zone ranges from ____.

A. 15 to 45 centimeters   B. 46 centimeters to 1.22 meters

C. 1.22 to 3.6 meters   D. larger than 3.6 meters

5. People from ____ are said to belong to polychronic people.

A. Austria   B. Germany   C. Switzerland   D. India

6. ____ are said to belong to the high-touch cultures.

A. The Americans   B. The Italians   C. The Germans   D The Brits

7. He said, "That's great" with an angry face. It's a kind of ____.

A. complementing   B. substituting   C. contradicting   D. regulating

8. To show number two, a person from ____ will hold up his thumb and index finger.

A. France   B. China   C. America   D the UK

9. People from ____ are taught to avoid eye contact with elders, teachers, and other people with status as a sign of respect.

A. North America   B. Latin America

C. the Mediterranean　　　　　　D. North Europe

10. Which one doesn't belong to the characteristics of monochronic people?

A. They make plans.　　　　　　B. They change plans.

C. They value time.　　　　　　D. They are committed to the job.

II. True or False

Directions: *Decide whether the statements are true (T) or false (F).*

1. According to one study, 93% of a message was conveyed by the speaker's nonverbal expressions. (　)

2. Universal emotions, such as happiness, fear, sadness are expressed in a similar nonverbal way throughout the world. (　)

3. The "O. K" gesture in the American culture means "zero" in Japan. (　)

4. In Britain, the thumbs-up sign can be used for hitch-hiking, asking for a free ride. (　)

5. When the verbal messages contradict the nonverbal messages, people tend to trust the verbal ones. (　)

6. Eye contact can be a way to regulate conversations, as breaking eye contact with someone is a way of "taking turns". (　)

7. In our personal lives, how we speak is relatively unimportant. (　)

8. The Thais like to touch babies or small children, and especially they like others to pat their children's head. (　)

9. When determining a worker's attitude about a situation, verbal symbols are more important than nonverbal symbols. (　)

10. When you are talking with an Arab, you should look at him in the eye. (　)

III. Translation

1. **Directions:** *Translate the following paragraph into Chinese.*

Nonverbal mistakes are often more difficult to avoid than verbal ones. For example, the amount of appropriate eye contact varies according to the country. When negotiating with the Japanese, I have learned to use intermittent eye contact across the bargaining table rather than staring directly. Southeast Asians also find an intense gaze unpleasant. While you may learn to use an indirect gaze in East and Southeast

Asia, you have to unlearn the lesson when doing business in the Mediterranean region, West Asia, and Latin America. These expressive people believe that "the eyes are the windows of the soul". They want to look you in the eye to demonstrate interest in the discussion and to show that they are honest and sincere. If you use indirect eye contact, you may be regarded as insincere—perhaps even dishonest.

2. **Directions:** *Translate the following paragraph into English.*

在中国文化中,红色通常象征着好运、长寿和幸福。在春节和其他喜庆场合,红色到处可见。人们把现金作为礼物送给家人或亲密朋友时,通常放在红信封里。红色在中国流行的另一个原因是人们把它与中国革命和共产党相联系。然而,红色并不总是代表好运与快乐。因为从前死者的名字常用红色书写,用红墨水写中国人名被看成是一种冒犯行为。

Chapter 7

Intercultural Communication Barriers

> Do not do unto others what you would not want others to do unto you.
>
> ——Analects of Confucius
>
> 己所不欲，勿施于人。
>
> ——《论语》
>
> Put oneself in somebody's shoes.
> 将心比心，换位思考。

本章导读

跨文化交际不仅受文化差异的影响，还受交际者个人心理因素的影响。个人的情感和态度会导致跨文化交际中出现误会、矛盾甚至冲突。此外，不同的价值观念和思维方式反映在语言表达上的差异也会产生跨文化交际障碍。了解这些障碍及其成因能够帮助我们克服障碍，促进跨文化交际的有效进行。本章主要介绍情感障碍、态度障碍和翻译障碍。情感障碍包括焦虑和不确定，以及假定一致性；态度障碍包括民族中心主义、文化定势、偏见和种族主义；翻译障碍主要包括词汇不对等、习语不对等、语法和句式不对等、经验不对等及概念不对等。

Learning Objectives

In this chapter, students will learn how to understand barriers caused by emotional, attitudinal, and translation problems, analyze reasons for emotional and attitudinal problems, and deal with some barriers caused by emotional, attitudinal, and translation problems.

Warm-up Activities

1. Have you experienced any awkwardness in intercultural interaction? If so, what did you feel? If not, what do you think may hinder intercultural communication?

2. In what way do you think we can facilitate intercultural communication?

Intercultural communication might offer us a new perspective and bring us personal gain. As we know, intercultural communication is not a simple process since it does not always go smoothly. To improve the quality of intercultural encounters, we have to be aware of what impedes them, which is assumed to be the first step to tackle barriers or obstacles in interactions between us and people from another culture. In this chapter, we'll talk about major intercultural communication barriers. They are emotional problems, attitudinal problems, and translation problems.

7.1 Emotional Problems

7.1.1 Anxiety and Uncertainty

Anxiety, as we all know, is a feeling of nervousness or worry. In the context of intercultural communication, it refers to the feeling of not knowing what one is expected to do, and focusing on that feeling and not being totally present in the communication transaction. It may also affect one's ability to communicate his ideas to others. You may have experienced meeting a person introduced by one of your friends. You may be highly occupied with the worry of behaving improperly due to knowing nothing about the new friend.

Uncertainty, as defined in *Collins Online Dictionary*, is a state of doubt about the future or about what is the right thing to do. It refers to our cognitive inability to explain our own or others' feelings and behaviors in interactions because of an ambiguous situation that evokes anxiety. Anxiety happens because of being afraid of failure in communication events, while uncertainty happens because we are unable to predict others' ideas and behaviors. Everyone who is involved in whatever intercultural communication events is likely to suffer from anxiety and uncertainty.

With respect to this problem, **Charles R. Berger and J. Calabrese,** professors of communication developed an **Uncertainty Reduction Theory (URT)** first presented in

1975, which can, in a way, be helpful. The communication **axioms** (原理) this theory has generated are clear and directly related to intercultural communication. **Berger and Calabrese** summarize this theory, "Central to the present theory is the assumption that when strangers meet, their primary concern is one of uncertainty reduction or increasing predictability about the behavior of both themselves and others in the interaction." According to the theory, all of us have a need to understand both the self and the other in interpersonal situations. Simply put, we have a desire to reduce the uncertainty built into every new meeting. However, "as our ability to predict which alternative or alternatives are likely to occur next decreases, uncertainty increases."

This uncertainty can take a number of forms, all of which can interfere with intercultural communication. First, there are behavioral questions that deal with how you should act during a particular situation and with a specific person. Should you shake hands or bow? Should you speak English or try your broken French? Should you offer a business card or wait for him or her to offer you a card? Should you ask questions about the person's family or avoid personal topics? In each of these instances, the uncertainty can cause stress. Second, there are a series of cognitive questions that can also bring about feelings of uncertainty and **hamper** (妨碍) predictability. How does the other person view time? How does the other person perceive women? How does the other person define status?

The essence of this uncertainty reduction theory is to gather information about the counterparts in intercultural encounters so as to predict their behaviors. This theory involves three kinds of strategies: passive strategies, active strategies, and interactive strategies. Following passive strategies, we observe the other person, either in situations where he or she is likely to change his or her behaviors to fit the situations as in a classroom, or where he or she is likely to act more naturally as in the stands at a football game or in a shopping mall. By using active strategies, we ask others about the person we're interested in or try to set up a situation where we can observe that person (e.g. taking the same class, sitting at a table away at dinner). As we can see, the passive strategies and active strategies are monitored individually, but interactive strategies engage two-way activities. We directly gather information by asking the other person questions about himself or herself. Or we actively tell the other person what he or she does not know about us. Asking questions and disclosing ourselves encourages our counterparts to reveal something equally important about themselves to us. In this way, more direct and accurate information about our counterparts helps reduce uncertainty and accordingly reduce anxiety.

(选自：严明. 大学英语跨文化交际教程 [M]. 北京：清华大学出版社, 2009.)

Questions for Discussion

1. Why was the Danish woman charged by New York City Police?
2. What made the woman do the same in New York City as in Copenhagen?

7.1.2 Assuming Similarity

Assuming similarity instead of difference turns out to be another barrier to intercultural interactions. It refers to the idea that people coming from another culture are more similar to you than they actually are or that another person's situation is more similar to yours than it in fact is. When you assume similarities between cultures you can be caught unaware of differences. This explains why people behave as they would in their home culture when they are in a new culture they know little, which may possibly incur communication failures. When you know nothing about a new culture, you might easily assume there are no differences and accordingly behave as you would in your home culture.

If a person assumes that the emotions displayed by the people from other cultures are similar to those displayed by himself, he might think they are lacking emotions or displaying emotions inappropriately when he sees those people behave differently from him in some situations. For example, a Chinese teacher gave her foreign colleague who taught at a high school in China a precious necklace made of crystal in her wedding ceremony. But two years later, when the Chinese teacher married, her college just gave her a silk handkerchief as the wedding gift. The Chinese teacher felt disappointed with their friendship. On the other hand, assuming difference instead of similarity can also hinder intercultural encounters or even cause conflicts because of one's neglecting what's in common between two cultures.

In 1997, a Danish woman left her 14-month-old baby girl in a stroller outside a Manhattan restaurant while she was inside dining with her husband. Other diners at the restaurant became concerned about the baby's safety and called New York City

Police. The woman was charged with endangering a child and was jailed for two nights. Her child was placed in foster care. The woman and the Danish **consulate** (领事) explained that leaving children unattended outside cafes is common in Denmark. Pictures were wired to the police showing numerous strollers parked outside cafes while parents were eating inside. The Danish woman assumed that Copenhagen was similar to New York—and what is commonly done in Copenhagen was also commonly done in New York.

7.2 Attitudinal Problems

Warm-up Activities

1. Can ethnocentrism be totally avoided in intercultural communication?
2. Does ethnocentrism always bring about negative consequences?

7.2.1 Ethnocentrism

People who are born and bred in any country are taught the preferred and unconscious ways to respond to the world. In China, we learned from our parents to bring gifts when visiting friends or relatives. We read from books that how happy we are to have friends coming from afar and come to a sense that hospitality helps to promote friendship. We are taught by teachers to respect the elderly and care for the young. We cannot deny that people generally perceive their own culturally-shaped behaviors or attitudes as natural and hence universal. But if people negatively judge another culture by the frame of their own, it will lead to ethnocentrism, referring to the belief that their culture is primary or even superior to others. It might well be the major barrier to intercultural communication.

The word "ethnocentrism" is derived from two Greek words: ethnos, for "nation"; and kentron, for "center". The word formation reveals that ethnocentrism happens when a particular nation sees itself as the center of the world. In other words, ethnocentrism refers to our tendency to identify within our group (e.g. ethnic or racial group, culture) and to evaluate outgroups and their members according to its standard.

Now read the following comparisons and think about which one is more correct than the other?

(1) Jews cover their heads when they pray, but Protestants do not.

(2) The Catholic speaks to God, the Buddhist has no god, and the Hindu has many gods.

(3) In parts of Turkey and Saudi Arabia, women cover their faces with veils, whereas women in the United States do not.

(4) Japanese bow to first-time met clients while Americans shake hands.

(5) Chinese address the seniors in neighborhoods like Ye Ye (grandpa) or Nai Nai (grandma), but the British address senior neighbors by their names directly.

The above examples suggest that ethnocentrism is not always deliberate. Ethnocentrism is assumed to be a function of how we are socialized. It is in one way or another embedded in our values, beliefs, norms, and behaviors. In this sense, ethnocentric attitude is more or less unavoidable in intercultural interactions.

Ethnocentric attitudes can be conscious or automatic, and all of us are thus likely to be ethnocentric in one way or another. The early Greek used the term "barbarians" to refer to those people living around them who did not speak Greek. The ancient Persian and Egyptians were considered by the Greeks to be inferior. Europe drew maps of the world with Europe at the center, and North Americans with the New World at the center. The British draw the Prime Meridian of Longitude(本初子午线) to run through Greenwich, near London. The Japanese word *ganjin* means "foreigner, a person who is not Japanese" with condescending (优越感) overtone. The Chinese, who called their country the Middle Kingdom, were convinced in ancient times that China was the center of the world.

Ethnocentrism can be positive if we are involved in **intracultural communication** (内文化交际) because it satisfies the need for **cohesiveness** (内聚力) and **solidarity** (团结) of a nation or cultural or ethnic group. Conforming to our shared traditions or customs, we feel safe and obtain the merits our culture brings to us. Don't we feel comfortable when we are treated generously as we treat others?

On the other hand, ethnocentric attitudes can result in problems or even conflicts when we are involved in intercultural communication. Ethnocentrism not only shapes narrow and defensive perspectives, but also normally generates stereotypes of members from other cultures, leading to rigid behaviors. And extreme ethnocentrism leads to a rejection of richness and knowledge of other cultures. It impedes communication and blocks the exchange of ideas and skills.

7.2.2 Stereotyping

People from a country are classified as a whole into a certain type based on certain characteristics without considering individual differences. The way we simplify or generalize these salient traits of cultural groups is called "stereotyping".

The word stereotyping was first used by a journalist, Walter Lippmann, in 1922 to describe judgement made about others on the basis of their ethnic group. Stereotyping is a natural process. Anyone can stereotype and anyone can be stereotyped. **Samovar and Porter** (2009) defined stereotyping as "a complex form of categorization that mentally organizes your experiences and guides your behaviors towards a particular group of people."

Stereotyping meets human beings' psychological need to categorize and classify. As is known to all, the world is so big, complex, and transitory that no one can know it in all its details. Although stereotyping brings convenience to some extent, it normally hinders intercultural communication because stereotypes **overgeneralize** (过于笼统地概括) and **oversimplify** (过于简单化) people's traits so that they ignore individual characteristics. For example, many people may have an impression that people from developed countries live in big houses, drive luxurious cars, and can always afford travelling around the world on holidays. People who think so generate their attitudes toward those people from the limited source of information. They didn't have any chance to expose themselves to the whole picture of developed nations where there are still poor people who can't get by on a daily basis. Stereotypes limit our deep understanding of another group of people. What's more, stereotypes create, repeat, and reinforce beliefs until they often become taken for "truth". For example, women were stereotyped as "housewives". Being confined to houses, they had been rejected in the workplace for centuries all over the world. The consequence of stereotyping is that the vast differences that exist among the members of any one group may not be taken into account in the interpretation of messages.

Generally speaking, stereotype is divided into four commonly seen types: racial stereotype, gender stereotype, cultural stereotype, and stereotype towards groups of individuals.

(1) Racial Stereotype

People may have certain stereotype towards a group just because of their ethnicity. For example, people tend to hold that all blacks are good at sports.

People may have certain stereotype towards a group just because of their ethnicity. For example, people tend to hold that all blacks are good at sports. In a study of black and white students at the University of Colorado at Boulder, Ryan (2014) found that blacks reported a stronger tendency to note certain stereotypical attributes in themselves (such as "dance well," "strong emotional bonds to family," and "financial support from athletic scholarships") and other attributes in whites (such as "high SAT math scores," "at least one parent has a college degree," and "spends money frivolously"). However, black students were more adept than their white counterparts at gauging the prevalence, as reported by the students, of these features in both groups—but particularly in whites. White students judged their own traits more accurately than those of black students.

These results support the theory that members of ethnic minority groups have a greater stake in understanding a more powerful majority population than majority members have in understanding minority groups, Ryan argues.

(2) Gender Stereotype

Gender stereotype means that people make inaccurate, overly simplistic generalizations of others based upon their gender. For example, many people always hold that men are strong and are breadwinners.

Many ads show mothers serving meals to their families, while very few show fathers doing this. Many newspaper photos, film, ads and TV programs show that men engaged in physically active pastimes such as sport, rock-climbing or canoeing, while few show women doing these things. Many magazine photographs and advertisements show teenage girls grooming themselves such as putting on make-up, brushing their hair and generally worrying about their appearance, whereas few shows teenage boys doing these things.

(3) Cultural Stereotype

People have cultural stereotype because of inaccurate, incomplete, or even wrong understanding of a certain culture. For example, fortune cookies are always associated with Chinese culture because they are often seen in Chinese restaurants in America.

But you will not find them in China. As a matter of fact, fortune cookies originated from Japan.

Cultural stereotyping limit management's ability to make best use of their employees' skills and help them develop new skills. Examples of cultural bias in the workplace include assuming that all Asians are good at math. If a manager sees John as an Asian person who is good with numbers but not people, he may never be given the opportunity to develop his people skills and he may eventually leave the company due to lack of opportunities.

Cultural stereotypes also affect employee morale and productivity. Employees are more likely to leave an organization if they believe that stereotypes determine how they are treated. Stereotypes lead to decreased productivity, dissatisfied customers and reduced revenues. They hinder open communication and teamwork and lead to a perception of in-groups and out-groups in which members guard information, using it as a form of power. Failing to include diverse employee perspectives and skills limits the company's creativity, problem-solving.

(4) Stereotype Towards Groups of Individuals

When people see a part of a picture and assume it is the whole picture of a certain group, it may lead to stereotyping. For example, people always associate librarians with such an image: an old lady, grey-haired, wearing a pair of glasses and always seeming to be serious.

There is a wide range of categories that are used to form stereotypes such as regions of the world, countries, races, religions, age, occupation, relational roles, physical characteristics and social class. For example, to say "All Chinese people like to practice Kung Fu" is a stereotype.

Age stereotype is that someone judges other people's behavior and appearance because of the age. The age can be simply classified into children, youngsters, adults and old-age people. Children are often described as innocent, naughty, for instance, people think only children like to play tricks. If an adult plays a trick on others, he will be thought to be "childish". Then, young people usually are stereotyped as impatient, rebellious and indulged in comfort. Thus, now more and more parents are enthusiastic to send their young sons and daughters to training camp in older to cultivate their good characteristics. Most obviously, young people, who are under 18, are not encouraged to fall in love with others for they have no experience so that they fail to handle love-related problems, which tends to have bad influence on their growth.

In terms of stereotype about occupation, most people just pay attention to its surface rather than penetrate into it. Most people want to be a teacher or doctor when they are young, because they are conveyed the idea that teachers and doctors are good jobs by the external world, having stable salary and bright prospects. While many people do not want to be engaged in farming, car or electric maintaining as they consider it a hard and dirty work without high income. These stereotypes will help children to set a goal so that they can work hard in these fields earlier.

(选自: 严明. 大学英语跨文化交际教程 [M]. 北京: 清华大学出版社, 2009.)

Samovar and Porter (2009) summed up the limitations of stereotypes as follows:

Stereotypes are a kind of filter—because they only allow in information that is consistent with information already held by the individual. It is not the act of classifying that creates intercultural problems; rather, it is assuming that all culture-specific information applies to all individuals from the cultural groups. Stereotypes also keep you from being successful as communicators because they are oversimplified, exaggerated, and overgeneralized. Stereotypes are resistant to change.

Stereotypes are not always negative. Sometimes people have positive ones on a group of people. But it does not necessarily lead to positive results or success in communications. For example, Chinese students tend to be stereotyped as being very diligent and good at math, which may foster the mutual respect among the people in intercultural communications. But what if a math teacher who holds this positive stereotype to a very high degree expects too much for the Chinese student who is literally not very good at math?

So far we have come to a conclusion that stereotypes, whether positive or negative, to a large extent, cause problems in intercultural interactions. But how do we acquire stereotypes? Stereotypes, like culture itself, are learned in a variety of ways. First, people learn stereotypes from their parents, relatives, and friends. Second, stereotypes develop through limited personal contact. Finally, many stereotypes are provided by the mass media.

Adler (1997) and Brislin (2000) gave some advice on how to overcome stereotyping. First, be aware of the existence of stereotyping; second, not to simplify one's thinking process; third, get in touch with people from various cultures; fourth, to find sufficient evidence and exceptions; fifth, describe an individual's behaviors instead of generalizing the comments over the whole community.

Warm-up Activities

1. How do stereotypes differ from prejudices? Can you give an example?
2. Can you give examples of some words used to show prejudice?

Prejudice

As an English proverb goes, birds of a feather flock together, which readily finds equivalence in Chinese, that is, "物以类聚，人以群分". It is by no means a coincidence. The proverb conveying the same meaning is found in nearly every culture. This seems to be the philosophy people use when selecting friends in most cases. There is an overwhelming tendency among all of us to seek out the people whom we consider to be like ourselves to a large degree. Like-minded people surely feel comfortable when talking about what both parties enjoy, which ends in not only promoting friendship but also yielding more personal interactions. Our inclination to choose friends and keep in touch with acquaintances that mirror our personality and interests should be obviously connected to intercultural communication. But the fact is that the culture that nurtures us with specialized patterns of communication and belief often separates us from people with a different background. The poet Emily Dickinson vividly described this separation when she wrote, "The Soul selects her own society—/Then—shuts the Door—/To her **divine** (神圣的) Majority—/Present no more." Her message is **crystalline** (明显的): Most of us prefer our own kind and avoid the unfamiliar. This tendency is the very reason that interpersonal bias was selected as a potential communication problem.

Seeking similarity, on one hand, strengthens the solidarity of in-groups, and on the other hand, separates "us" from "them", the members of out-groups. People act out prejudice when labeling the behaviors, customs, and speech of out-group people "strange" and "inferior", and even avoiding and/or withdrawing from contact with the disliked groups.

Prejudice refers to the irrational dislike, suspicion, or hatred of a particular group, race, religion, or sexual orientation. Prejudice involves an unfair, biased, or intolerant attitude towards another group of people or an individual from the group. Growing from stereotype, prejudice is either negative or positive attitude or emotions towards a group or its individuals. Positive prejudice seldom incurs failures or adversity in intercultural communication as negative prejudice does.

It seems confusing to tell prejudice from stereotype. To make things easier, we can simply say that stereotyping is cognition without conscious awareness, while prejudice is an attitude which is readily applied to communicative behaviors, without always leading to an action.

If a Chinese were not accommodated by his foreign friend in the manner of Chinese people's hospitality, he would create a stereotype of foreigners' being indifferent, feel discontent or even disappointed with them, form such a prejudice that they are not worth making friends with, and accordingly be very likely to stay away from them or refuse to communicate with them, which is discrimination.

This example finds its theoretical explanation in the logical forms of prejudice formulated by **Ronald Smith** as follows. Ronald Smith views prejudice as a moral attitude, and it usually takes the following process of formation:

Prejudice, like stereotype, is also acquired. It is precedent or a prejudgment based on previous decisions and experiences, which becomes unchangeable even when people are confronted with new experience or evidence, according to **Gordon Allport**. Prejudice is expressed mainly in five ways. First, it can be expressed through **antilocution** (仇恨言论) which involves talking about a member of the target group in negative and stereotypic terms. Someone would be engaged in this form of prejudice if he or she told a friend, "Those Germans did it once, so we can never trust any of them ever again." Second, people act out prejudice when they avoid and/or withdraw from contact with the disliked group. Third, when discrimination is the expression of prejudice, the prejudiced person undertakes to exclude all members of the group in question from certain types of employment, residential housing, political rights, educational and recreational opportunities, churches, hospitals, or some other types of social institutions. Often in cases of discrimination, we observe ethnocentrism, stereotyping, and prejudice coming together in a type of fanaticism that completely obstructs any form of successful intercultural communication. Fourth, when prejudice moves to the next level of expression, we often see **physical attacks** (肢体冲突). Fifth, the most alarming form of prejudice is **extermination** (灭绝). This expression of prejudice leads to acts of physical violence against the out-group.

Since prejudice has so many negative consequences, how can we kick it off to facilitate intercultural communications? First, we should accept that we have prejudice towards other people so as to be alert of prejudice by reflecting our own prejudiced attitude. Second, involve ourselves in communications with more people to improve the understanding of various cultures. Third, be very cautious about and avoid using language with a tint of prejudice or discrimination.

Now let's compare the inappropriate expressions with their appropriate versions.

	inappropriate expressions	appropriate expressions
(美国) 黑人	black	African American
残疾人	handicapped	the physically challenged
穷人	poor people	the needy, the economically disadvantaged
男同性恋者	homosexual	gay
看门人	janitor	custodian
清洁工	dustman	sanitation engineer
长相丑的	ugly	plain looking
老人	old person, the elderly	senior citizen
学习成绩差的学生	retarded student	exceptional student
盲人	blind people	the visually challenged

(选自：祖晓梅. 跨文化交际 [M]. 北京：外语教学与研究出版社，2015：196.)

Using appropriate expressions can largely reduce the risk of being offensive in intercultural communication. To sign up for some courses or training programs is another supplementary strategy to reduce prejudice and foster intercultural interactions. Apart from the above-mentioned, to have access to more sources of information helps a lot.

Warm-up Activities

1. Can you think of some examples of racism on social media?
2. What may forge racism?

Racism

According to **Brislin** (1988), prejudice can be expressed in **red-neck racism** ("红脖人"型种族主义) and **symbolic racism** (象征型种族主义). In Brislin's words it refers to the belief "that members of a given cultural group are inferior according to some imagined standard and that the group members are not worthy of decent treatment". A case in point is the prejudice many held against indigenous groups all over the world throughout the history. Brislin points out that symbolic racism occurs when members of one culture have negative feelings about another culture because they believe the "outside culture is a threat to their group".

It can be generalized that racism refers to any policy, practice, belief, or attitude that attributes characteristics or status to individuals based on their races. It goes further than a specific kind of prejudice, for it also involves the exercise of power. Racism exists worldwide. In some Western countries, race is seen as a continuum rather than mutually exclusive categories. Racism appears in songs, insults and malicious humor, employment ads written to discourage non-white applicants.

Elliot Aronson's illustration of how prejudiced people see the world fully explains racism. If Mr. Bigot sees a well-dressed European American protestant sitting on a park bench and sunning himself or herself at three o'clock on a Wednesday afternoon, he thinks nothing of it. If he sees a well-dressed African American man doing the same thing, he is liable to leap to the conclusion that the person is unemployed and he becomes infuriated because he assumes that his hard-earned taxes are paying that shiftless good-for-nothing welfare subsidies to keep the African American man in good clothes. If Mr. Bigot passes a European American's house and notices that a trashcan is overturned and some garbage is strewn about, he is apt to conclude that a stray dog has been searching for food. If he passes an African American's house and notices the same thing, he is inclined to become annoyed, and to assert that "those people live like pigs". Not only does prejudice influence his conclusions, his erroneous conclusions justify and intensify his negative feelings.

At the culture level, racism denies the existence of the culture of a particular group; for example, the denial that African Americans represent a unique and distinct culture that is separate from European American culture and all African cultures. Cultural racism also involves the rejection by one group of the beliefs and values of another, such as the "negative evaluations by whites of black cultural values".

So far we have learned that ethnocentrism, stereotyping, prejudice and racism hinder or even **jeopardize** (危害) intercultural interactions. But what causes the persistence of these attitudinal problems? There are various reasons. And we'll have a look at the widely acknowledged six reasons:

(1) Socialization

Ethnocentrism, stereotyping, prejudice and racism are learned, many of which are passed on from parents to children, sometimes in subtle messages such as "we don't associate with people like that" or "be careful when you are with them".

(2) Social Benefits

Expressing ethnocentrism, stereotyping, prejudice and racism may bring support from others who share them. For example, it is difficult for people to break away from the prejudices of their families and friends, as rejecting the prejudice can be perceived as breaking away from the association.

(3) Economic Benefits

Ethnocentrism, stereotyping, prejudice, and racism can be strong when there is direct competition. When Chinese immigrants worked on building the transcontinental railroad across the United States when jobs were plentiful, Chinese were perceived as being hardworking, industrious, and law-abiding. But after the railroad was completed and jobs dwindled, Chinese were perceived as being crafty and stupid.

(4) Psychological Benefits

Ethnocentrism, stereotyping, prejudice, and racism can be used to generate a feeling of superiority and to explain a complex world in terms of simple causes as in saying "those people are the source of all our problems".

In order to undo the tendency of racism, stereotyping, prejudice, we must become empathetic—be curious, open-minded, inclusive, sensitive, and tolerant to differences and ambiguity; respect and value others; be always ready to take alternative perspectives, hold a pluricultural attitude, embrace the ethic of concern for others, and concern for both self and other in human interaction and relationships.

Being empathetic is **reciprocal** (互惠互利的) and **bidirectional** (双向的). It is the starting point, prerequisite as well as the guarantee of intercultural dialogue on an equal footing that creates harmonious relationships, self-cultivation and reconstruction through critical self-reflection, and the human life community on a global scale.

An empathetic person is willing to step outside their own perspective to appreciate others and concern for truth and precision in human interaction analysis. Empathy opens a new way of life. It leads to personal change as the individual penetrates deeply enough into the inside of a foreign culture and thus becomes a richer person in the heart. He shifts readily from one language to another, from one set of habits, attitudes and values to another. Thus he is in a position to look at problems from more than one viewpoint and to see the essential ethnocentrism of each.

However, it is worth noting that learning to see from another perspective and to be capable of empathetic projection always needs sincerity, mutual trust, mutual respect, mutual tolerance and mutual acceptance. Mutual understanding, accepting differences and seeking common ground or the practice of being concerned for both self and other form the basis for moving beyond stereotypes and prejudices.

7.3 Translation Problems

Warm-up Activities
1. Can you think of some Chinese words that don't have English equivalents?
2. Can you think of some English idioms that have equivalent meanings in Chinese language?
3. Why do you think there are some misunderstandings in translation from one language to another?
4. How can problems in translation due to lack of equivalence be avoided or tackled?

Language is assumed to be the most obvious barrier to intercultural communication. Knowing the language of a culture is undoubtedly the prerequisite for fully understanding the culture. There is no doubt that people who speak the same language feel safer and more comfortable than those who do not share a common language in interactions. But it does not mean that speaking the same language guarantees the smoothness of intercultural communication. Vocabulary differences in English used in the United States and Great Britain provide the strong evidence. For example, American people tend to use "knock up" to mean "to **impregnate** (使……怀孕) ". When an Englishman from England who travelled to the United States asked the hotel clerk to provide a morning call service by asking, "Would you please knock me up at 6: 30?" The clerk would be embarrassed or even feel insulted. Linguistic symbols are nearly arbitrary. They are conventions by which certain sounds are attached to certain objects and events, which signify the social aspects of language. Therefore, we say language, to a certain degree, reflects unique aspects of its culture. In another word, culture is conveyed in language. Since every culture has its unique characteristics, a certain word or concept may not have an exact counterpart in another language. In this sense, language can be a barrier to intercultural communication.

　　In dealing with the problem of not sharing a common language, translation plays a critical part. Language translation is not only difficult; it can be inept and have extreme consequences. Near the end of World War II, after Italy and Germany surrendered, the Allies sent Japan an ultimatum to surrender. Japan's Premier announced that his government would "mokusatsu" the surrender ultimatum. "Mokusatsu" was an unfortunate word choice because it could mean both to consider and to take notice of. The Premier, speaking in Japanese, apparently meant that the government would consider the surrender ultimatum. But, the English language translators in Japan's overseas broadcasting agency used the "to take notice of" meaning of "mokusatsu". Consequently, the world heard that Japan had rejected the surrender ultimatum rather than that Japan was considering the ultimatum. This mistranslation led the United States to assume Japan was unwilling to surrender and the atomic bombing of Hiroshima and Nagasaki followed. Quite possibly if the other meaning had been selected in the translation process, the atomic bomb would not have been used in World War II.

　　Due to uniqueness in respective four subsystems (phonology, morphology, syntax, and semantics) of a certain language, people from different cultural backgrounds encounter translation problems generally in the following five aspects: the lack of equivalences in vocabulary, idioms, grammar and syntax, experiences and concepts.

7.3.1　Lack of Vocabulary Equivalence

The first barrier is the lack of vocabulary equivalence. It occurs when there are no words in one language that correspond precisely with the meaning of words in another.

As the famous example shows, the Arctic people have a great variety of words for "snow" due to the geographical environment there which is not shared with other areas. In the same vein, when people of different cultures do not share a lot in customs and traditions, they may have different understandings of the meaning of a certain word as well as its associative meanings.

Some color words in English culture have different connotations from those in Chinese culture. "Yellow" in some contexts means "obscene". When we say "扫黄" and translate it as "fight against yellow", it makes no sense to English speakers. Likewise, when Americans say "yellow-bellied" and "yellow streak", Chinese people cannot figure out that it really means being cowardly.

Some fruit words can have different meanings from another culture. For example, "You are a lemon." If you think you are "柠檬精" as what the internet buzzword means, you are misunderstanding it. In fact, "a lemon" means something not as good or as useful as it should be, or someone who looks shy or foolish or even useless. For example, He took a little test drive and agreed the car was a lemon. (Chinese meaning: 他试驾了一下，认为这车不行。) I just stood there like a lemon. (Chinese meaning: 我就傻乎乎地站在那儿。)

Another challenge in terms of vocabulary is that some English words have many collocations in which meanings vary. As can be seen, the meaning of a certain word heavily depends on the collocations and its context. Take the word "apple" as an example. Check this sentence: "The Big Apple is the city full of challenges and opportunities". "the Big Apple" refers to New York City. Here, "apple" implies wealth, treasure and opportunities. Here is another example to prove it. "Born with a magical piece of jade in his mouth, Jia Baoyu is the apple of the family's eye." However, "apple" does not always mean something good or valuable. If we say "Stop talking rudely like that. You really look like a wise apple." In this context, "wise apple" does not have positive meaning. Instead, it means a smug, self-conceited person who always annoys others. If we don't know the fact that the same word means differently in different contexts, communications will be hindered.

7.3.2 Lack of Idiomatic Equivalence

The second barrier is a lack of idiomatic equivalence. According to *Collins Online Dictionary*, an idiom is a group of words which have a different meaning when used together from the one they would have if you took the meaning of each word separately. The meaning of an idiom is highly attached to culture and conventions. Cultural commonalities generate equivalence between English and Chinese idioms. For example,

(1)"药补不如食补"——Diet cares more than the doctors.

(2)"大树底下好乘凉"—— A good tree is a good shelter.

(3)"善有善报"——Do well and have well.

(4)"宁做林中鸟,不当笼中鸟"——Better be bird of the wood than bird of the cage.

(5)"丢脸"——lose face

Despite the similarities, there are endless established and conventional expressions which are exclusively understandable to their own culture. It is rather challenging for speakers of another culture to understand their meanings and usages. The English language is known to particularly replete with idioms. For example, "I tried any means to stay calm before the interview, but it was like water off a duck's back." According to the context, "be like water off a duck's back" means "be of no use". When learning English idioms, we have to keep this rule in mind that words in idioms must be bound together and cannot be replaced with others. Here is another example. Right before you take the final exam, your friend says to you, "Keep your shirt on, buddy. You can make it after such hard work." You may have guessed out what this idiom "keep your shirt on" means. It means "Don't worry!" or "Take it easy." Again, the idiom "the old man kicked off the bucket", to English native speakers, means "the old man died." But if this idiom is translated word for word, the intended meaning will be lost. These examples explain why non-English speakers, although they know every single word in the conversation, can hardly understand what English speakers mean when talking to them.

It is the same case in Chinese idioms. When it comes to interpreting Chinese idioms in English, literal translation is basically not a good option, for the images and connotations forged in two cultures have no equivalent functions. Take a look at the literal translation of the Chinese idiom"有钱能使鬼推磨". "With money, you can make the devil turn the millstone". In English, "devil" symbolizes "the evil" or "the vicious". It does not convey message of being powerful and not being controlled by the alive as it does in the Chinese expression "鬼". In the phrase "turn the millstone", "turn" simply means "to make the millstone moves," which misses out the message of "toil" and "drudgery". Therefore, "Money makes the mare go" or "Money is a good servant" may make sense to English speakers in English cultural context. Another example may further explain why the literal translation does not make sense. If the Chinese idiom "跳进黄河也洗不清" is interpreted as "One cannot be cleaned if one takes a bath in the Yellow River", the speakers of English culture would be confused. So it is obvious that the version "One cannot clean up his fame if it is put on him" can be more explicit and understandable.

7.3.3 Lack of Grammatical-Syntactical Equivalence

The third barrier is the lack of grammatical-syntactical equivalence. Syntax is the arrangement of words to form phrases and sentences. Languages differ in their syntactic(句法的) structures. In English, word order is important because it conveys meaning. The syntax of the English language gives a different meaning to these two sentences: "The dog bit the man" and "The man bit the dog." In Latin, however, the subject and object of a sentence are indicated by word endings rather than word order. Linguists agree that the grammatical categories of one language cannot be used to describe another language. Languages differ in the numbers and kinds of grammatical categories they have and how these categories are indicated. Thus, the information that in English would be expressed as "The dog bit the man" would be "Dog bite(s) man" in Chinese. In Chinese, the tense of the verb need not be indicated, but it must be in English, although it can be brought in by using a time word such as "now" or "yesterday".

Differences in syntax and grammar among languages make us believe that to learn a foreign language is more than to learn the vocabulary of that language merely. Take learning English as an example: a high proficiency of English vocabulary does not necessarily lead to an advanced ability to construct the English words into meaningful sentences. Also, mother tongue can strongly interfere with the sentence structure strong. So, the lack of grammatical-syntactical equivalence can be another translation problem. For example, in Chinese, we can say "今天，我们学校来了一位新校长。" But in English, the sentence "Today, our school comes a new president" is grammatically and syntactically wrong.

Grammatical and syntactic mistakes are also frequently seen in the translation of passive sentence patterns. Take this sentence as an example, "The peace was restored." Can we translate it as "安静被恢复了"? The passive expression certainly is not accepted in Chinese. In the same vein, the Chinese sentence "衣服洗了" cannot be directly translated as "The clothes have washed". From the aforementioned, we know that syntactic patterns are not always equivalent in Chinese and English. Translation is supposed to conform to how the target language expresses itself.

In addition, we often need to understand a language's grammar and syntax to understand the meaning of words. For example, words in English can be nouns, verbs or adjectives depending on their position in a sentence. In English, people can say "plan a table" and "table a plan", or "book a place" and "place a book", or "lift a thumb" and "thumb a lift".

7.3.4 Lack of Experiential Equivalence

The fourth barrier is the lack of experiential equivalence. The following case may help deepen the perception of this problem. A university professor from America came to visit a university in China. When he was introduced to official leaders of different ranks in the university, such as "科长", "处长", the interpreter had trouble in finding in corresponding words in English, for there is no such a title in American administration system. If an object or experience does not exist in one culture, it is difficult to translate words referring to that object or experience into that language when no words may exist for them. Examples of this kind are in the long list. In 2015, the former Vice Chairman of the National People's Congress Foreign Affairs Committee Fu Ying once remarked at a Press Conference, "要学习在世界的中央舞台长袖善舞肯定是需要时间的". In Chinese culture, "长袖" literally means long sleeves of ancient or classical costumes worn by artists or dancers in dancing performances. "长

袖善舞" can be explained as to perform skillfully and gracefully. But in the culture of English speaking countries, there is no such an object. So to make English speakers understand this figure of speech, this sentence was translated as "It will take time for us to master the steps necessary to waltz gracefully across the global stage. "

There are many things or objects that are exclusive to Chinese culture, such as "炕", "太极", "衙门", "四合院", "漕运", "水墨画", "粽子", "状元", "唐装", etc. On the other hand, there are objects or experiences that exclusively exist in English culture which may make no sense to Chinese people. For example, "motel", "parliament", "monarchy", "clone", "copy", "mini", "T-shirt", "coffee", "pudding", etc. When translating these terms, we can use literal translation or transliteration and simultaneously attach the adequate explanation to it in order to achieve clarity and accuracy. It is worth mentioning that when a cultural image or object is widely acknowledged or accepted in another culture, explanation will not be necessary.

7.3.5 Lack of Conceptual Equivalence

The fifth barrier is the lack of conceptual equivalence, which is the rather challenging problem. It refers to abstract ideas that may not exist in the same fashion in diverse languages. It is hard to find a precise one among English words—relationship, connection, obligation, and dependency to indicate the Chinese concept "guanxi (关系)". As we all know, "Chinese Dream" reflects the expectation and determination for the rejuvenation of the Chinese nation, which has been the greatest dream of the Chinese people since the beginning of modern times. In common effort, Chinese people aim to make the country prosperous and strong and see that the people are happy.

Another commonly-accepted example is the concept of the Chinese word "天". In one of the classical Chinese literary works, *A Dream of Red Mansions* (《红楼梦》), there is such an utterance "谋事在人，成事在天" said by Liu Laolao in Chapter Six. David Hawkes translated it as "Man proposes, God disposes." Though "God" makes sense to English readers, they might assume that Liu Laolao is a Christian. But in Chinese translators Yang Xianyi and Dai Naidie's version, "God" is replaced with "Heaven", which reveals the fact that ancient Chinese belief in heaven dominated everything with the almighty power. Expressions like "三个代

表", "不折腾", "熊孩子", "单身狗", etc. convey no equivalent concepts in English language and culture. In the same vein, "Waterloo", "Uncle Sam", "Big Apple", "crow", "dog", "owl", "white elephant" and the word "Dutch" have respective connotations which are not found in Chinese language. When translating the words or terms with different cultural connotations, we need to make efforts to achieve the functional equivalence which may make sense to speakers of target language. For example, in Chinese, we say "吹牛", but in English "to talk horse" transmits the same message. In Chinese, we say "瘦的像只猴子", but in English, "as thin as a shadow". Figurative uses of "饿的像只狼" in Chinese and "as hungry as a bear" in English are also the appropriate counterparts.

To deal with the problem of conceptual equivalence, the translators must be the masters of both languages and cultures. If so, the functional equivalence could be maximized. There is a practical technique for green-hand translators to improve translation, that is, to use back translation. Back translation involves first translating into the second language, then translating back into the first language, and then comparing the result to the original. Often, the process can prevent us from making translation problems.

Key Terms

anxiety and uncertainty	焦虑和不确定性
Uncertainty Reduction Theory (URT)	不确定性减少理论
ethnocentrism	民族中心主义
stereotype	定势
racial stereotype	种族定势
gender stereotype	性别定势
cultural stereotype	文化定势
prejudice	偏见
discrimination	歧视
racism	种族主义
pluriculturalism	多元文化主义
vocabulary equivalence	词汇对等
idiomatic equivalence	习语对等

grammatical-syntactical equivalence	语法和句法对等
experiential equivalence	经验对等
conceptual equivalence	概念对等

Notes

1. **Charles R. Berger** (Ph. D., Michigan State University), a professor in the Department of Communication at the University of California, Davis. His research interests include message production processes and the processing of threat-related messages by intuitive and rational systems. He is currently a member of several editorial boards of communication journals. Berger has published a three-digit integer's worth of articles and book chapters. Among the books, he has published are *Language and Social Knowledge: Uncertainty in Interpersonal Relations* (with James J. Bradac) and *Social Cognition and Communication* (with Michael E. Roloff). He also co-edited the first edition of the *Handbook of Communication Science* (with Steven H. Chaffee) and *Communication and Social Influence Processes* (with Michael Burgoon). He together with Richard J. Calabrese introduced Uncertainty Reduction Theory in 1975 in a paper entitled *Some Exploration in Initial Interaction and Beyond: Toward a Developmental Theory of Interpersonal Communication.*

   查尔斯·R. 伯杰（密歇根州立大学博士），加州大学戴维斯分校传播系教授。研究方向包括信息生产过程，通过直觉与理性系统处理与威胁相关的信息。现为几家传播学学术期刊编委会成员。伯杰教授发表百余篇学术文章。其著作包括《语言与社会知识：人际关系中的不确定性》（与 James J. Bradac 合著），《社会认知与沟通》（与 Michael E. Roloff 合著）。与 Steven H. Chaffee 合编《传播学手册》（第一辑），与 Michael Burgoon 合编《传播与社会影响过程》。伯杰教授与理查德·J. 卡拉布雷塞（Richard J. Calabrese）于 1975 年共同发表了一篇名为《初次交往及后续交往之探索：人际交际发展理论》的论文，提出"不确定性减少理论"。

2. **Morton Klass,** a professor of Anthropology at Barnard College, Columbia University. His previous books include *East Indians in Trinidad, Caste: The Emergence of the South Asian Social System*, and *Ordered Universes: Approaches to the Anthropology of Religion.*

莫顿·克拉斯，哥伦比亚大学巴纳德学院人类学教授。他出版的著作包括《特立尼达拉岛的东印度人，种姓：南亚社会体系的产生》、《有序的世界：宗教人类学研究方法》。

3. **Walter Lippmann** (1889-1974), an American writer, reporter, and political commentator famous for being among the first to introduce the concept of Cold War, coining the term "stereotype" in the modern psychological meaning, and critiquing media and democracy in his newspaper column and several books, most notably his 1922 book *Public Opinion*. After graduating from Harvard, he co-founded the influential liberal magazine *The New Republic* in 1913. In 1931 Lippmann started writing a column "Today and Tomorrow" in the New York Herald Tribune, which was syndicated in more than 250 newspapers worldwide and won two Pulitzer Prizes (1958, 1962). Throughout his 60-year career, Lippmann was highly praised and known as the Father of Modern Journalism.

沃尔特·李普曼（1889—1974），美国作家、记者、政治评论员。他是首批提出"冷战"概念的学者之一，创造了现代心理学意义上的"定势"这一术语，在其报纸专栏及几部著作中批判媒体和民主，最为引人注目的是其1922年出版的著作《公众舆论》。李普曼毕业于哈佛大学，于1913年与人共同创办具有影响力的自由派杂志《新共和》。1931年，在《纽约先驱论坛报》上开设"今日与明日"专栏，所写专栏被国内外250家报刊转载，并于1958年和1962年两次斩获普利策奖。在长达60年的新闻职业生涯中，李普曼享有很高声誉，被尊为"现代新闻学之父"。

4. **Larry A. Samovar,** a professor at the Department of Communication, San Diego State University, a leading authority on research and writing in the field of intercultural communication. He has published more than 100 articles in the academic circle and at international conferences and has published more than 13 books. His monograph on communication, co-authored with Richard E. Porter, has been republished many times. Samovar is an activist and a consultant to both the governments and the private sectors.

拉里·A. 萨莫瓦尔，美国圣地亚哥州立大学传播学院教授，跨文化交际研究和写作方面的权威人物。他在学术圈内和国际会议上发表了一百多篇学术论文，出版著作有13部之多。他与理查德·E. 波特合著的传播学专著多次再版。萨莫瓦尔热心社会活动，长期担任政府和私人部门的咨询顾问。

Chapter 7　Intercultural Communication Barriers

5. **Richard E. Porter,** a professor Emeritus of the Department of Communication Studies at California State University, Long Beach, USA, has long been a researcher and an author of more than 16 books on intercultural communication. He has long been collaborating with Larry A. Samovar in the field of intercultural communication.

    理查德·E. 波特, 美国加州州立大学长滩分校传播研究系名誉退休教授,长期从事跨文化交际方面的研究与著述,出版著作有 16 部之多。他与拉里·A. 萨莫瓦尔长期合作编著跨文化交际领域的著作。

6. **Nancy J. Adler,** a professor of International Management at McGill University in Montreal, Canada. She conducts research on global leadership, cross-cultural management, and women as global leaders and managers. She has authored more than 100 articles and produced the film, *A Portable Life*. Her book, *International Dimensions of Organizational Behavior* (4th ed., 2002), has over a quarter million copies in print in multiple languages. In addition to her research and writing, Dr. Adler consults with major global companies and government organizations on projects in Asia, Europe, North and South America, and the Middle East. Canada has honored Professor Adler as one of the country's top teachers from among professors in all disciplines at all universities.

    南希·J. 阿德勒, 加拿大蒙特利尔麦吉尔大学国际管理学教授,研究领域主要为全球领导力、跨文化管理、女性作为全球领导者和管理者。她至今发表百余篇文章,并且创作一部电影《便携式生活》。她的著作《组织行为学的国际维度》(第四版,2002 年)被译为多国语言,发行超过 25 万册。除研究与著述外,阿德勒博士还与亚洲、欧洲、北美和南美洲以及中东项目中一些主要的全球公司及政府组织合作。加拿大曾授予阿德勒教授全国高校顶级教师称号。

7. **Richard Brislin,** a professor Emeritus at the University of Hawaii at Manoa. He is a distinguished scholar and an educator in the areas of cross-cultural psychology, management, training, and communication. Brislin reviews submissions for over ten professional journals and five major textbook publishers. He develops materials for use in cross-cultural training programs. One of his books, *The Art of Getting Things Done: A Practical Guide to the Use of Power*, was a book of the Month Club selection in 1992.

    理查德·布雷斯林, 夏威夷大学马诺阿主校名誉退休教授,跨文化心理学、管理、培训和传播领域的杰出学者和教育者。布雷斯林教授被十余家学术期刊聘为评审专家,是 5 本主要教科书的出版人。他还研发了跨文化培训项目资料。其专著《做事的艺术:行使权力实用指南》曾入选 1992 年美国"每月读书会"推荐书目。

8. **Elliot Aronson,** an American psychologist. He is listed among the 100 most eminent psychologists of the 20th century and is best known for the invention of the Jigsaw Classroom as a method of reducing interethnic hostility and prejudice. He is also known for his research on cognitive dissonance and his influential social psychology textbooks. In his (1972) text, *The Social Animal,* (now in its 11th edition), he stated Aronson's First Law: "People who do crazy things are not necessarily crazy." He is the only person in the 120-year history of the American Psychological Association to have won all three of its major awards: for writing, for teaching, and for research. In 2007, he received the William James Award for Lifetime Achievement from the Association for Psychological Science. He officially retired in 1994 but continues to teach and write.

   埃利奥特·阿伦森,美国心理学家,20 世纪 100 位杰出的心理学家之一。他发明了"拼图式课堂"以减少不同种族间的敌意和偏见,并因此而闻名。他在认知失调方面的研究及编写的颇具影响力的社会心理学教科书也使他声名远扬。在 1972 年出版的著作《社会性动物》(现为第 11 版)中,他提出了"阿伦森第一法则":"做出疯狂举动的人不一定是疯狂的"。他是美国心理协会 120 年的历史上唯一一名荣获著书立说、教学和科研三项主要大奖的学者。2007 年,荣获美国心理协会颁发的威廉姆斯·詹姆斯终身成就奖。阿伦森教授 1994 年退休后,继续教书、写作。

9. **Judith Martin** has studied at the Universite de Grenoble in France. She received her doctorate at the Pennsylvania State University. By background and training, she is a social scientist who has focused on intercultural communication on an interpersonal level and has studied how people's communication is affected as they move or sojourn between international locations.

   朱迪思·马丁曾就读于法国格勒诺布尔大学,于宾夕法尼亚州立大学获得博士学位。教育背景和所受培训使其成为一名社会学家,专注于开展人际交往层面上跨文化交际及人们的交际如何受跨国移民或旅居的影响等方面的研究。

10. **Thomas Nakayama** has studied at the University de Paris and various universities in the United States. He received his doctorate from the University of Iowa. By background and training, he is a critical rhetorician who views intercultural communication in a social context.

    托马斯·那卡雅玛曾就读于巴黎大学及美国的多所大学，于爱荷华大学获得博士学位。教育背景和所受培训使其成为一名批判性的修辞学家，主要研究社会背景下的跨文化交际。

11. **David Hawkes** (1923–2009), a British Sinologist and Redologist. His major achievement was to translate one of the four classic Chinese literary works, *A Dream of Red Mansions* (a complete version of 120 chapters), which he named *The Story of the Stone*. This was the first complete English version and also a great event in the history of Western Sinology and in the translation circle. Hawkes has made great contributions to introducing Chinese literature to the world. Hawkes is also famous for his research on *The Verse of Chu* and Dufu's poems. Among his translation works, *The Verse of Chu: Songs of the South—Selected Poems of Ancient China* and *A Little Primer of Tu Fu* are of great importance.

    戴维·霍克思（1923—2009），英国汉学家、红学家。他的重大成就是翻译一百二十回的《红楼梦》全译本，他名之为《石头记》，这是英语世界第一个《红楼梦》全译本，也是西方汉学史和翻译界的一件大事。霍克思为中国文学走向世界做出了重大贡献。霍克思也以专研楚辞、杜诗著名，所译《楚辞·南方之歌：中国古代诗歌选》和《杜诗初阶》，在全世界颇有影响。

12. **Yang Xianyi and Dai Naidie (Gladys Tayler)**

    Yang Xianyi (1915–2009), a Chinese literary translator. Yang and his wife Dai Naidie (1919–1999) produced a number of quality translations. The works translated include classical Chinese poetry, such classic works as Cao Xueqin's *A Dream of Red Mansions*, Wu Jingzi's *The Scholars*, Liu E's *Mr. Decadent: Notes Taken in an Outing*, also known as *The Travels of Lao Can*, and some of Lu Xun's stories. Yang was also the first one to render the *Odyssey* into Chinese (prose) from the ancient Greek original. He also translated Aristophanes's *Ornites*, Virgil's *Georgics*, *La chanson de Roland* and Bernard

Shaw's *Pygmalion* into Chinese.

杨宪益和戴乃迭

杨宪益（1915—2009），中国文学翻译家。与其夫人戴乃迭（1919—1999）共同完成了多部杰出译作，其中包括中国古典诗歌、古典文学名著如曹雪芹的《红楼梦》，吴敬梓的《儒林外史》，刘鹗的《老残游记》，以及部分鲁迅的作品。杨宪益也是将古希腊原著《奥德赛》以散文体译成中文的第一人。其翻译的西方文学作品还包括阿里斯托芬的《鸟》，维吉尔的《农事集》《罗兰之歌》，以及萧伯纳的《卖花女》。

Case 1

Scenario 1

The other day, Wang Xin, a sophomore in Beijing, received a text message from his friend, He Lin, who is studying in America. He Lin told Wang Xin that his roommate would travel to Beijing this summer and asked whether Wang Xin would like to pick up his American friend Jerry at the airport. Wang Xin agreed to help and prepared a lot of topics. But when he met Jerry, he couldn't think of anything to talk about except for simple greetings. On the way to the hotel, Wang Xin and Jerry barely talked. The atmosphere was very embarrassing.

After taking Jerry to the hotel, Wang Xin told his friend He Lin about the embarrassment. Wang Xin confessed that he was afraid of failure in communication with Jerry because he was unable to predict Jerry's ideas and behaviors and consequently he chose not to talk. To Jerry, the same holds true.

Questions for Discussion

1. In this case, both Wang Xin and Jerry felt anxious and uncertain. How do we understand the feelings?

2. If you were Wang Xin, what would you do to overcome anxiety and uncertainty?

Scenario 2

Learning about Wang Xin's feeling, He Lin recommended the effective strategies he used to reduce anxiety and uncertainty when he first encountered his roommate Jerry. That is, to talk about his own life on campus and ask Jerry about his life.

Taking He Lin's advice, Wang Xin became confident of the interaction with Jerry. Harboring some common questions, Wang Xin invited Jerry to a welcome dinner. This time, the dinner went very well with them asking and answering questions a lot. So at the end of the dinner, Wang Xin took the initiative to show Jerry around Houhai. During this trip, Wang Xin bought Beijing snacks and beers for Jerry and even paid the taxi to the hotel for Jerry. But when Wang Xin relayed all this to He Lin in a tone of excitement later, He Lin told him that his warm-heartedness discomforted Jerry and made him very frustrated. Wang Xin was totally confused.

Questions for Discussion

1. Why do you think Wang Xin's hospitality made Jerry uncomfortable?
2. If you were Jerry, what would you do before going to China?

Scenario 3

Wang Xin was very upset with Jerry. The next day, he filled his another friend in on Jerry's response to his hospitality. He said, "American people are really cold-blooded."

 Questions for Discussion

1. What do you think of Wang Xin's comments on Americans?
2. If you were Wang Xin's friend, what would you say to him?

Scenario 4

After one month's stay in China, Jerry had to go back to the U. S. Learning about this, Wang Xin decided to call Jerry and hoped to resolve their misunderstanding. He suggested having a dinner together. And of course they made a deal on splitting the bill. During this dinner, Wang Xin extended his willingness to make friends with Jerry. But when he wanted to express his feeling with Chinese idiom "不打不相识", he could not come up with any English equivalence.

Questions for Discussion

1. What do you think of Wang Xin's taking the initiative to promote intercultural interaction between him and Jerry?
2. How do you translate Chinese idiom "不打不相识"?

Case 2

In 1913, members of an American Indian tribe challenged the degree of control that Congress exercised over tribal affairs. In its decision, the Supreme Court ruled:

Always living in separate and isolated communities, adhering to primitive modes of life, largely influenced by superstition and fetishism, and chiefly governed according to crude customs inherited from their ancestors, these American Indians are essentially a simple, uninformed and inferior people. As a superior and civilized nation, the U. S. government has both the power and the duty of exercising a fostering care and protection over all dependent Indian communities within its borders.

 Questions for Discussion

1. What message does it transmit in the Supreme Court's decision?
2. What does this expression "both the power and the duty of exercising a fostering care and protection over all dependent Indian communities within its borders" really mean?

Case 3

Amy Cooper, who worked in an investment company, took her dog into Central Park on Memorial Day; Christian Cooper, an African-American man going bird watching, urged Amy Cooper to leash her dog, as required by the park's rules, but she got on her cell, all hysterical and threatened to tell police that Christian Cooper was threatening her. Christian Cooper, the black man filmed the white woman and just wanted the video to speak for itself. When police arrived, they determined that the two Coopers (who are not related) engaged in a verbal dispute and no one was arrested or given a summons, according to an NYPD spokesperson. After the incident, Christian Cooper's sister posted the video which went viral on Twitter. Amy Cooper was fired from her job at an investment firm and she surrendered her cocker spaniel to the animal rescue where she'd adopted it.

"It's a little bit of frenzy, and I am uncomfortable with that," Christian said in an interview with *The New York Times*. "If our goal is to change the underlying factors, I am not sure that this young woman having her life completely torn apart serves that goal."

In an appearance on CNN, he said he considers the woman's actions racist, but he urged people who were outraged by it to stay civil. "I find it strange that people who were upset that...that she tried to bring death by cop down on my head, would then turn around and try to put death threats on her head. Where is the logic in that?" he said. "Where does that make any kind of sense?" He said death threats against her "should stop immediately."

 Questions for Discussion

1. What do you think of Amy Cooper's response to Christian Cooper's urge?
2. Why do you think Christian urged the outraged people to stay civil?

Case 4

With a long history, Sichuan cuisine has had great fame and enjoyed good reputation both at home and abroad. However, due to various reasons such as a wide range of ingredients, varied seasonings, diverse cooking techniques, great varieties, different naming methods, and profound cultural background, many regional cultures in names of Sichuan dishes don't have any equivalent English expressions, which brings great difficulties to the English translations and affects its development and dissemination abroad.

Chinese-English names of the same Sichuan dishes are chosen for analysis to study whether Sichuan regional culture concerning such aspects as regional ingredients, regional cooking techniques, regional tastes, regional cultural allusions and so on is translated properly or not between two authoritative works: *Enjoy Culinary Delights* (《美食译苑》) and *Sichuan Cuisine* (《中国川菜》) from the translation principles of sememe maximum approximation, cultural transmission, briefness, aesthetic effect and creation, under the background of cross-cultural communication, in order to shed some light on the translation of Chinese dishes. The better versions or the suggested versions are as follows.

Chinese dish	Literal Translation	Suggested version
泡椒凤爪	Chicken Feet with Pickled Peppers	Pickled-Chili-Flavored Chicken Feet
虫草鸭	Duck Soup with Aweto	Steamed Duck with Caterpillar Fungus
红烧肉	Red-Braised Pork Belly	Browned Braised Pork Belly
米粉肉	Steamed Pork Belly with Rice Flour	Steamed Pork Belly Coated with Rice Flour
干煸牛肉丝	Sauteed Shredded Beef with Chinese Pepper	Dry-Fried Beef Slivers
火爆腰花	Quick-Fried Pork Kidneys	Stir-Fried Pig Kidney

 Questions for Discussion

1. What factors should be taken into consideration in Chinese dishes translation?
2. What are the guiding principles in Chinese dishes translation?

Further Reading

Passage 1

The original form of Chinese character 恕(shu), empathy, is in the form of 𢡛, which is etymologically (语源上) composed of the pictographs of 女(nǚ), woman on the top and 心(xin), heart, at the bottom. In this way, the character 𢡛 is given the meaning of a woman and her heart, which symbolizes tenderness, tolerance, womanly care and obedience. Later, the character 𢡛 is transformed into the **ideographic** (表意的) form of 恕(shu), which is etymologically composed of 如(ru) on the top, meaning "as if" or resemblance and 心(xin), heart at the bottom. The character 恕(shu) thus included the notion that in interaction with others one should act with a woman's heart, i.e. with womanly care and love. So, 恕(shu) means projecting self, in terms of the whole person—heart (emotion, compassion), mind, and behavior—into other, thus taking the perspective of others.

The practice of 恕(shu), empathy, is reciprocal or bidirectional. In human relationships and interactions, one must first move from other to self in order to clarify self. That is, it is only once one has moved from other to self in order to clarify self that one can move in the opposite direction and project self into other, so that one can decide what is appropriate to do. In this self-projecting process, the self is not the model by the standard of which all others are evaluated. This means one is expected to walk in the shoes of others, taking the perspective of others in thinking as well as in feeling and behavior. Confucius considered empathy in this regard as the unifying ethical principle that one acts on to the end of his days. It is through the practice of empathy that one establishes himself while establishing others.

According to Confucian holistic humanism, humans should observe the moral and ethical principle, the golden rule: "Do not do unto others what you would not want others to do unto you. " There is a different version of the golden rule from the West: "Do unto others as you would have them do unto you, "or "Treat others with the concern and kindness you would like them to show toward you. " What is more, the golden rule is augmented by Confucius ethical principle or what is called the social and moral responsibility by Tu Weiming, which goes, "In order to establish ourselves, we must help others to establish themselves; in order to enlarge ourselves, we must help others to enlarge themselves. " As a moral and ethical principle of self-other reciprocity and self-other incorporation, this social and moral ethic calls for concern and responsibility not only for others but also for self. This holistic Confucian humanism is obviously morally and ethically open-minded and inclusive in nature.

Projecting self into other and taking the perspective of others cognitively, affectively and communicatively lead to avoidance, reduction, rejection and critique of stereotypes, prejudice, and ethnocentrism.

However, affectively, empathy is different from sympathy, in the sense that empathy involves the shifting of one's stance or perspective while sympathy does not. Sympathy allows the sharing of feeling of the other but it allows no shift of stance and perspective. An empathetic person willingly projects himself or herself into the experience of the other, to feel, think, and behave in ways which allow him to know what it is to be the other and to view the world through the frame of reference of the other. An empathetic person suspends analysis, evaluation, and judgment from within his or her own frame of reference and sets aside his or her own values and norms at least temporarily. The Western golden rule "Do onto others as you would have them do unto you, " according to Milton Bennett is not empathy but sympathy. What is more, if one adopts the essentialist or rationalist world view and regards other as "either like or similar to self" or "irrelevant to self" and thus judges and evaluates other with this being-for-self ethic as the standard, one is likely to impose his or her own decisions, wills, and perspectives upon other. This sympathy will inevitably lead to ethnocentrism or even worse.

An empathetic person is one who trusts and commits to others, emphatically listen to others, tends first or temporarily to describe rather than judge the behavior of others so that he may reduce and avoid the tendency of leaping hastily to inadequate conclusions without sufficient data or imposing his or her own stance upon others. Walking in the shoes of the other forms the core of the development of intercultural sensitivity as it allows the other to feel psychologically secure and comfortable as they know that they are being listened to, understood, appreciated, and respected as equals.

Empathy involves, through intercultural interaction, communication and dialogue in terms of mediation and negotiation on an equal footing, as well as critical self-reflection, mutual learning and redefining, and active adaptation as extensive exposure to different world views which leads to the development of a more pluralistic orientation, and thus results in the internalization of two or the more alternative cultural references and the commitment to their co-existence within the self.

(选自 Jia Yuxin. Experiencing Global Intercultural Communication. Foreign Language Teaching and Research Press, 2019: 191–192, 206–208.)

Questions for Discussion

1. According to Confucius, how is "empathy" explained? What is the significance of "empathy"?

2. How do we understand holistic Confucian humanism? What is the essence of holistic Confucian humanism?

3. What is the essential difference between empathy and sympathy?

Passage 2

The Essence of Chinese Culture Is "Hehe"—Harmony and Cooperation

Today, the world is by no means trouble-free. Regional flashpoints, local conflicts and terrorist attacks continue to flare up. Global economic recovery lacks speed and momentum. Some people are even pessimistic about the future of the world. It is common sense that with increasing connectivity, no one can remain immune from such negative factors. Yet, how should we ride out these storms? Particularly for major countries, it is a must to bear responsibility and take bold actions.

Facing such a situation, China states it has been pursuing the greater good for humanity, based on President Xi Jinping's Thought on diplomacy for a new era, which is grounded on "Hehe" or Harmony and Cooperation. What's the origin of Harmony and Cooperation? How has it evolved? What does it mean?

First, where does "Hehe" come? Going back millennia, there were so many dynasties and rulers in the history of China. Yet, having gone through ups and downs, the country is home to 56 ethnic groups, as if a garden where different local cultures blossom together. An ancient Chinese saying references the vast ocean embracing all rivers running into it. So does China.

Specifically, "Hehe" can be traced back to Confucian thought on harmony, much of which stresses three principal harmonious relationships. First, harmony between human and nature. In Chinese culture, human life is part and parcel of nature. Second, harmony among people. In Confucius' eyes, an individual cannot live without community and society. Interpersonal harmony, hence, is crucial for us. Third, harmony within oneself. Chinese thinking highlights that people should not only understand the external world but more importantly, uplift their internal state of mind or pursue the inner world of "Junzi", also known as a virtuous man.

All of the above mirrors the essence of Chinese culture and resonates with universal human values. This is perhaps why Confucian thought in the 21st century still retains the interest of not only the Chinese but also people in other parts of the world.

Then, what does "Hehe" mean? The concept is still embodied in Chinese people's daily lives. Take two examples. One is about Chinese cuisine, authentic Kung Pao Chicken involves multiple layers of flavor like being sweet, sour, salty, and spicy, but combines all these complementary or even opposing flavors so "harmoniously". Thus, its name has been spread globally.

Another is Traditional Chinese Medicine (TCM). It offers a holistic picture and worldview, which means that our bodies coordinate with the environment and the universe. Our visceral(内脏的) organs comprise a physical universe in which they also need to be in harmony with each other. Therefore, "Hehe" has been already reflected much in Chinese people's everyday lives.

But, now, due to trade frictions and political tensions, uncertainties and destabilizing factors seem to crop up every day. Should we opt for confrontation or cooperation? Should we opt for harm or harmony? Problems are rising, hence, so is the need for cooperation and harmony, "Hehe". This is the time. This is the place. We are the decision-makers.

(选自 https://news.cgtn.com/news/3d3d414e3363444f33457a6333566d54/index.html.)

 Questions for Discussion

1. What is the essence of Chinese culture?

2. What does "Hehe" stand for? What is the origin of this concept?

3. How is "Hehe" embodied in Chinese people's lives in the modern age? Give some examples.

Passage 3

The West is Trying to Put Pressure on Chinese Culture

The massive Western offensive on China continues and is gaining momentum. The coronavirus pandemic has become the White House's new trump card in the struggle against the strengthening of China and the growth of its influence in the world.

The pandemic, which hit Western countries very hard, temporarily disconnected Europe from American influence, but this did not last long, and today the Europeans are again dancing to the tune of Washington.

On the eve it became known that Sweden drove out of the country the Chinese institutions and schools of Confucius. The coronavirus has nothing to do with it; the institutes were expelled for another reason. According to the Swedish side, these humanitarian structures that taught the Chinese language and promoted Chinese culture supposedly served as an instrument of influence for Beijing.

Note that, unlike Western NGOs, the Confucius institutions operating in many countries of the world do not interfere in the affairs of the host states, or in the matters of their domestic policy, do not dictate to the local authorities what to do, and do not speculate on human rights and international law.

Confucius Institutes are a network of international cultural and educational centers. The functions of these structures include language training, holding scientific conferences, popularizing Chinese culture, testing, organizing internships in China and so on.

By the way, for already a decade, namely since 2011, the Confucius Institute has been successfully operating at Baku State University. It was created at the Faculty of Oriental Studies of BSU in partnership with China's Anhui University. The Azerbaijani side has no complaints about this structure.

The Chinese NGO does not go beyond its goals and objectives, which are exclusively humanitarian and cultural. This cannot be said of the structures created and financed by the governments of Western countries. All of them act supposedly "independently", but in fact, they are financed from state budgets and serve political purposes.

Take the same United States Agency for International Development (USAID). The organization was created allegedly to provide humanitarian assistance, but the real goal of its creators is to intervene in the internal affairs of other countries and support the strengthening of American influence.

In principle, to some extent, Americans can be understood. In recent years, China has truly turned into a powerful country in terms of its economy. The secret of China's success in its advancement in the world is that this state does not take away anything from anyone and does not dictate conditions to anyone, it simply offers the best conditions. Yes, this is called soft power, but so many countries will prefer soft power as opposed to the tough and brazen policies of the White House. China advances its interests by economic forces, giving benefits to partners, while the U. S. uses exclusively political methods, disregarding the interests of partners. This is a very serious difference, and before the pandemic, Washington was not able to convince its allies of the need for a massive attack on Beijing. Now, at his service was the coronavirus, with which Donald Trump and his team are trying to beat the Chinese. But these weapons are unreliable and in the post-pandemic period, when the countries of the world begin the struggle for their economies, they will stop working.

But let us return to Sweden. Confucius institutions themselves probably did not even imagine that, by organizing Chinese language courses, they were believed to actually encroach on the most sacred thing—European freedom and democracy. But what does SIDA, the Swedish government agency for assisting developing countries, do? No, we will not say anything, perhaps the structure has the noblest goals, but for some reason they are realized in Russia, which the United States hates. SIDA's multi-million-dollar aid package to Georgia and Ukraine somehow looks strange, and with the aggravation of relations between Moscow and Minsk—and to Belarus.

Or take the infamous Freedom House, an American NGO created as a club that clears the way for American interests. The organization has actually devalued the concept of human rights and freedoms, turning them into an object of speculation and a weapon of pressure on governments disliked by the White House.

Can someone blame the Chinese institutions for something like this? In addition to the demagogy dictated by the U. S. , Sweden itself is not able to present any realistic arguments supporting the accusations made.

And the Chinese language is better to continue to study. Because China has repeatedly shown the world an example of how to get out of crises, to get on their feet in the most difficult situations. The Chinese have coped with the coronavirus better than many others and today help other countries. And the fact is that the pandemic which hit the West is not a problem of Confucius institutions.

Be that as it may, Trump will not be able to "turn off" China. The hysteria associated with coronavirus in Europe will eventually pass, and Europeans will again begin to incline to what is beneficial to themselves, and not the United States. The trade war declared by the Americans on Beijing before the pandemic, as you know, hit the economies of the Western countries themselves, bringing Washington nothing but moral satisfaction.

And finally, the wise advice of Confucius to the West: If you hate, then you have been defeated…

(选自 https://news. cgtn. com/news/2020-04-27/The-West-is-trying-to-put-pressure-on-Chinese-culture-Q1Ns69JgfS/index. html.)

Questions for Discussion

1. What is the secret of China's success in its advancement in the world?

2. Do you think learning Chinese language is beneficial to tackle challenging problems encountering the world?

3. How do you understand the Confucius thought: If you hate, then you have been defeated?

Exercises

I. Word-filling

Directions: *Fill in the blanks with the proper words.*
1. Anxiety refers to the ____ of not knowing what one is expected to do, and focusing on that feeling and not being totally present in the communication transaction.
2. Ethnocentrism refers to the belief that their culture is primary or even ____ to others'.
3. Stereotyping is used to describe ____ made about others on the basis of their ethnic group membership.
4. Prejudice involves an unfair, biased, or intolerant ____ towards another group of people or an individual from the group.
5. Racism refers to any policy, practice, belief, or attitude that attributes characteristics or status to individuals based on their ____.
6. Persistence of these attitudinal problems is caused by socialization, social benefits, ____ benefits and psychological benefits.
7. People from different cultures may have different understandings of the meaning of a certain word as well as its ____ meanings.
8. An idiom is a group of words which have a ____ meaning when used together from the one they would have if you took the meaning of each word separately.
9. If an object or experience does not exist in your culture, it is ____ to translate words referring to that object or experience into that language when no words may exist for them.
10. Lack of ____ equivalence refers to abstract ideas that may not exist in the same fashion in diverse languages.

II. Multiple Choices

Directions: *Choose the best answer for each question.*

1. What strategies does the Uncertainty Reduction Theory involve?

A. Interactive strategies;

B. Active strategies;

C. Passive strategies;

D. Above all.

2. Which one is not ethnocentric attitude?

A. Lifestyles in other cultures are not as valid as those in my culture.

B. I have little respect for the values and customs of other cultures.

C. My culture should be the role model for other cultures.

D. People of other cultures are different from me.

3. Which one cannot be used to overcome stereotyping?

A. To get in touch with people from various cultures;

B. To assume that you have no stereotypes of others;

C. To find sufficient evidence and exceptions;

D. To describe an individual's behaviors instead of generalizing traits over the whole community.

4. Which one of the following strategies is not effective to avoid prejudice?

A. To reflect our own prejudiced attitude;

B. To involve ourselves in communications with more people;

C. To stay away from talking to the people from other cultures;

D. To avoid using language with a tint of prejudice or discrimination.

5. Which of the following statements about racism is wrong?

A. Racism goes further than a specific kind of prejudice.

B. Racism involves the exercise of power.

C. Racism exists only in some areas.

D. Racism denies the existence of the culture of a particular group.

III. True or False

Directions: *Decide whether the following statements are true or false.*

1. Uncertainty means that we only fail to explain others' feelings and behaviors in interactions.

2. Both assuming similarities and assuming difficulties hinder intercultural com-

munication.

3. Extreme ethnocentrism leads to a rejection of richness and knowledge of other cultures.

4. Stereotypes are always negative which may evoke conflicts in intercultural communication events.

5. Often in cases of discrimination, we observe ethnocentrism, stereotyping, and prejudice coming together.

6. Negative evaluations by whites of black cultural values reflect stereotyping.

7. It is easy for people to break away from the prejudices of their families and friends as long as they are aware of having prejudices.

8. If we don't know the fact that the same word means differently in different contexts, communications will be hindered.

9. A high proficiency of English vocabulary leads to an advanced ability to construct the English words into meaningful sentences.

10. We can use literal translation or transliteration and simultaneously attach the adequate explanation to it in order to achieve clarity and accuracy.

IV. Translation

A. **Directions:** *Translate the following paragraph into English.*

子贡问曰："有一言而可以终身行之者乎？"子曰："其恕乎！己所不欲，勿施于人。"自己不愿意的，不要强加给别人。这是孔子所提倡的"恕道"（推己及人的原则），以自己的心意推测、理解别人的心意，亦即今之所谓设身处地，换位思考。其哲学基础是"性相近"（人的本性是相近的）。它是儒家处理人与人关系的重要原则，如今也被引申为反对强权政治的国际关系原则，其基本精神是仁爱、平等与宽容。

B. **Directions:** *Translate the following paragraph into Chinese.*

We need to commit to mutual opening up that features shared benefits. COVID-19 is a stark reminder that all countries are in a community with a shared future. No one can stay immune in a major crisis. Solidarity and cooperation is the right choice to make in meeting challenges. We must uphold the principle of mutually beneficial cooperation. We need to build trust rather than second-guess each other; we need to join hands rather than throw punches at each other; and we need to consult rather than slander each other. Bearing in mind the common interests that bind us all, countries need to work together to make economic globalization more open, inclusive and balanced for the benefits of all.

Chapter 8

Intercultural Adaptation

> Human beings draw close to one another by their common nature, but habits and customs keep them apart.
>
> 君子和而不同，小人同而不和。
>
> ——《论语·子路》

本章导读

跨文化适应是一个复杂、动态的发展过程。本章从文化适应、文化冲击等概念入手，继而详细介绍人们在离开本土文化而与另一种文化碰撞时将会经历的不同阶段，旨在帮助学习者了解跨文化适应中会遇到的各种不适，提前做好充分的准备。本章最后一部分则为学习者提供了跨文化适应策略，从而帮助学习者更好地参与和适应跨文化交际活动。

Learning Objectives

In this chapter, students will learn how to know the concept of acculturation and its four degrees, understand the concept, factors and effects of culture shock, and master the strategies of intercultural adaption.

Warm-up Activities

1. Have you ever experienced living or studying in a new cultural environment, such as, another city or a foreign country?

2. What is your first impression about the new culture?

3. What challenged you most in the process of adjusting to the new environment?

4. What strategies do you think you could use to help overcome the obstacles?

8.1 Introduction

Have you ever watched or heard about a movie *Avatar*? It tells a story about a group of human beings who are sent to the moon named Pandora for a unique mission. The hero of the movie is a former Marine, Jake Sully. And one thing that may impress most audience, among all the exciting plots might be how Jack links his human mind to a body of Avatar and has to recondition his mind anew, leading to the bond with the native tribe, which had its own language and culture.

Actually, when one leaves one's home culture and enters a new cultural environment, it may be quite similar to a human being entering the alien world of Pandora in the movie *Avatar*, and it is quite natural for this person to encounter some difficulties in cross cultural communication. This process of adjusting to a fresh culture is known as intercultural adaptation.

As Kim (1988) puts it, "Individuals enter an unfamiliar culture with the culture communication competence that they have internalized in their home country. The internalized cultural imprinting that governs individuals' identity and behavior remains largely unrecognized, unquestioned, and unchanged until they encounter people with different cultural attributes." Then people may have certain mental, emotional, and physical discomfort. How long its impact lasts before the normality returns mainly depends on how adaptable the individuals are when situated in the new environment of the host culture. It's most obvious that one has to adapt one's behavior to the customs and expectations of the host country. This is not to deny one's own culture but to respect that of others. Another responsibility one has is to remain open in order to become aware of similarities and differences—to learn rather than to judge.

8.2 Acculturation

When people from one culture enter a new culture, they are faced with a different set of values, behavioral patterns, and a different verbal and nonverbal communication system. In most cases, they are affected by the new surroundings. They get to learn and adopt the norms and values of the new culture. And they must find a new source of livelihood and build a new life. This adaptation to the new **host culture** (主体文化) is called acculturation. It describes what happens when people from one culture enter a different culture.

There are different levels of acculturation based on two independent dimensions. The first dimension concerns one's adoption or rejection of the host culture. The second once deals with the retention or rejection of one's home culture. Along these two dimensions, acculturation can be categorized into four degrees: assimilation, integration, separation, and marginalization.

8.2.1 Assimilation

Assimilation is a process in which individuals are absorbed into the dominant culture, adopting the cultural norms of the host culture over their original culture. In this case, individuals lose their original cultural identity as they acquire a new identity in the host culture. During the process of assimilation, they not only adopt the language of the host culture but also adapt to the customs and attitude, the basic rules and norms of the host culture. There is an ongoing effort to approach the dominant culture while discontinuing the values, beliefs, and behavior patterns associated with their native culture.

8.2.2 Integration

Different from assimilation, which usually leads to the loss of individuals' home culture, integration refers to a situation in which people are able to adopt the cultural norms of the host culture while maintaining identity with their native culture. It usually occurs when migrants have an interest both in maintaining their original culture and language and in having daily interaction with the dominant groups. It differs from assimilation in that it involves a greater interest in maintaining one's own cultural identity. Integration leads to and is often synonymous with biculturalism. In this process, people take part in activities to interact with the dominant culture with less stress or conflict. To be sure, their successful integration of cultural skills and norms does not mean that they reject their native cultural identity. In fact, it is the bicultural identity that leads to a successful life in a bicultural context.

8.2.3 Separation

In this process, people reject the host culture or prefer low levels of interaction with the host culture in favor of preserving a close connection with their native culture. In this case, people may resist acculturation with the dominant culture and choose not to identify with the host cultural group. At the same time, they have strong desire to maintain their home cultural identity. A typical example is the **Amish** (阿米什人), who came to the United States from Europe in the 18th century. They maintain their own way of life and identity and avoid prolonged contact with other groups. The Amish do not participate in U.S. popular culture. They are best known for their simple living, plain dress, and reluctance to adopt many conveniences of modern technology. They don't have televisions or radios. Nor do they go to movies or read mainstream newspapers or books. They choose separation, and the dominant society respects their choice.

8.2.4 Marginalization

Marginalization occurs when individuals choose to reject both their native culture and the dominant host culture. In many cases, marginalized people give up their home culture and hope to acculturate in the dominant culture, only to find that they are not accepted by the host culture. These persons experience alienation from both the home culture and the host culture. Often, they feel a sense of abandonment. For example, the punks are a marginalized group.

Actually, people sometimes combine different modes of acculturation. Their levels of acculturation can differ between their private and public life. An individual may reject the values and norms of the dominant culture in his private life (that is, separation), whereas he might adapt to the dominant culture in public parts of his life (that is, integration or assimilation). He or she may desire economic assimilation (via employment), linguistic integration (that is, bilingualism), and social separation (via marrying someone from the same group and socializing only with members of their own group).

8.3 Culture Shock

As Oberg puts it, "Culture shock is precipitated by the anxiety that results from losing all our familiar signs and symbols of social intercourse . " He found that human beings experience the same feelings when they travel to or live in a different country or culture and that culture shock is almost like a disease; it has a cause, symptoms, and a cure. Although the reactions associated with culture shock vary from individual to individual, most of the literature in the area of culture shock suggests that people normally go through four periods stages: honeymoon period, crisis period, adjustment period, and biculturalism period.

Culture shock is a great concern to everyone who is or will be experiencing another culture. What happens to us when we first go into a new cultural setting? Actually, learning to live in a new and different environment is usually both exciting and stressful. When we enter a new culture, our first reaction is excitement. However, this excitement gradually wears off. We may not find big differences in this new culture: people in that culture wake up in the morning, drive their cars to work, pick up the kids from school, sit down and eat dinner, watch some TV, and then go to bed. But it's the little things: they drive different cars, eat different foods, and watch different sports. At this time, we realize that we are confronted with a different cultural environment. It is a combination of unfamiliar stimuli and a loss of familiar signs, signals, practices and customs of social intercourse. These differences between our home culture and the new culture then result in a variety of emotions, including loneliness, feelings of not fitting in, anxiety, depression, and stress.

The term culture shock is used to describe the feelings of individuals when they encounter different social norms, values, beliefs, and ways of doing. It is virtually a communication problem. It involves the depressed feelings accompanying a lack of understanding of the verbal and nonverbal communication of the host culture, its customs, as well as its value systems. It happens when we have to deal with a huge number of new things which are difficult to understand and interpret because the cultural context has changed. Things taken for granted at home need to be constantly monitored in the new culture in order to ensure some degree of understanding.

For example, in the movie *Treatment*, there are a huge number of conflicts among characters: the feelings of not fitting in of the grandpa when he arrived in the United States, the anxiety of Xu Datong when his boss and friend refused to help him in the court, and the confusion of Americans about traditional Chinese treatment Gua Sha. All these reflect the culture shock due to the differences between Chinese culture and American culture.

We are unlikely to experience culture shock suddenly from a single event. It is more likely that we will feel it gradually, from our day-in and day-out experience. It occurs in the social encounters, social situations, social episodes, or social transactions between **sojourners** (旅居者) and host nationals. It is the reaction of sojourners to problems encountered in the dealings with the host members. In other words, we experience culture shock when we are away from many familiar cultural cues and patterns, when we live or work in an ambiguous environment for an extended period of time, when our values and beliefs are questioned in a new environment, and when we are continually expected to perform with appropriate skills and speed before we are able to understand clearly the rules of performance.

Factors of Culture Shock

An individual reared in one culture may find it difficult to interpret and react to a situation in another culture. Any changes in climate, food, living condition, language, population, social roles can foster culture shock.

(1) Language Shock

When we are unfamiliar with the host language, language shock may occur. If we do not understand the language, we lose the ability to adjust ourselves to the new environment. As we struggle with learning a new language, we find ourselves at a loss. Just like in the movie *Treatment*, when the grandpa found English was the main language used in his son's family, he just felt quite uneasy and couldn't fit in. There is constant mental and emotional stress when we have to consciously think about how to express ourselves in the target language and when we are not able to convey the message we would like to impart in the way we want. There is also the humiliation of not being able to express ourselves in a way that agrees with our intellectual level, societal role, and status.

(2) Transition Shock

Another common shock we may experience is transition shock. It is used to describe the distress we experience when trying to cope with the multitude of changes required by the host culture. We may feel confused about what is normal and appropriate behavior and under which conditions. We are not sure about how and whom to greet, when to show thanks, when and how to accept and refuse invitations, how to take conversational turns, and where and how to obtain essential information and basic necessities. It is a problem for us to understand people in the host culture.

(3) Role Shock

Sometimes, when we enter an ambiguous new culture, we may even feel loss of personal status and make efforts to switch our role in order to fit and function well in the host culture. This is called role shock.

(4) Education Shock

For international students, education shock frequently happens when they try to adapt themselves to academic life, especially when the learning situation is new and distressing.

In a new culture, familiar cues guiding social interaction are often no longer operable. For example, North Americans experiencing the bargaining at a bazaar in China may perceive the Chinese as demanding and deceitful. Rather than identifying such bargaining behavior as accepted and expected within a given cultural context, North Americans are more likely to have certain misunderstanding of such behavior. Neither Canadians nor Americans are accustomed to bargaining, except perhaps at a car dealership; in North America, unlike in China and many other cultures, bargaining is not viewed as an accepted and expected social convention or custom.

(5) Effects of Culture Shock

①Negative Effects

Since culture shock is a traumatic experience that an induvial may encounter when entering a different culture, we can experience both physical and psychological symptoms. We may feel uncomfortable with the food, bedding, dishes in the new culture; we may feel stressed on health and safety; and we may be afraid of physical contact with anyone in the new culture.

Culture shock may lead to some physical outcomes, such as headaches, stomachaches, dizziness, and unsettledness. Sometimes, people suffering from culture shock even seek to suppress the bad feelings with too much eating, drinking or sleeping.

In addition to the physical problems, culture shock brings about psychological problems, either. The common ones are **insomnia** (失眠), fatigue, isolation and loneliness, homesickness, **disorientation** (迷失方向), self-doubt, nervousness, depression, frustration with hosts, criticism of new culture, **irritability** (易怒), moments hostility, and outbreaks of suppressed anger.

The newcomers often experience overloaded information. They make efforts to understand all the new information of the different culture. At the end of a day confronting many cultural patterns, they are mentally and often physically exhausted. The great concern over every aspect of life may even result in the abuse of alcohol and drugs or a decline in work quality.

The reaction to culture shock may differ greatly from person to person. Some personality traits are associated with less culture shock or culture shock of a shorter duration. For some, it may take only a few weeks to work through the distress due to the cultural differences they experience; for others, it may take a long period of time to overcome the frustration of culture shock. Individuals who are open-minded, outgoing, and emotionally stable tend to adjust better and more quickly in new cultural situations.

Overall, the degree of culture shock and the length of the shock experience depend in large part on an individual's personality and psychological makeup. In very serious cases, the only way to eliminate the problem caused by culture shock may be to return to familiar surroundings, just like the grandpa in the movie *Treatment*, who chose to return to China after a series of cultural conflicts.

② Constructive Effects

As we mentioned above, culture shock usually leaves us a negative impression. Undoubtedly, it does constitute a misbalancing experience. The feeling of uncertainty may even cause great stress and discomfort. However, we can also view culture shock from a constructive perspective. Actually, there are some positive outcomes of culture shock, which help with individual growth.

Culture shock provides a learning opportunity that demands new ideas and new responses in coping with a constantly changing environment. Gradually, it can offer us a new set of behavioral responses to future unfamiliar situations. In the movie *Be There or Be Square*, Li Qing was confronted with many obstacles shortly after she arrived in the United States. However, she didn't choose to return to China. Instead, she made up her mind to learn English and to get used to the life there.

For most of us, culture shock brings about a high but not extreme level of anxiety that causes us to learn about a new culture and learn about ourselves. The personal anxiety aroused in culture shock will help us to increase the amount of learning to a certain degree. Learning how to behave from negative cultural feedback can give us a sense of challenge and achievement as a result of dealing with people from very different backgrounds. Therefore, culture shock is valuable as a personal learning process and can push people to learn about themselves.

8.4 Intercultural Adaptation

Compared with culture shock, which is a relatively short-term discomfort due to the unfamiliarity of surroundings and a lack of familiar cues in the environment, intercultural adaptation refers to a long-term adaptation process into a new culture, the process of increasing our level of fitness to meet the demands of a new cultural environment. In other words, intercultural adaptation is a process of dealing with maladjustment within a host culture.

Adjusting to a new culture is an ongoing process with many ups and downs. We may experience different stages in the intercultural adaptation due to cultural differences. In order to better adapt to the new culture and overcome culture shock, it is necessary for us to have a detailed understanding of the process of intercultural adaptation.

There have been a number of researches in stages of intercultural adaptation process over the years. One of the earliest was a simple model called the U-curve. U-curve pattern begins with high effect, followed by a drop in satisfaction, and end with a period of recovery and full adjustment. Generally, U-curve comprises four stages: honeymoon period, crisis period, adjustment period, and biculturalism period.

8.4.1 Honeymoon Period

Honeymoon period is the first phase of intercultural adaptation. In this stage, we are fascinated by all the new things we encounter in the host culture. We love the food, the scenery and the people, and we are interested in seeing and doing as much as possible. We are still viewing the new environment from our own cultural perspective, just like tourists. That's why this stage is also referred to as the tourist phase. Our curiosity in this stage often provides us with a feeling of excitement when we detect the similarities and differences between the home culture and the new culture. We tend to neglect the differences and keep our cultural status and identity by focusing on the similarities between the host culture and our own culture. We usually take positive reaction to stress we felt when encountering cultural differences. This is the stage usually experienced by people who stay only briefly in other cultures, whether for leisure travel or for business.

8.4.2 Crisis Period

Gradually, however, these positive feelings begin to change. Then, we enter the second stage, crisis period. It is also called the hostility or frustration stage. During this stage, we experience what is called culture shock. We must directly face the challenges of the new culture on a day-to-day basis. We begin to feel overwhelmed and confounded by the values, beliefs, behaviors, and lifestyles of the new culture. Activities that we take for granted suddenly become problems we cannot understand or overcome.

Such problems often lead to a feeling of rejecting or being rejected by the host culture. We increasingly sense that we are different and isolated and experience a growing sense of disorientation and worry. When we cannot overcome these problems, we will be confronted with severe depression, which will ruin our life in the new environment.

8.4.3 Adjustment Period

The third period is adjustment period. This period is also referred to as the recovery stage. Efforts to cope with the problems in the crisis period gradually provide us with new ways to live in the new culture. During this stage, we eventually realize that the problems are due not to deliberate attempts by the natives, but to a real difference in values, beliefs, and behaviors. Therefore, we develop a positive attitude toward solving our problems and actively seek out effective problem-solving and conflict resolution strategies. We begin to learn how to respond and adapt appropriately to the new environment by following the social and cultural norms of the host nation. We also learn to appreciate and respect the new culture and to develop sensitivity toward cultural differences.

Typically, the adjustment phase is slow. In this gradual period, we get a sense of control and effectiveness so much so that we not only improve our ability to survive in the new culture without the assistance of cultural cues from the home culture, but also mark a growth in our personal flexibility.

8.4.4 Biculturalism Period

Biculturalism period or the mastery stage is the last stage of the U-curve pattern. In this stage, we may still experience occasional anxiety and frustration, but we have cultivated an understanding of the host culture and can begin to work and play in the new environment with a feeling of enjoyment. We have nearly recovered from the culture shock and developed our independent attitude and behaviors. Feeling comfortable with dual cultural identity, we are able to enjoy and appreciate the contrasts of two cultures.

In this stage, we actively engage in the culture with our new problem-solving and conflict resolution tools with some degree of success. We develop a level of competency in communicating with the natives. So, we are healthy psychologically, having a sense of integration with the host culture.

8.5 Strategies of Intercultural Adaptation

Tip 1 Assume the Principle of Difference

If you want to adapt to the new culture, you must try to understand that things are simply going to be different in your new culture and that the way you are accustomed to doing things is not the only way. Remember that your perceptual context is biased in favor of your culture and your in-group. How you perceive your host culture is not objective or neutral. All of the verbal and nonverbal messages encoded and decoded are filtered through your cultural, **microcultural** (微观文化), environmental, socio-relational, and perceptual **filters** (感知滤波器). These filters bias and color your expectations, which will certainly be violated as you interact with your host culture.

Tip 2　Study the Host Culture

What you can do is to study the host culture. You can read about the new culture, attend seminars, watch movies, and socialize with host nationals in order to know their culture. If possible, interview friends or colleagues who have travelled or lived in that culture.

Tip 3　Study the Local Environment

In addition to studying about the general culture, try to learn as much as you can about the local environment in which you will live—such as where to buy favorite foods, where to find physicians, where schools are located, how public transportation operates (if there is any), or how to fill prescriptions. Taken-for-granted operations that you unconsciously perform in your day-to-day lives will be different in the host culture.

Tip 4　Learn Basic Verbal and Nonverbal Language Skills

You should also learn some basic verbal and nonverbal language skills. If you are not fluent in the language of your host culture, it is a good idea to familiarize yourself with their verbal and nonverbal language. Attach labels to the various items of your home in the language of the host culture. Practicing functional and frequently used phrases will help you perform basic survival tactics. Keep in mind that common verbal colloquialisms can be wildly misinterpreted across cultures. Find out nonverbal language skills as an aid.

Tip 5　Develop Intercultural Relationships

The best way to get to know and understand another culture is to establish relationships with host nationals, who know the norms and subtleties of their culture and can be of great help in your learning and understanding them. You will learn more about another culture by initiating and developing relationships with host nationals in your own country than you will be traveling to their country and staying in Western hotels and seeing the countryside on a tour bus with a translator.

Tip 6　Maintain an Intimate Social Network

Meanwhile, don't give up your social network in your home culture. Close interpersonal relations can provide positive feedbacks on matters related to your self-esteem and emotional needs.

Tip 7　Anticipate Failure Events

Finally, you have to be fully prepared for unsuccessful moments in cultural adaptation. Regardless of how hard you make efforts, there will be frustrations and depressions. Therefore, it would be better for you to anticipate failure events before you start.

These are the tips for your intercultural adaptation. Please keep in mind: Cultures are dynamic and ever-changing. We are living in a global village today and have many chances to meet another culture different from our own. Hopefully, what has been discussed in this chapter can help you be better prepared and motivated to avoid culture shock and engage in intercultural adaptation.

Key Terms

acculturation	文化适应
assimilation	同化
integration	融合
separation	分隔
marginalization	边缘化
culture shock	文化冲击
U-curve pattern	曲线模式
honeymoon period	蜜月期
crisis period	挫折期
adjustment period	适应期
biculturalism period	二元文化期

Notes

1. **Host culture** is the opposite to home culture. The former refers to the culture of a foreign country in which people are living or temporarily living or the culture of

other countries that they hope to acquire, while the latter refers to the original mainstream culture of the birthplace.

目的语文化与本国文化相对。前者指在国外居住或暂时居住时该国文化或希望习得的别国文化，后者指出生地原有的主流文化。

2. **The Amish** are members of a religious group in the US who live in a simple traditional way that often involves farming and no modern technology.

阿米什人是美国基督教的一个支派，他们过着简朴传统的生活，从事农业，拒绝现代科技。

3. *Treatment* is a film directed by Zheng Xiaolong and starred by Liang Jiahui, Jiang Wenli and Zhu Xu. It was produced in 2001. Taking the misunderstanding caused by traditional Chinese medicine therapy—Gua Sha as the main line, the film tells the story of Chinese people falling into various hardships due to the cultural conflicts between the East and the West, and how they finally break through the dilemma because of people's sincerity and love.

《刮痧》是由郑晓龙执导，由梁家辉、蒋雯丽、朱旭主演，于2001年出品的一部电影。该片以中医刮痧疗法产生的误会为主线，讲述了华人在国外由于东西方文化的冲突而陷入种种困境，最后又因人们的诚恳与爱心，最终冲破困境的故事。

Case 1

The Story of Xiao Zhang

Xiao Zhang took the course of Intercultural Communication and found that one third of his classmates were international students. At first, he felt both excited and nervous because he had never spoken to foreigners in English in real life. During the first few lectures, he always sat in a row with his Chinese classmates, and he was not the only one, all the Chinese students in this class did not sit next to international students. Besides, he felt that it was difficult to follow the professor, who lectured in English only. He sometimes couldn't catch up with the teacher. And he hated to take part in classroom activities in English. Seeing international students interact with teachers in English, he felt awkward and unable to join them. Several weeks later, he got gradually used to the atmosphere and began to greet international students in English. Occasionally, he would sit next to international students. His anxiety and fear faded away. After class, he even tried to have private communication with foreign students in English. However, most international students preferred to talk to him in Chinese after class.

 Questions for Discussion

1. What attitudes did Xiao Zhang hold toward the international students at the beginning of the course?

2. How do you interpret the purpose of the international students chatting with Xiao Zhang in Chinese after class?

3. Which mode(s) of acculturation do Xiao Zhang and the international students represent?

Case 2

Culture Shock

When I first came to the states, I was unprepared to live there, that's why I always suffer from stress because of culture shock. I feel that student-teacher relationships in North American are not the same as they were in Hong Kong. Hong Kong students often have high regard for their teachers. In Hong Kong, students never call their teacher by their first name, because it is not respectful to the teacher. Also, they hesitate to ask or to answer questions in class because they don't want to lose their face in showing their ignorance in front of the class, and sometimes because their English is not good enough to form a clear question. And if they give the wrong answer, it not only humiliates them but also brings shame on their families. Hong Kong students were taught to be modest and not to display their knowledge freely until being specially called for. All these things can lead to misunderstanding since my teachers thought that I was too shy, or stupid, or abnormal. Sometimes when being directly asked for some questions, unlike American students, which are more creative and can always give a fast answer, I have to take a long time to think the question over, because I was afraid to give the incorrect answer. Teachers often feel uncomfortable with my silence and tend to interpret my silence as an indicator of my inability to answer a question. It's a normal thing that American teachers expect Asian students to ask them to explain something difficult. However, Hong Kong students don't do this as we have seen earlier. Moreover, their feedback sometimes leads to more misunderstanding. When teachers see their students listen to them in smiling or head nodding, they imagine that these students understand thesubject very well. In reality, some students mask their emotions and just act like that to be polite, since they think that if they would ask question, the teachers would be hurt for their teaching was not clear enough for the class.

(选自 https://wenku.baidu.com/view/49f1beeba900b52acfc789eb172ded630b1c983b.html.)

 Questions for Discussion

1. Why do most Asian students hesitate to ask or to answer questions in class?

2. What will teachers interpret the author's silence?

Case 3

Philips Lighting Company

The vice president of human resources in a district of Philips Lighting Corporation comes from America. He talks with a Chinese employee who is considered to have the potential ability. He would like to learn the employee's personal career goal for the next five years and the position he hopes to achieve. The Chinese employee did not answer the question directly, but began to talk about the company's future plan, the company's promotion system, and his current position in the organization instead. The vice president was a little puzzled, and he became impatient before he finished speaking, because the same thing had happened several times before. "I just want to know the employee's personal goal in the next five years, and what kind of position he wants to take at Philips, but why can't he offer me a clear answer?" After the conversation, the vice president couldn't help complaining to the human resources director. "Why is this foreign president so aggressive?" The employees who were under pressure during the conversation also wanted to complain to the director.

The human resources director knows exactly the misunderstanding lies in the different communication methods. Although he tried very hard to explain it to both parties, it is still difficult for them to completely eliminate the problems that have arisen.

(选自 https://wenku. baidu. com/view/52e838e55a1b6bd97f1922791688848 68762b8be. html.)

 Questions for Discussion

1. Why is the foreign president so angry?

2. Why is there a misunderstanding between the vice president and the employee?

Case 4

Thumbs up

Thumbs up is perhaps the most common of hand gestures and one that has been used for thousands of years. The signal for approval or agreement is commonly found in European and American cultures as a sign of approval or that things are going according to plan. The gesture is so prevalent that it is a common emoji and is commonly used in social media and customer service ratings to indicate satisfaction.

However, in many Islamic and Asian countries, it is considered a major insult. In Australia, the gesture also means all is fine unless the user moves it up and down which transfers the gesture to an insult.

The thumbs down gesture is also commonly used in America, but less so in many other countries. The gesture obviously means the opposite of "thumbs up", however in many cultures it is considered to be very rude and arrogant.

(选自 https://englishlive. ef. com/blog/english-in-the-real-world/hand-gestures/.)

 Questions for Discussion

1. What is perhaps the most common of hand gestures and one that has been used for thousands of years?

2. What does "thumbs up" mean in many Islamic and Asian countries?

3. Why the gestures for "thumbs down" is less commonly used in many other

countries except America?

Further Reading
Passage 1

Deepening Exchanges and Mutual Learning Among Civilizations For an Asian Community with a Shared Future

First, we need to respect each other and treat each other as equals. All civilizations are rooted in their unique cultural environment. Each embodies the wisdom and vision of a country or nation, and each is valuable for being uniquely its own. Civilizations only vary from each other, just as human beings are different only in terms of skin color and the language used. No civilization is superior over others. The thought that one's own race and civilization are superior and the inclination to remold or replace other civilizations are just stupid. To act them out will only bring catastrophic consequences. If human civilizations are reduced to only one single color or one single model, the world would become a stereotype and too dull a place to live in. What we need is to respect each other as equals and say no to hubris and prejudice. We need to deepen the understanding of the difference between one's own civilization and others', and work to promote interaction, dialogue and harmony among civilizations.

Second, we need to uphold the beauty of each civilization and the diversity of civilizations in the world. Each civilization is the crystallization of human creation, and each is beautiful in its own way. The aspiration for all that is beautiful is a common pursuit of humanity that nothing can hold back. Civilizations don't have to clash with each other; what is needed are the eyes to see the beauty in all civilizations. We should keep our own civilizations dynamic and create conditions for other civilizations to flourish. Together we can make the garden of world civilizations colorful and vibrant.

Third, we need to stay open and inclusive and draw on each other's strengths. All living organisms in the human body must renew themselves through metabolism; otherwise, life would come to an end. The same is true for civilizations. Long-term self-isolation will cause a civilization to decline, while exchanges and mutual learning will sustain its development. A civilization can flourish only through exchanges and mutual learnings with other civilizations. Such exchanges and mutual learning should be reciprocal, equal-footed, diversified and multi-dimensional; they should not be coercive, imposed, one-dimensional or one-way. We need to be broad-minded and strive to remove all barriers to cultural exchanges. We need to be inclusive and always seek nourishment from other civilizations to promote the common development of Asian civilizations through exchanges and mutual learning.

(选自习近平在亚洲文明对话大会开幕式上的主旨演讲——《深化文明交流互鉴　共建亚洲命运共同体》)

 Questions for Discussion

1. Is there any race or civilization superior over others? Why or why not?

2. Do different civilizations have to clash with each other? Why or why not?

3. Why does the author compare civilizations with living organisms in the human body?

Passage 2

Toward Peace and Development for All

Globalization is an unstoppable trend. It is neither "Westernization" nor "Easternization". It should not follow the law of the jungle, still less the winner-takes-all approach. The UN should uphold the principle of extensive consultation, joint contribution and shared benefits and rebalance economic globalization so that it will be more open, inclusive, and beneficial to all.

The UN must remain a facilitator of exchanges between civilizations. It is the diversity of civilizations that gives our global village its vitality. We should raise the awareness about its importance and be more than willing to respect, protect and promote such diversity.

Civilizations can complement each other in the course of seeking common ground. They can also make progress together through exchanges and mutual learnings. We should encourage different civilizations, cultures and countries to flourish together through interactions and healthy competition. In this regard, the UNESCO and the UN Alliance of Civilizations have a big role to play.

We should encourage and respect the efforts of countries to choose development paths that suit their national conditions. Countries with different systems and paths should respect and learn from each other to achieve common progress. The UN should serve as a platform for harmonious co-existence between countries with different systems and a bridge for dialogue and exchange.

(选自外交部部长王毅在第 72 届联合国大会一般性辩论上的演讲 ——《人人得享和平与发展》)

Questions for Discussion

1. What should UN do so that globalization can be more open, inclusive, and beneficial to all?

2. What gives our global village its vitality, according to the passage?

3. What organizations will play a big role in the flourishment of different civilizations?

Passage 3

Forging a Strong Partnership to Enhance Prosperity of Asia

The youth represent hope and the future. I am glad to see that the saplings of friendship and cooperation between China and Singapore so carefully nurtured by past generations of the leaders of the two countries have grown into luxuriant trees laden with fruits. The baton of China-Singapore friendship needs to be passed on to you, the younger generation of the two countries, and it is you who will carry forward this friendship. Last July, several Singaporean college students in their early 20s joined a "Looking China" program to learn about China through taking photographs, a program that took them to Northwest China. There, they captured images of modern China through camera lens and experienced and shared the Chinese culture with others by watching the local Qinqiang Opera, eating Lanzhou hand-pulled noodle and taking a river trip on sheepskin rafts. Two Chinese students studying at the National University of Singapore spent an entire year filming the personal stories and dreams of 50 Singaporeans. I am sure you know many similar anecdotes of such people-to-people exchanges.

As a Chinese saying goes, instead of complaining that one's talents go unrecognized, one should learn to appreciate the wisdom of others. I hope the young people in both China and Singapore will learn more about the history and culture of both countries as well as each other's personal aspirations. Learn from each other, deepen your friendship, carry forward China-Singapore friendship, and be a new force driving the growth of China-Singapore relations. This is my hope for you.

Looking ahead, I believe that Asia is once again taking the lead in promoting the development of history. Asia is our homeland, and is where our future lies. China stands ready to work with Singapore and other neighbors as well as all the other countries in the world to usher in a new era of all-round cooperation and turn Asia into our beautiful homeland.

（选自习近平在新加坡国立大学的演讲——《深化合作伙伴关系共建亚洲美好家园》）

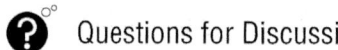 Questions for Discussion

1. Whose responsibility is it to carry forward China-Singapore friendship?

2. What program did several Singaporean college students joined last July and what did they learn through this program?

3. What does President Xi hope the young people in both China and Singapore to learn from each other?

Passage 4

Civilizations have become richer and more colorful with exchanges and mutual learning. Such exchanges and mutual learning form an important drive for human progress and global peace and development.

First, civilizations have come in different colors, and such diversity has made exchanges and mutual learning among civilizations relevant and valuable. Just as the sunlight has seven colors, our world is a place of dazzling colors. A civilization is the collective memory of a country or a nation. Throughout history, mankind have created and developed many colorful civilizations, from earlier days of primitive hunting to the period of agriculture, and from booming industrial revolution to the information society. Together, they present a magnificent genetic map of the exciting march of human civilizations.

Second, civilizations are equal, and such equality has made exchanges and mutual learning among civilizations possible. All human civilizations are equal in terms of value. They all have their respective strengths and shortcomings. There is no perfect civilization in the world. Nor is there a civilization that is devoid of any merit. No one civilization can be judged superior to another.

Third, civilizations are inclusive, and such inclusiveness has given exchanges and mutual learning among civilizations the needed drive to move forward. The ocean is vast for it refuses no rivers. All civilizations are crystallizations of mankind's hard work and wisdom. Every civilization is unique. Copying other civilizations mechanically or blindly is like cutting one's toes just to fit his shoes, which is not only impossible but also highly detrimental. All achievements of civilizations deserve our respect and must be treasured.

History also tells us that only by interacting with and learning from others can a civilization enjoy full vitality. If all civilizations can uphold inclusiveness, the so-called "clash of civilizations" will be out of the question and the harmony of civilizations will become reality. This is like what we Chinese often say, "radish or cabbage, each to his own delight."

Today, we live in a world with different cultures, ethnic groups, skin colors, religions and social systems, and the people of various countries have become members of an intimate community of shared destiny.

The Chinese have long come to appreciate the wisdom of "harmony without uniformity".

There are 200-odd countries and regions, over 2,500 ethnic groups and a multitude of religions in the world today. We can hardly imagine if this world has only one lifestyle, one language, one kind of music and one style of costume.

Victor Hugo once said, "There is a prospect greater than the sea, and it is the sky; there is a prospect greater than the sky, and it is the human soul." Indeed, we need a mind that is broader than the sky as we approach different civilizations. Civilizations are like water, moistening everything silently. We should encourage different civilizations to respect each other and live in harmony, so that exchanges and mutual learning between civilizations will become a bridge promoting friendship between people around the world, an engine driving progress of human society, and a bond cementing world peace. We should draw wisdom and nourishment and seek spiritual support and psychological consolation from various civilizations, and work together to tackle the challenges facing mankind.

（选自习近平在联合国教科文组织总部的演讲）

 Questions for Discussion

1. What forms an important drive for human progress and global peace and development, according to the passage?

2. What has made exchanges and mutual learning among civilizations possible?

3. Why does President Xi mention a Chinese saying "radish or cabbage, each to his own delight"?

Exercises

I. True or False

Directions: *Decide whether the following statements are true or false.*

1. Assimilation refers to the process in which individuals are absorbed into the dominant culture, adopting the cultural norms of the host culture over their original culture. (   )

2. Separation occurs when individuals choose to reject both their native culture and the dominant host culture. (   )

3. The term culture shock is used to describe the feelings of individuals when they encounter different social norms, values, beliefs, and ways of doing. (   )

4. Any changes in climate, food, living condition, language, population, social roles can foster culture shock. (   )

5. When international students try to adapt themselves to academic life, especially when the learning situation is new and distressing, transitional shock frequently happens. (   )

6. Culture shock only leads to negative effects since it is a traumatic experience

that an induvial may encounter when entering a different culture. (　)

7. Adjusting to new culture is an ongoing process with many ups and downs. (　)
8. U-curve pattern of cultural adaptation comprises three stages: honeymoon period, crisis period, and adjustment period. (　)
9. To handle culture shock and adapt ourselves to the host culture, we should give up our social network in the home culture. (　)
10. The following tips can help us adapt to the new culture: assume the principle of difference, study the host culture and learn basic verbal and nonverbal language skills. (　)

II. Matching

Directions: *Match the following words and expressions with the correct Chinese.*

1. crisis period   A. 蜜月期
2. host culture   B. 文化适应
3. marginalization   C. 阿米什人
4. honeymoon period   D. 挫折期
5. acculturation   E. 文化冲击
6. assimilation   F. 双重文化身份
7. bicultural identity   G. 目的国文化
8. integration   H. 同化
9. culture shock   I. 边缘化
10. the Amish   J. 融合

III. Translation

A. **Directions:** *Translate the following paragraph into Chinese.*

When people travel to a country different from their own, they will experience culture shock. The term describes a traveler's feelings of bewilderment when the environment and culture change from the one that he or she is familiar with. The unfamiliar surroundings, foreign language and strange habits of a new country can all contribute to a feeling of uneasiness and confusion. It is not only those who travel and live abroad who get culture shock. Any change in surroundings can bring about these feelings. If a person leaves home for the first time and goes to college, for example, then the new environment and new experiences may be a shock to this person.

  B. **Directions:** *Translate the following paragraph into English.*

  跨文化交际能力是当代社会必须具备的一项能力。随着世界经济的快速发展和教育全球化的深入，不同民族、不同国家、不同种族的人与人之间的交流达到了前所未有的水平。不同的文化背景造成人们行为习惯或说话方式大不相同，交际中不可避免地会出现大量的冲突和矛盾。这是因为人们生活在不同的社会背景之中，他们的教育方式、行为习惯、社会风俗、价值观念以及历史文化都各不相同，因而在交流和沟通中就会产生比较大的困难和阻碍。想要在交际中减少不必要的文化冲突，需努力提高自身的跨文化交际能力。

Chapter 9

Intercultural Communication Competence

> Seeing from the different part, neighbors become far distant; but seeing from the similar part, all myriad are to be a unity.
> —— *Dechong Fu of the first section in Zhuangzi*
>
> 自其异者视之,肝胆楚越也;自其同者视之,万物皆一也。
> ——《庄子·内篇·德充符》

本章导读

跨文化交际能力是交际者进行跨文化交际时所必须具备的一项综合能力。具有跨文化交际能力的人,能够无障碍地理解另一种文化,进而恰当、高效地与人进行沟通。本章将分析培养跨文化交际能力的迫切需要,介绍交际能力和跨文化交际能力的概念及定义,说明跨文化交际能力的构成要素,列举提高跨文化交际能力的策略和技巧,最后阐释"人类命运共同体"的内涵及如何构建。

Learning Objectives

In this chapter, students will learn how to: understand the definition and components of intercultural communication competence, develop intercultural communication competence, and understand the concept of "a community with a shared future for mankind".

Warm-up Activities

Why do we need to develop intercultural communication competence in modern society?

Chapter 9　Intercultural Communication Competence

9.1　Imperative for Intercultural Communication Competence

As the interactive web of human societies strengthens, the world is now shrinking into a "global village". The "global village" is an image that is used to describe the web of interconnections that modern technologies have created. Communication media like WeChat, QQ, and Facebook now make it possible to establish virtually **instantaneous** (即时的) links to people who are thousands of miles away. Modern transportation systems also help to create the global village. Geographical distance is no longer an obstacle to intercultural communication. In this world, people of different cultural backgrounds mix together and come to depend on one another closely. Our lives are influenced or even shaped by decisions made by others and events that take place somewhere in the world and our decisions and the events which take place in our culture also affect or shape others wherever they are. You have a lot of opportunities to experience actual communication with people from different cultures, a foreigner asking way to you. No matter whether you are in business, government agencies, or educational institutions, you need to be competent in intercultural communication. Intercultural communication competence is now more vital than ever due to **economic, demographic**(人口结构的), social justice, and cultural transmission concerns.

9.1.1　Economic Concern

Globalization refers to the fact that different cultures and economic systems around the world are becoming connected and similar to each other because of the influence of large multinational companies and improved communication. It involves social, economic and cultural changes. With the development of globalization, no country is completely self-sufficient. Many of our products, from the cars we drive to the clothes we wear, are designed or manufactured by foreign companies. Since the reform and opening up, China has had increasingly frequent contacts with other countries and created many miracles in economic development. Chinese economy has integrated into the world economy and become an important member of it. Multinational corporations and joint ventures' contributions cannot be unnoticed as they take part in various international economic activities in China. All participants in business bring their ways of thinking and acting into the business arena. Cultural differences and conflicts are inevitably a big problem. Some Chinese employees leave their foreign employers because they feel they don't get cultural identity they hope to have. The companies will have to face a brain drain if they don't solve cultural conflicts no matter how good pay, benefits, and working conditions they can provide. Therefore, the companies should have some knowledge about Chinese culture which is characteristic of Confucianism so as to localize their business administration. On the other hand, the Chinese employees working in foreign companies should gain some understanding of the companies' native culture or at least of the ways their foreign colleagues and superiors behave so that they can avoid misunderstandings to a certain extent while working together with them. Broadly speaking, the economic success of many countries increasingly relies on individual and collective abilities to communicate competently with people from other cultures. Equally, their economic relationships require global interdependence and intercultural communication competence.

9.1.2 Demographic Concern

The economic globalization gives rise to cultural globalization. With the influence of globalization, the local culture of every ethnic group is actively and openly communicating with various other cultures, which makes the world culture as a whole demonstrate general as well as particular feature. In the era of cultural globalization, almost all nations are involved in cultural exchange, promoting the cultural development at the same time. It is clear that many countries, including China, are now multicultural societies. There is an increasing pattern of cross-border movements, which is changing the distribution of people across the globe. While many Chinese people go to study or work abroad, a great number of foreign people are attracted by Chinese culture and come to experience and appreciate it by traveling, working, or residing in China. Some of them even find Chinese spouses. Such demographic change requires a heightened emphasis on intercultural communication competence so as to avoid cultural conflicts and to promote mutual understanding.

9.1.3 Social Justice Concern

Cultural groups throughout the world are dependent on each other so that culture is one of the most important global communication issues that humans face. The need to understand and appreciate those who differ from us has never been more important. If we could not understand other cultures or have prejudice against their beliefs or values, we might have misunderstandings, conflicts, quarrels, fights, and even wars as a consequence. So, both social justice and world peace depend on the communicators' intercultural communication competence.

9.1.4 Cultural Transmission Concern

As China integrates into the international community in all aspects, it attracts more and more concern from all over the world and its mysterious culture is very appealing to other countries. The glorious and **awe-inspiring** (令人惊叹的) Forbidden City, Temple of Heaven, the elegant porcelain, calligraphy, and drawing works of art all show the vitality of Chinese culture. To promote the transmission of Chinese culture, you should develop intercultural communication competence by enhancing the ability to acquire new knowledge of a culture and cultural practices, to recognize cultural differences, and to adapt to the differences. You should be aware of your cultural identity when communicating with people of different cultural backgrounds. In addition to understanding the society and culture of the foreign (language) countries, you should learn to introduce China's national conditions, history, and culture to the outside world so that the world knows better about China.

9.2 Communication Competence vs. Intercultural Communication Competence

9.2.1 Communication Competence

The concept of "communication competence" or "communicative competence" was first put forward by American sociolinguist **Hymes**, who argued that it is not only grammatical competence but also the ability to use language appropriately that should be paid attention to in language acquisition. According to him, communication competence is the ability to convey information, exchange thoughts, and communicate emotions verbally or nonverbally. It involves the ability to express by speaking and writing as well as the ability to interpret by listening and reading.

The concept has been developed by scholars for decades but there is still some disagreement on how best to define and measure communication competence. In this book, we would define competent communication according to American psychologist **Brian H. Spitzberg,** who defines it as interaction that is perceived as effective in fulfilling certain rewarding objectives and is also appropriate to the context in which the interaction occurs.

The key words in the definition are "appropriate" and "effective". The appropriateness of one action depends on the communication contexts and the relationship between the communicators. The "appropriate action" in one situation might be inappropriate in another. The action of one party must conform to the other's social and cultural norms and behavioral expectations. The "effectiveness" depends on whether the communicative goals are achieved.

Spitzberg summarizes four kinds of communication influenced by appropriateness and effectiveness: minimizing communication, **sufficing** (足够的) communication, maximizing communication, and optimizing communication. Minimizing communication refers to communication which is neither appropriate nor effective. Sufficing communication is appropriate but ineffective, which meets the fundamental demands of the communicative situation but does not accomplish any communicative goals. Maximizing communication refers to communication which reaches expected goals but in an inappropriate way. The behaviors may be fierce words or even fraud. Optimizing communication is appropriate and effective, which achieves communicative objectives and conforms to the expectations of communicators in a certain situation.

For example, it is not appropriate to greet a foreigner with the utterance of "Where are you going?" The appropriate way is to say "How are you?" But if the **interlocutor** (谈话对象) utters "How are you?" the interaction is not effective even though it does not offend the **recipient** (接受者). The "effectiveness" presupposes grammatical correctness as well as the right use of rhetorical techniques. Competent interpersonal communication results in the appropriate actions of the communicators which fit the expectations and demands of the situation and effective behaviors which achieve desired personal outcomes.

The relationship between the communicators also influences the appropriateness of communication. People may establish a new relationship by violating communication norms. For example, according to the rule, colleagues should only talk about work during office hours, but their talks often involve personal matters and other topics irrelevant to their jobs in practice. Such talks are not appropriate to the context but are acceptable with regards to the colleagues' personal relationship.

9.2.2 Intercultural Communication Competence

When interaction crosses cultural boundaries, it requires the communicators to have intercultural communication competence. Intercultural communication is a kind of interaction which takes place between individuals or groups of different cultural backgrounds. In intercultural interaction, the lack of similarity increases the difficulty of successful communication. The factors that influence the results of communication include differences in language, culture, world view, and values.

Another factor that affects intercultural communication competence is context, which involves the relationship between the communicators, the place where the communication occurs, the objectives of the communication as well as the communicators' social and communicative roles. It is relatively easy to communicate with an interlocutor of the same cultural background because both parties use the same symbol system and each of them is aware of the other party's expectations of his/her behavior. It is much more difficult for communicators of different cultural backgrounds to communicate in that they lack sufficient knowledge about each other's culture and do not know what behavior is appropriate in a certain context, which will possibly cause their anxiety. The lack of knowledge and the negative emotion of anxiety may give rise to inappropriate communicative skills, negative motives and attitudes, causing intercultural interaction to fail.

For example, in the U.S., business negotiation is a very formal way of communication, which is usually conducted at a meeting room, where both sides of the negotiation are seated face to face. Therefore, American people will think it informal for both sides of Arabian negotiators to sit on the ground in a mixed way or think it inappropriate for Finnish people to negotiate while taking a sauna bath. In Arabian and Finnish cultures, however, people do so to ease the tension of competing and maintain harmonious relationships.

Intercultural communication competence is an inner power, which can be enhanced through the acquisition of cultural knowledge and application of communicative skills to behaviors. Communicators with strong intercultural competence behave appropriately in accordance with the social norms and their relationships and effectively achieve communicative goals.

Then what is intercultural communication competence? The definition of intercultural communication competence is quite similar to that of communication competence in that it also concerns appropriateness and effectiveness, but it puts more emphasis on the relationship between the communicators and the cultural situation they are in. The **construct** (结构成分) of the definition has evolved over years. Accordingly, the teaching objective of intercultural communication has changed from "familiarizing students with foreign cultures" to "cultivating cultural awareness" and finally to "enhancing intercultural communication competence". "Familiarizing students with foreign cultures" mainly refers to the teaching of cultural knowledge. "Cultivating cultural awareness" is based on the mastery of some cultural knowledge, which involves insights into and attitudes towards other cultures. "Enhancing intercultural communication competence" is the behavior in real-life communication after possessing cultural awareness. The three stages of teaching objective just correspond to the three aspects of knowledge, skills and awareness of intercultural communication.

In the past few years, scholars have gradually reached an agreement to some extent on intercultural communication competence. **Chen Guoming** defines intercultural communication competence as "the ability to effectively and appropriately complete a communicative behavior to get the expected response". **Lusting & Koester** believe that successful intercultural communication is regarded as an appropriate and effective behavior which occurs in a particular situation. It requires rich knowledge, rational motive, and skillful action. **Brian H. Spitzberg** points out that intercultural communication competence is assessed on the basis of one action's appropriateness and effectiveness in a given situation. **Wiseman** defines it as the knowledge, motive, and skills needed to communicate appropriately and effectively with a person from a different culture.

9.3 Byram's Model of ICC

According to Michael Byram, to successfully communicate with a person from a different country or culture, the communicator must possess fundamental knowledge about the geographical position and political climate of the other party's country. Thus he can avoid being innocent in communication and can show respect to the country or culture. He should also possess knowledge of his country or culture, which is an important way to maintain his cultural identity. Without explicit cultural identities, the two parties cannot possibly communicate or understand each other well. Byram believes successful communication needs to reach two kinds of objectives: effective information exchange and the establishing and maintenance of good relationships, both of which are related to attitudes.

While certain knowledge has a positive impact on communication, its success or failure to some extent hinges on the communicator's attitudes towards foreign people and their cultures as well as whether he is willing to communicate. If the communicator rejects other cultures or is unwilling to communicate, he will not succeed in communicating, let alone establish a good relationship with the interlocutor even if he has a wealth of communicative knowledge. Knowledge and attitudes are preconditions, while skills exhibited in communication are an important factor contributing to successful communication. Byram classifies skills as the skills of interpreting and relating and the skills of discovery and interaction. The former refers to the ability to analyze the information of one's own culture and that of the interlocutor's culture as well as to relate the two types of information. The latter refers to the ability to discover cultural information in communicative or non-communicative contexts. The three factors of knowledge, attitudes, and skills can be obtained through experiencing, thinking, and education.

Based on the preliminary reflections, Byram proposes a model of intercultural communication competence in terms of objectives. The model includes five factors which are attitudes, knowledge, skills of interpreting and relating, skills of discovery and interaction, and critical cultural awareness.

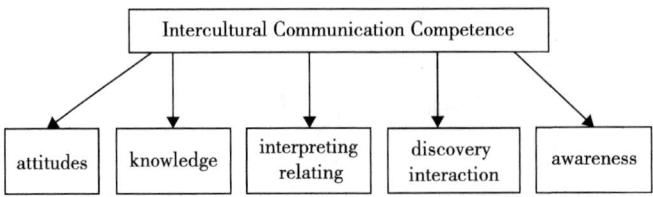

9.3.1 Attitudes

Attitudes here are towards people who are considered different with regard to the cultural meanings, beliefs and behaviors. Such attitudes are in many cases prejudice or stereotype, and are often negative, causing interaction to be unsuccessful. As a matter of fact, even positive prejudice can hinder mutual understanding. The ideal attitudes are curiosity and openness, readiness to suspend disbelief about other cultures and belief about one's own. To be specific, they include (1) willingness to seek out or take up opportunities to engage with otherness in a relationship of equality; (2) interest in discovering other perspectives on the interpretation of familiar and unfamiliar phenomena both in one's own and in other cultures and cultural practices; (3) willingness to question the values and presuppositions in cultural practices and products in one's own environment; (4) readiness to experience the different stages of adaptation to and interaction with another culture during a period of residence; (5) readiness to engage with the conventions and rites of verbal and nonverbal communication and interaction.

This kind of learner with such attitudes will constantly question and observe, try anything new rather than cling to the familiar things while studying in another country. The learner is willing to use the language in a lesson and ask questions about something in a textbook at the end of it, or enjoys talking about what he has heard about another country. The learner becomes fully engaged with his environment instead of living almost enclosed in the links with home.

The attitudes factor and other factors are interdependent. Impossible though it is to interpret and relate entirely values free, raising the awareness about one's own values helps to avoid biased interpretation. The relationship between attitudes and knowledge is not the simple cause and effect. Nevertheless, it is probably easier to relativize one's own meanings, beliefs and behaviors by comparing with others' than to decenter and distance oneself from the natural and unchangeable processes of socialization. Thirdly, if the communicator has attitudes of openness and curiosity, he will find it less difficult to operate the skills of discovery and interaction. Finally, relativizing one's own and valuing others' meanings, beliefs, and behaviors conduces to developing critical cultural awareness.

9.3.2 Knowledge

The knowledge needed for intercultural communication can be divided into two categories. The first one comprises knowledge about "social groups and their products and practices in one's own and in one's interlocutor's country". As it is acquired through primary and secondary socialization, this knowledge is always present in a more or less refined degree, some of it being conscious, some unconscious. It includes knowledge of the shared beliefs, behaviors and meanings of the social group one belongs to and of diverse identities (national, regional, social etc.). Knowledge about other countries is usually relational, it is acquired through one's own socialization and known through the perspective of one's own culture. It is therefore important to know about relationships between one's own and one's interlocutor's country and how to maintain them, about possible causes of misunderstandings and about the perspectives on each other's countries' national memories.

The second category refers to knowledge that is a precondition for successful interaction, but is not acquired automatically. This is declarative knowledge of "the general processes of societal and individual interaction", which leads to the awareness that one is a product of one's own socialization and includes knowledge of the processes and institutions of socialization, of social distinctions and of institutions which affect the living conditions in one's own and in one's interlocutor's country. It should be complemented by procedural knowledge of how to act in specific circumstances.

9.3.3 Skills of Interpreting and Relating

Skills of interpreting and relating are the ability to interpret a document or event from another culture, to explain it and relate it to documents or events from one's own. They include the ability to (1) identify ethnocentric perspectives in a document or event and explain their origins; (2) identify areas of misunderstanding and dysfunction in an interaction and explain them in terms of each of the cultural systems present; (3) mediate between conflicting interpretations of phenomena.

Documents depicting another culture—television reports or language learning textbooks—may claim to give an "impartial" or "objective" account. Readers of them need interpret them in relationship with their own and identify ethnocentrism in them with existing knowledge about how ethnocentric perspectives are acquired in socialization. The interpretation includes handling dysfunctions and contradictions so as to resolve them where possible. The skills can be distinguished from the skills of discovery and interaction in that they do not necessarily involve with an interlocutor. Consequently, the individual can decide when to interpret, not constrained by the demands of social interaction.

9.3.4 Skills of Discovery and Interaction

Skills of discovery and interaction are the ability to acquire new knowledge of a culture and cultural practices and the ability to operate knowledge, attitudes and skills under the constraints of real-time communication and interaction. They include the ability to (1) elicit from an interlocutor the concepts and values of documents or events and to develop an explanatory system **susceptible** (可能……的) of application to other phenomena; (2) identify significant references within and across cultures and elicit their significance and connotations; (3) identify similar and dissimilar processes of interaction, verbal and nonverbal, and negotiate an appropriate use of them in specific circumstances; (4) use in real-time an appropriate combination of knowledge, skills, and attitudes to interact with interlocutors from a different country and culture, taking into consideration the degree of one's existing familiarity with the country and culture and the extent of difference between one's own and the other; (5) identify contemporary and past relationships between one's own and the other culture and country; (6) identify and make use of public and private institutions which facilitate contact with other countries and cultures; (7) use in real-time knowledge, skills, and attitudes for mediation between interlocutors of one's own and a foreign culture.

These skills enable some people to quickly understand a new cultural environment and to interact in increasingly rich and complex ways with people whose culture is unfamiliar to them. The skill of discovery may be operated either in the individual's own time or in social interaction. It works where the individual has no or only a partial existing knowledge framework. It is the skill of building up specific knowledge as well as an understanding of the beliefs, meanings, and behaviors which are inherent in documents or interactions. One mode of discovery is through social interaction, but this adds **constraints** (限制) of time and mutual perceptions and attitudes. Then the skill of interaction comes into play to manage these constraints in particular circumstances with specific interlocutors. The individual needs to draw upon their existing knowledge, have attitudes which sustain sensitivity to others, operate the skills of discovery and interpretation, establish relationships, manage dysfunctions, and act as a mediator between people of different origins and identities.

9.3.5 Critical Cultural Awareness

Critical cultural awareness is an ability to evaluate critically and on the basis of explicit criteria perspectives, practices, and products in one's own and other cultures and countries. It includes the ability to (1) identify and interpret explicit or implicit values in documents and events in one's own and other cultures; (2) make an evaluative analysis of the documents and events which refers to an explicit perspective and criteria; (3) interact and mediate in intercultural exchanges in accordance with explicit criteria, negotiating where necessary a degree of acceptance of them by drawing upon one's knowledge, skills, and attitudes.

The components of intercultural competence are interdependent in various ways. The willingness to relativize one's own and to value others' experience is a precondition for a conscious control of biased interpretation. An attitude of openness also facilitates the discovery of new knowledge and interaction with foreign cultures. Inversely, the readiness to relativize one's own culture depends on an analysis of one's own socialization based on critical cultural awareness. A similar relation exists between the attitudes factor and knowledge about other cultures since the latter enables one to distance oneself from one's own socialization through comparison. The components of knowledge are in turn preconditions for the skills of interpreting and relating as this draw upon existing knowledge. So do the skills of discovery and interaction, by which knowledge of other cultures can be augmented and refined.

9.4 Components of Intercultural Communication Competence

The components of intercultural communication competence can be broadly classified as individual components and contextual components, the former of which include motivation, attitudes, knowledge, behaviors and skills.

9.4.1 Individual Components

(1) Motivation

According to **Gudykunst,** motivation is made up of a number of needs: for a sense of security as a human being; for a sense of predictability; for a sense of group inclusion; for a sense of a common shared world; for symbolic material **gratification** (满足); to avoid **diffuse** (不清楚的) anxiety; and to sustain our self-conceptions. Motivation is the overall set of emotional associations that people have as they expect to or actually get involved in intercultural communication.

In the "global village", there are still many people lacking motivation to know about others. Some may be members of powerful groups who often think they are superior to others and don't need to know much about other cultures. Some are uncomfortable, anxious, uncertain, and fearful about intercultural communication. Others fail to have motivation to communicate across cultures because of historical events or political environments.

Motivation is an important aspect of intercultural communication competence. If you are not motivated to communicate with others, it probably doesn't matter what knowledge or skills you possess. As a result, you'd better first examine your motivation to reach out to others who are culturally different if you want to develop intercultural communication competence.

(2) Attitudes

Attitudes of tolerance for ambiguity, empathy, and nonjudgmentalness are helpful for cultivating intercultural communication competence.

① Tolerance for Ambiguity

Tolerance for ambiguity refers to the ability to perceive and tolerate uncertain situations. When an individual regards an ambiguous situation as desirable rather than source of threat, he is considered to possess such ability. The cultures of different countries or ethnic groups in the world are quite different from each other, lacking absolute equivalence. Many cultural products such as Chinese knot and cultural practices like traditional Chinese festivals, for example, cannot be found in other countries. Tolerance for ambiguity is one of the most difficult abilities to develop since people have a natural preference for predictability and fear for uncertainty. It requires us to be open when we interact with people who look different from us and who behave in ways that are strange to us whether we are abroad or at home. In other word, if you can handle situations you do not immediately understand, then you probably have a high tolerance for ambiguity.

Some factors may influence tolerance for ambiguity: nature and upbringing, education, self-confidence, early experiences, and optimism. You can develop tolerance for ambiguity by remembering that even in the toughest situation, there are always two principles you can rely on.

Firstly, you can always control your response to a situation. Your reaction is your choice.

Secondly, recognizing what you can and can't control will increase the likelihood of a successful outcome and lower your anxiety.

②Empathy

The concept of empathy is used to refer to a wide range of psychological capacities that are thought of as being central for what constitutes humans as social creatures. It allows us to know what other people are thinking and feeling, to emotionally engage with them, to share their thoughts and feelings, and to care for their well-being. Empathetic attitude is culture-bound. We cannot really view the world through another person's eyes without knowing something about his experiences and life. Cultural empathy requires the intercultural communicator, who has grown up in an environment where the local culture is very influentials, to get rid of the impact of local culture and to think in a way people think in another culture so as to find out the common ground connecting the two cultures.

There are two levels of empathy in intercultural communication: pragma-linguistic empathy and socio-pragmatic empathy. The former refers to the situation when the speaker deliberately expresses he thoughts and intentions and the listener tries to understand the speaker from the speaker's standpoint. The latter involves the two parties' socio-cultural backgrounds, interpersonal relationships, and the context. It requires the communicators to respect the backgrounds, social manners, and customs of each other. Chinese people are inclined to ask about the name, place of origin, age, salary and family members, while British and American people would not take those as the subject of a talk. Chinese people are not accustomed to hugging or kissing in an encounter with unfamiliar interlocutors, while the British and American people regard them as a very common way of greeting. The languages and cultures in the world are so numerous that there are not two as similar as showing the same social reality. As a consequence, all the communicators should follow the principle of empathy in intercultural communication. They must try to understand not only what others say but also how they feel.

③ Nonjudgmentalness

"Nonjudgmental" means of, relating to, or denoting an attitude, approach, etc. that is open and not incorporating a judgment one way or another. In intercultural communication, we are supposed to avoid judgments based on our personal and especially moral standards, but it is very hard to achieve.

To develop a nonjudgmental attitude, we should distinguish three levels of information processing: description, interpretation and evaluation. Descriptive statements convey factual information described or clarified without expressing feelings or judging. For instance, "The sun rises in the east and sets in the west". Interpretive statements are descriptions with interpretations, e. g. the interpretation on some data. Evaluative statements clarify how we feel about something, which are based on an assessment of the values, qualities, and significance of a particular person or thing. The statement that "This transfer is misleading because it suggests that foreign language learners should model themselves on first language speakers" is evaluative. Among the three, only descriptive statements are nonjudgmental in that they are the sole statements not influenced by subjective emotions or prejudices. It is impossible to always stay at the descriptive level but it is important to be aware when we are describing, when we are interpreting and when we are evaluating.

(3) Knowledge

The important knowledge includes the information about universal culture and specific culture. The various cultures in the world have common ground in moral creeds and their practices. Even the nonadjacent places which have never had any cultural contact may have many similar codes of conduct. For example, theft, violence, and murder are forbidden in all cultures. As people's self-consciousness awakens, they become concerned more about social norms like justice, honesty, sympathy, humanity, and "Do not do onto others what you do not want others do onto you". Generally speaking, the core values of universal culture are accepted by all people in the world. The knowledge about universal culture provides insights into the intercultural communication process abstractly and can help communicators make sense of cultural practices no matter what cultures are involved.

The knowledge about specific culture is used to understand a particular culture. Such knowledge includes information about what maintains the culture's uniqueness and what are the predominant cultural patterns. It involves how much you know about your own and your interlocutor's culture. It refers to the cognitive information you are supposed to have about other people, the context of communication, the criteria of appropriateness operating in a specific culture, or at least some of dominant values and beliefs in your interlocutor's culture. Besides, you should be able to distinguish individualistic from collectivistic culture, high-context from low-context culture, high from low power distance culture, high-uncertainty-avoidance from low-uncertainty-avoidance culture, and judge which culture your interlocutor comes from.

If you have such knowledge, you are more likely to be successful in intercultural communication. And if you don't, you will find it impossible to interpret correctly the meanings of other people's messages, nor will you be able to behave appropriately and effectively in a particular context. To successfully acquire knowledge, you need to overcome such barriers as cognitive simplicity rigidity and ethnocentrism. If you are cognitively simplistic and rigid in intercultural communication, you tend to process information about persons from different cultures based on your overgeneralization or prejudice.

Ethnocentrism, coined by **William Graham Sumner,** is the perception that one's ethnic group is the center of everything, against which all other groups are judged. People often take it for granted that the values, social norms and language of their ethnic group are superior to others' or others' are all related to theirs. The person who holds ethnocentric standpoint holds negative attitudes towards other groups and thus is not perceived as competent. The reasonable viewpoint is decentering, which maintains that cultures can only be understood relative to another; there is no absolute standard of rightness or goodness that can be applied to cultural behavior. Decentering involves the view that all cultures are of equal value.

We can't know everything about all cultures or develop relationships with people from all cultural groups. Therefore, it's important to acquire some general knowledge about cultural differences and some specific knowledge concerning certain cultures.

(4) Behaviors and Skills

Communication is a kind of behavior and communication competence is reflected in specific communicative behaviors. Behavioral competence includes (1) all the skills for obtaining useful information and solving problems; (2) the ability to mediate and communicate appropriately; (3) the strategic ability to overcome cultural differences and achieve communicative goals with proper strategies. There seem to be two levels of behavioral competence: the macro level and the micro level. The former includes many behaviors that are common in all cultures, such as being respectful, being polite, showing interest, and acting friendly. The latter is the implementation of general behaviors in specific cultures. It is significant for you to realize these different levels of behaviors and be able to adapt to them.

9.4.2 Contextual Components

Language is a social phenomenon. It cannot be used without a certain context, just like plants cannot live without air and water. Therefore, when we learn a language, we should not only try to acquire knowledge in **phonetics** (语音学), **lexicology** (词汇学) and grammar, but more importantly understand the language and use it properly in a particular context.

To put it simply, context is language environment. It can be classified as situational context and cultural context. The former is the factors which influence speech acts in an actual situation, including participants, setting (time, place), utterances' degree of formality, medium of communication, topic and register. The latter includes cultural customs and social norms.

Cultural customs refer to the modes of life people pass down from generation to generation and the collective habits people have in language, behavior and mentality. Social norms are the rules and restrictions on communication. Cultural context involves the traditional culture, customs, religious belief and even literary quotations, covering almost all aspects of our life. Context plays a complementary role in the understanding of deep meanings and implications. For example, a not so familiar person pays a visit to your house. It is very cold, the guest has a mild cold, and the windows of your house are open. The guest say, "It is so cold today!" If you take it as a normal statement and think the guest just wants to tell you the fact that the weather is cold, then you are wrong. He is actually asking you to close the windows implicitly. Such hint is the additional information the context provides.

To be a good intercultural communicator, you should be sensitive to the contexts of communication and take on appropriate modes of behavior accordingly.

9.5 How to Achieve Intercultural Communication Competence

Warm-up Activities
What should we do as citizens living in the "global village"?

According to **Jia Yuxin,** a competent intercultural communicator should be able to effectively mediate between cultures and effectively negotiate on an equal footing between different, even opposite cultures in the multicultural world.

Then how to achieve that goal and become a global citizen? Here we aim at becoming a "global citizen" instead of "native speaker" or "near-native speaker" though it has long been the objective for foreign language learners to have the same mastery over a language as a native speaker. In fact, it is wrong to use the native speaker as a model because it creates an impossible target and consequently inevitable failure.

On one hand, foreign language learners and native speakers learn and acquire a language under very different conditions. Literature shows that few if any bilinguals are perfect in linguistic competence, even less so in sociolinguistic or sociocultural competence. On the other hand, were it possible, it would create the wrong kind of competence. It would imply that a learner should temporally forget one language in order to blend into another linguistic environment, to be accepted as a native speaker by other native speakers. It also suggests separating from one's own culture and acquiring a native sociocultural competence and a new sociocultural identity. The stress involved in this process could be permanently damaging. The more desirable outcome is to be a learner with the ability to see and manage the relationships between themselves and their own cultural beliefs, behaviors and meanings and those of their interlocutors, a global citizen, someone that embraces multiple identities, of which the global identity is the most important and perfect. To that end, you can adopt the following strategies.

9.5.1 Desire to Learn and Adjust

The desire to learn and adjust to a new culture is the first step towards successful intercultural communication. Only when you are willing to learn the language, acquire knowledge about the culture and the process of communication will you perceive other people and their cultures objectively and behave appropriately in actual communication.

9.5.2 Decentering

"Ethnic" refers to cultural heritage, and "centrism" refers to the central starting point or the tendency of people to put their own group at the center. "Ethnocentrism" basically refers to judging other groups from one's own cultural point of view, or misinterpreting other cultures because one uses the concepts of his own culture. Ethnocentrism can lead to making false assumptions about others' ways based on one's own limited experience. The key word is assumptions, because we are not even aware that we are being ethnocentric.

There are two reasons accounting for people's being ethnocentric: one is their limited life experience. People will never be able to experience every life situation of everyone around the world, so assumptions about life have to be based on existing limited experience. It is normal to assume things and interpret new experience and others' behavior on the basis of one's own experience.

Another is their lack of cross-cultural awareness. According to Haney's view, cross-cultural awareness means a sensitive cognition towards cultural elements of one who attends intercultural communication. Ways of expression differ from others if the speakers come from different culture backgrounds. Thus, successful interpreting is the result of accurate comprehension and reconstruction and application of various skills and techniques in a professional manner and to a professional standard that will be achieved at both discourse and cultural level.

9.5.3 Cognitive Complexity

Cognitive complexity may be defined as the tendency to **construe** (理解) social behavior in a multidimensional way, such that a more cognitively complex individual has a more **versatile** (全面的) system for perceiving the behavior of others than a less cognitively complex person does. People who can see a wide variety of things about another person in contrast to seeing only limited details can usually communicate more effectively. So, if you want to make better and more accurate judgments about others, try to see as various aspects as possible about them.

9.5.4 High Self-esteem and Confidence

Self-esteem and confidence psychologically enhance intercultural communication competence. If you have high self-esteem, you like yourself, you think that you are a valuable person, and therefore you behave confidently. Confidence can help you adjust to a new environment and perform well. As a Chinese person, we have ample reasons to have confidence in the path, theory, system, and culture of socialism with Chinese characteristics. Since the 18th National Congress of the Communist Party of China, President Xi Jinping has mentioned traditional Chinese culture on many occasions, expressing his recognition of and respect for Chinese culture and its ideological value system, showing Chinese government and Chinese people's high spirits and ambition, improving Chinese nation's cultural confidence. Cultural confidence is a nation and a political party's high appreciation of and active practice on its cultural value. With self-esteem and confidence in Chinese culture, we can proudly carry forward China's civilization in intercultural communication and see how it is seen from the perspective of the interlocutor.

9.5.5 Innovativeness

If you are innovative, you are able to develop and accept new ideas, willing to experiment with new approaches and especially willing to learn. You will take up opportunities to learn about the meanings, beliefs and values etc. of another culture. That will contribute to the development of your intercultural communication competence.

9.5.6 Respect for People

Respect for people also helps you to build strong and healthy interpersonal relationships, enabling you to be interculturally competent. When you respect the person you communicate with, you will feel at ease and be willing to get to know about him/her. Thus, you will tend to dispel misunderstandings and achieve appropriate and effective interaction.

In addition to the strategies, here are some tips for you to improve your intercultural communication competence.

Firstly, emphasize the areas of similarity with others while accepting differing opinions. Premier Zhou put forward the idea of seeking common ground while reserving differences as one of the five principles for peaceful coexistence among different nations at the Bandung Conference. This principle can be applied to intercultural communication. If you can stress **commonality** (共同点), you will improve the interpersonal relationship. At the same time, you should remain open and receptive because **dogmatism** (教条主义) blocks intercultural communication.

Secondly, make your verbal messages consistent with your nonverbal messages. If there are noticeable differences between your verbal and nonverbal messages, you will **discredit** (使……丧失信誉) yourself and ruin your relationships with other people after all.

Thirdly, avoid dominating conversations or being submissive in conversations. Pay attention to how much you talk while communicating in a group. If you keep talking and dominate the communication, that may make your interlocutors feel bored or even have bad impact on your interpersonal relationships. The effective way of communication is to listen to others, invite their explanations, and show genuine interest in what they are saying. On the other hand, you shouldn't be overly submissive because if so, people may either think that you have nothing to contribute or have no interest in talking with them, which will possibly result in communication breakdown and intercultural relationship failure.

9.6 Intercultural Communication Toward a Community with a Shared Future for Mankind

Warm-up Activities

Find the meaning of "a community with a shared future for mankind" in the dictionary or on the Internet and share your understanding of it with your partner.

China put forward the initiative of jointly building a community with a shared future for humanity and an open, inclusive, clean and beautiful world that enjoys lasting peace, universal security and common prosperity. This initiative is not an empty slogan, nor an illusionary utopia. It is a blueprint for mankind's future based on a keen understanding of history and the trend of times, in line with the long-term and shared interests of humanity. This proposal has hence received high recognition and acclaim from the international community, and shown strong vigor and vitality. More importantly, it is of great significance to the development of the world.

In 2013, President Xi Jinping put forward the proposal of building a community with a shared future for mankind. As China's friendly cooperation with other countries in the world, the proposal is obtaining more and more people's support and approval.

The concept has become a high-frequency term of China's diplomacy. Its connotation, framework, and scope have also been gradually developed and improved. On October 18, 2017, President Xi proclaimed in the report to the 19th National Congress of the Communist Party of China (CPC). In his keynote speech at the CPC in Dialogue with World Political Parties High-Level Meeting on December 1, 2017, President Xi elaborated the concept comprehensively and systematically, and put forward a Chinese proposal based on two questions – to build a what kind of world and how to build this world, and called on all humankind to work together to build a better world.

9.6.1 The Connotation of the Thought of "a Community with a Shared Future for Mankind"

Man is a kind of social existence. Since the moment when human beings evolved from animals, they have lived a kind of community life. Only in the community can people survive and develop.

Today's world is in a period of great development, reform and adjustment. Peace and development are still the themes of the times. Meanwhile, there are many uncertainties in the world. In this context, President Xi scientifically grasped the general trend of world development, profoundly revealed the characteristics and laws of the development of international relations today, and put forward the important thought of building a community with a shared future for mankind. The thought has shown China's wisdom and China's determination to promote world peace and development and to solve common problems facing human society. It is in line with the common and long-term interests of people all over the world.

The core of the thought is building a world of lasting peace, universal security, common prosperity, openness, inclusiveness, cleanliness and beauty. This fully shows that we should focus on promoting the construction of a community with a shared future for mankind from five aspects of politics, security, economy, culture and ecology.

9.6.2 Political Concern

In politics, we should respect each other and consult on an equal footing, resolutely abandon the Cold War mentality and power politics, and take a new road of state-to-state dialogue rather than confrontation, partnership rather than alliance. China's rise will promote world peace. It will not be a maker of international conflicts or engage in monopoly and bullying. Under the guidance of this new concept of communication, China has established different forms of partnership with many countries and regional organizations, basically forming a global partnership network.

9.6.3 Secure Concern

In terms of security, we should resolve disputes through dialogue, resolve differences through consultation, deal with traditional and nontraditional security threats comprehensively, and oppose all forms of terrorism. The international community should advocate the concept of comprehensive, common and cooperative security, so that our global village can become a grand stage for common development, rather than an arena for competing with each other. Moreover, we should not confuse a region or even the world out of selfish motives. Peace rather than war, cooperation rather than confrontation, and win-win rather than zero sum are the eternal themes of peace, progress and development of human society.

9.6.4 Economic Concern

Economically, we should work together to promote trade and investment liberalization and facilitation, and promote economic globalization towards a more open, inclusive, balanced and win-win direction. All countries should jointly maintain world peace, promote development with peace, and consolidate peace with development. Many countries are a link in the international production chain so that orders in one country affect employment in another, investment of one country promotes the development of infrastructure construction of another country, and a country's economic problems will also form a chain reaction. It's hard for a country to detach itself from our interconnected world.

9.6.5 Cultural Concern

In terms of culture, we should respect the diversity of world civilizations, and replace the estrangement of civilization with the exchange of civilization, overcome the clash of civilization through mutual learning, and transcend the superiority of civilizations through coexistence. In Chinese culture, differences, even opposites are complementary rather than competitive or threatening to each other, while in the Western culture, all the things in the universe are divided into exclusive subject and object, human and nature, self and other. One of the profound secrets to Chinese culture is tolerance and integration. It fully respects the diversity of world cultures, strengthens dialogue among civilizations and promotes cultural harmony in the spirit of harmony without uniformity. As *The Book of Rites* puts, "It is this same system of laws by which all created things are produced and developed themselves each in its order and system without injuring one another; that the operations of Nature take their course without conflict or confusion." Different civilizations embody the wisdom and contribution of different nationalities, and there is no difference of the superior and the inferior, let alone the good and bad. Differences among civilizations should not be the source of world conflicts, but the driving force for the progress of human civilization.

We should promote communication and dialogue among civilizations, draw on each other's strengths through competition and comparison, and achieve common development through exchanges and mutual learning. Through this, exchanges and mutual learning among civilizations can serve as a bridge of friendship between peoples and a driving force for the progress of human society.

9.6.6 Ecological Concern

In terms of ecology, we should adhere to environmental friendliness, cooperate to cope with climate change, and protect the earth homeland on which human beings depend for survival. The building of ecological civilization is related to the future of mankind. It is necessary to solve the contradictions brought about by industrial civilization and realize the sustainable development of the world with the aim of harmonious coexistence of man and nature. We should pursue green, low-carbon, circular and sustainable development, take actions to address new challenges such as climate change, and explore a path of civilized development featuring increased production, a prosperous life and a sound ecology.

We only have one earth, and if it is destroyed, we can go nowhere. If all kinds of resources on earth are exhausted, it will be difficult for us to replenish them elsewhere. We should carefully protect the earth, its ecological environment and make the planet better for future generations.

To build a community with a shared future for mankind, we should: (1) interact with people of different cultures through intercultural dialogue; (2) understand and accept the differences between the East and West cultures; (3) seek common values and ethics across the East and West.

(1) Interacting through Intercultural Dialogue

The community with a shared future for mankind is not a community which consists of people who are always together, but a community whose members have mutual access to one another and are ready for each other. Harmony with diversity is the ultimate goal of intercultural communication. To transcend cultural differences and achieve harmony, we must learn to communicate through intercultural dialogue on an equal footing. It not only enriches one's own culture but is very likely to build a culture from a third perspective, which contains the core values and ethics needed in a community with a shared future for mankind.

The precondition for intercultural dialogue is mutual trust which enables us to interact with others in true partnerships. Only when our interlocutors feel our understanding and appreciation will they actively get involved in a mutually beneficial business transaction or interpersonal and intercultural dialogue. Trust enables us to accept others as an end rather than as a means to an end. However, trust cannot be taken for granted. Mistrust may occur when one party from an individualistic culture, like American culture, looks for hidden meanings in communication with people from the East. When an American who values direct and explicit communication talks with a person from the East who is supposed to always favor indirect and implicit interaction, the American inclines to look for hidden meanings. In many cases, such attempt will not succeed and cause communication to fail.

(2) Understanding Cultural Differences

When communicating with people from different cultures, we should take into account the differences between the two cultures in order to avoid misunderstanding. According to Hofstede's cultural dimension theory, there are five basic cultural dimensions used to measure and compare cultural differences, including collectivism and individualism, power distance, uncertainty avoidance, masculinity and femininity, long-term orientation and short-term orientation.

China is a typical collectivist country, and Chinese culture emphasizes the role of "us". In Chinese culture, we often pursue collective honor and value, and we value interpersonal relationship very much as well. On the contrary, the United States is a typical country with strong individualistic culture, which puts more emphasis on "you", "I" and "he". In American culture, people tend to pursue personal independence, freedom and value creation.

Hofstede's power distance refers to the degree to which people accept the unequal distribution of power. Generally speaking, American culture is greatly influenced by Christian thought. People believe that power is granted by God, and at the same time, they accept God's supervision, and everyone is equal before God. While China is greatly influenced by Confucianism and believes that power is granted by heaven and has an irresistible binding force on the people.

Uncertainty avoidance refers to a society's tolerance for uncertainties and ambiguous situations. China is a typical high-uncertainty country, accustomed to following the rules, and also a collectivist culture, which pays special attention to harmonious relations. The United States is a country of low uncertainty, and they are often afraid of rules or risks.

According to Hofstede's survey, countries like Japan, China, Austria, Venezuela, Italy and Switzerland are considered to be cultures with high masculinity index. Whereas countries like Sweden, Norway, Netherlands, Denmark and Yugoslavia are among the cultures with high femininity index. In masculine cultures, both men and women are relatively tough, and their social gender roles are clearly distinct. Men are supposed to be assertive, tough, and focus on material success, whereas women are supposed to be more modest, tender and concerned with family life. In feminine cultures, social gender roles overlap. In these cultures, no one should fight or no one should be too ambitious. Everyone is concerned with maintaining good relationships with others. Both men and women are supposed to be modest, tender, and concerned with the quality of life.

Time orientation mainly emphasizes the time orientation of different cultural groups, that is, the focus of different cultures on the development of things. Long-term oriented culture emphasizes the continuity of the past and the future, referring to the accumulation of time in the process of development. People in this culture usually think that experience and inheritance are very important, advocating history as a reference for the present and future. China is a country with long-term cultural orientation which has extensive and profound culture, and attaches great importance to the heritage of history. People in short-term oriented culture focus on the present and are good at planning for the future. They do not think that experience and history play an important role in future development, they pay more attention to innovative development in the future.

(3) Seeking Common Ground

Despite the differences, people have been learning from each other since long time ago and mutually defining each other through intercultural communication. They are co-creating the global village and making joint efforts to accomplish the goal of a community with a shared future in the new era. The various cultures, the Chinese and Western cultures in particular, also have common ground. People in both cultures not only care for the children of their own, but those of others, not only respect their own elders but those of others. People are expected to care about people they know and like as well as those who are unknown to them. This human nature is commonly shared. The extended love and concern for others connect people closely so that solidarity and fraternity are developed among people, which is the foundation for a community with a shared future. Fraternity, a functional equivalent of community, reveals people's intent to form a global village and to forge bonds between the fragmented world we experience in our physical existence and the imagined community in our mind.

 Key Terms

communication competence	交际能力
minimizing communication	最小交际
sufficing communication	足够交际
maximizing communication	最大交际
optimizing communication	最优交际
intercultural communication competence	跨文化交际能力
attitude	态度
knowledge	知识
critical cultural awareness	批判文化意识
individual component	个体要素
motivation	动力
tolerance for ambiguity	模糊容忍度
empathy	移情
non-judgmentalness	非主观性
behaviors and skills	行为与技能
contextual component	语境要素
cultural custom	文化习俗
social norm	社会规范
cultural context	文化语境
decenter	去中心性
cognitive complexity	认知复杂性
innovativeness	创新性

| high self-esteem and confidence | 高度自尊自信 |
| win-win | 双赢的 |

 Notes

1. **D. H. Hymes,** an American sociolinguist. He first put forward the concept of "communicative competence" in the 1970s directed against Chomsky's concept of "competence". His works include *American Structuralism, Ethnography, Linguistics, Narrative Inequality, Foundations in Sociolinguistics* and so on.

   D. H. 海姆斯, 美国社会语言学家,于20世纪70年代针对乔姆斯基的"语言能力"这一概念的缺陷首次提出交际能力的概念。其著作包括《美国结构主义》《人种志、语言学、叙述不平等》《社会语言学基础》等。

2. **Brian H. Spitzberg,** a Senate distinguished emeritus professor of the School of Communication in San Diego State University (SDSU). His works include *Handbook of Interpersonal Competence Research, The Dark Side of Interpersonal Communication, The Communication Capstone* and so on.

   布莱恩 H. 施皮茨贝格, 美国圣地亚哥州立大学交流学院参议院名誉特聘教授。其著作包括《人际交往能力研究指南》《人际交流阴暗面》及《交际巅峰》等。

3. **Chen Guoming,** a professor of Department of Communication, University of Rhode Island, chair professor of Hundred Talents Program, South China University of Technology, Secretary General of International Association for Intercultural Communication Studies. His works include *Foundations of Intercultural Communication* and so on.

   陈国明, 美国罗德岛大学传播系教授,华南理工大学百人计划讲座教授,国际跨文化传播研究学会秘书长,其著作包括《跨文化交际学》等。

4. **Myron W. Lustig,** an emeritus professor of the school of communication at San Diego State University (SDSU). He is a former editor of *Communication Reports* and is currently on the editorial boards of several intercultural communication journals. Dr. Lustig has written nine books or book revisions, over 30 scholarly research articles, and numerous conference papers.

   迈伦 W. 鲁斯蒂格, 美国圣地亚哥州立大学交流学院的名誉教授。他曾是《传播报告》的编辑,后来在几家跨文化交流期刊的编委会工作。鲁斯蒂格博士撰写并修订的书籍共有9本,发表了30多篇学术研究文章和大量的会议论文。

5. **Dr. Jolene Koester,** president of California State University, Northridge. Known nationally for her leadership in higher education, she currently serves on the board of directors of NAFSA, an association of international educators. She is also a past chair of the Board of Directors for the American Association of State Colleges and Universities, a former president of the Western States Communication Association.

   茉莲妮·凯斯特博士曾是美国加州州立大学北岭分校的校长。她在高等教育领域的领导地位闻名全国,目前担任一个国际教育家协会NAFSA的董事会成员。她也是美国州立学院和大学协会董事会的前任主席,西部各州通讯协会的前任主席。

6. **Richard Wiseman,** a professor of psychology at the University of Hertfordshire. His works include *Quirkology, The Luck Factor, Night School, 59 Seconds* and so on.

   理查德·怀斯曼,赫特福德大学的心理学教授。其著作包括《怪咖心理学》《幸运配方》《夜校》《59秒》等。

7. **Michael Byram,** an emeritus professor at Durham University (UK) and a guest professor at University of Luxembourg. He is also a visiting professor at Beijing Language and Culture University and consultant professor at Harbin Institute of Technology. His works include *Teaching and Assessing Intercultural Communicative Competence, From Foreign Language Education to Education for Intercultural Citizenship, Language and Culture Pedagogy From a National to a Transnational Paradigm, Developing Intercultural Competence in Practice* and so on.

   迈克尔·拜拉姆,英国杜伦大学名誉教授、卢森堡大学客座教授,同时也是北京语言文化大学客座教授,哈尔滨工业大学顾问教授。其著作包括《跨文化交际能力的教学与评估》《从外语教育到跨文化公民教育》《语言文化教育方法论——从国家范式到跨国范式的转变》《在实践中培养跨文化能力》等。

8. **William B. Gudykunst,** a tenured professor in the Department of Speech Communication at California State University, Fullerton, USA. He is one of the leading

scholars in the field of intercultural communication. His last book, *Theorizing About Intercultural Communication*, contains a series of core theories put forward by many authoritative scholars in this field, which can be said to be a theoretical treasure house of intercultural communication research.

威廉 B. 古迪昆斯特，美国加利福尼亚州立大学富勒顿分校言语交际系终身教授，是跨文化交际研究领域的泰斗之一。他生前的最后一部著作《跨文化交际理论建构》包含了该领域众多权威学者提出的一系列核心理论，可以说是跨文化交际研究的一个理论宝库。

9. **William Graham Sumner,** an American sociologist and economist, one of the founders of American sociology. His works include *Folkways: A Study of the Sociological Importance of Usages, Manners, Customs, Mores and Morals*, *East Side-West Side: Organizing Crime in New York* and so on.

威廉姆·萨姆纳，美国社会学家、经济学家、美国社会学奠基人之一。主要著作有《民俗论》《东区—西区：纽约的组织犯罪》等。

10. **Jia Yuxin,** a famous expert in intercultural communication, director of the International Association for Intercultural Communication Study, and the current president of the China Association for Intercultural Communication. His works include *Intercultural Communication*, *Theory and Practice of Intercultural Communication*, *Intercultural Communication Research* and so on.

贾玉新教授，著名的跨文化交际学专家，曾任国际跨文化交际研究学会的主任理事、现任中国跨文化交际学会会长。其著作包括《跨文化交际学》《跨文化交际理论探讨与实践》《跨文化交际研究》等。

11. **Zero-sum game** derives from game theory. It is a game in which one player wins and the other loses, but the total score is always zero. As opposed to "zero sum", the concept of "win-win" is used in the 21st century. The basic theory of "win-win" is to "benefit oneself" rather than "harm others", and to achieve a satisfactory result through negotiation and cooperation.

零和游戏源于博弈论（game theory），是指一项游戏中，游戏者有输有赢，一方所赢正是另一方所输，而游戏的总成绩永远为零。与"零和"对应，21世纪也常用"双赢"概念。"双赢"的基本理论就是"利己"不"损人"，通过谈判、合作达到皆大欢喜的结果。

12. **Tao**, the way, is metaphor for the path along which Heaven, earth, and the myr-

iad things must travel and general norm that they must observe.

道乃天地万物必行之路之隐喻。

Case 1

Charles, an American businessman, was sent to Thailand by the company to manage its branch. Roy, manager assistant of Thai side, was a rare talent who was smart and capable. But he had been frequently late recently. Charles decided to do something to remind him. After much deliberation, he had four strategies for dealing with the problem.

A. To talk to Roy privately, ask him why he was late, and tell him he had to get to work on time.

B. To ignore the problem.

C. To criticize him in public when he is late next time.

D. In a private conversation, to indicate that he would like to ask Roy to help with the problem of frequent lateness among company employees, and ask Roy for advice on how to deal with it.

 Questions for Discussion

Which strategy would you take if you were Charles? And why?

Make your choice based on your understanding of the appropriateness and effectiveness of communication.

Case 2

Last semester, I went to the US as an exchange student. The experience was exciting and precious to me.

I took the course of American literature by William Canale, an American professor who was well-known for his rich knowledge as well as his strictness in evaluating papers but I was confident that I could write papers meeting his standards. My experience, however, proved what I have learned was far from enough.

One day, he assigned us to write a research paper about the short story "To Build a Fire" and he told us that we could make an appointment with him for advice to improve our paper. I quickly finished my paper and took it to him for his advice. After reading my paper, William gave his comment as follows: "The paper was interesting and unusual. The ideas of your paper were brave. I almost agreed with your ideas. I would suggest that you find some material in the library. These are only a few minor comments and it is up to you to make the decision." I regarded these words as compliments, which meant my paper met his standards. But unexpectedly, I received a very low grade and was asked to rewrite my paper. I was confused and asked some other students in this class about the reason for my low grade. After a long discussion, we figured out that the main reason was that I failed to understand what the professor meant in his indirect comment. His words of "interesting" and "unusual" were in fact his tactful response to something he did not understand or like. He said that only to avoid hurting my feeling. What he really meant by "brave" was pretty close to unreasonable, stupid and thus unacceptable rather than courageous. His suggestion of "finding some material in the library" was not only a suggestion as I had understood but implied that I should have used some material from the books in the library, not just from the Internet. And his words "almost agreed" which seemed approval of my ideas possibly meant strange and they were just a kind of encouragement.

Later, when I got well-acquainted with him, I was able to attribute the misunderstanding or misinterpretation to his personal traits. I understood that people even from the same culture talk differently. It seems that he was complimenting me, but in fact he was pointing out my weakness. Frankly, at the beginning when I realized what he meant I felt really disgraced and in fact offended. I wonder why he could not have been straightforward and pointed out my shortcomings directly. Now I know that I was to blame. I have been learning English for many years; I used to think I can understand people from the West with whatever English and culture I have learned. I hadn't expected that a person in a low-context culture could be so indirect in communication. Americans are not all alike. Now I realized, after this event and many others, the importance of intercultural learning. Overgeneralizing others may easily lead to misunderstanding or even worse result. The only thing we can and should do is to broaden our mind, to embrace more categories, and to be sensitive to individual differences.

Questions for Discussion

1. Who is to blame in this case? And why?
2. What lesson do you learn from the case?

Further Reading

Passage 1

To Explore Mars Is a Meaningful Mission

The successful launch of the probe Tianwen 1 on Thursday in Wenchang, South China's Hainan Province, marks the beginning of the country's endeavors to find out more about Mars.

The probe is named after a poem by ancient Chinese poet Qu Yuan (340–278 BC), which is titled *the Quest for Heavenly Truth or Questions to Heaven*. The poem asks many of the questions that people did not know the answers to at the time. China's first Mars probe Tianwen 1 is meant to help provide answers to questions scientists today have about Mars.

Tianwen 1 is another example of the "strange arts" that can be employed to know more about our solar system and the universe we inhabit. The probe will travel about seven months before it reaches Mars, where it will deploy a **rover** (漫游者) to roam the surface. The rover will conduct scientific investigations into the planet's soil, geological structure, environment and possibly water.

Despite the fact that **NASA** ((美国) 国家航空和航天局) has already sent four rovers to the Red Planet, and is planning the launch of a fifth named Perseverance this year, China's first Mars mission shows how much progress Chinese space scientists and engineers have made in a relatively short space of time.

Given the complex technologies needed for the development of the probe and rover, the successful launch marks a remarkable breakthrough for China in outer space exploration technology. It also suggests that China is catching up with the United States and Russia in terms of its space technology development.

Mars is said to bear some similarities to Earth, which means it could provide many of the resources humans need. Despite the rovers launched by the US and Russia, there is a long way to go before the mysteries of Mars are unraveled, let alone the successful exploitation of its resources. China's mission to the Red Planet is therefore of significance to humankind's exploration of outer space. The country is expected to launch a larger probe to Mars around 2030 which will bring samples back to earth.

China has long maintained that the international community join hands to realize the peaceful exploration of outer space, and China will add to the peaceful exploration of outer space by sharing what it learns with the rest of the world. China is open and inclusive in the development of its space technology not least because it believes that the exploration of outer space should help build a community with a shared future for mankind.

(选自 https://www.chinadaily.com.cn/a/202007/23/WS5f19889ba31083481725bb6f.html.)

 Questions for Discussion

1. Why was Mars probe Tianwen 1 launched?
2. How long will the probe travel before it reaches Mars?
3. What does the successful launch suggest?

Passage 2

Post-Pandemic Recovery Must Be Green

It is imperative countries fulfill their commitments to reduce emissions. In the face of the pandemic, climate change, or any other global challenge, no country is exempt and all must stand together.

Many states have taken and will continue to take active actions to try and limit the global temperature rise. Currently, 114 countries in the world have announced that they will give an enhanced **Nationally Determined Contribution** (NDC) **target** (国家自主贡献目标), and 121 countries promised carbon **neutrality** (碳中和) by 2050.

Although the novel **coronavirus crisis** (新冠危机) has disrupted the normal economic and social development of countries, the green and low-carbon development trend as determined in the Paris Agreement is irreversible, and tackling climate change remains high on the agenda of global governance and the socioeconomic development of countries.

China attaches great importance to climate change, and takes the fight against climate change as the important strategic measure for high-quality sustainable development at the forefront of building a community with a shared future for humankind. The positive policies and actions taken by China have achieved remarkable results and the country has realized its 2020 commitments in advance.

China's GDP in 2019 more than **quadrupled** (使……成为四倍) that in 2005, while CO_2 emissions per unit of GDP were reduced by 48.1 percent from 2005, equivalent to about a reduction of 5.62 billion tons of CO_2 emissions. The percentage of **non-fossil fuels** (非化石燃料) in primary energy consumption reached 15.3 percent. The total installed capacity of renewable energy accounts for about 30.4 percent of the total worldwide and the increase accounts for 32.2 percent of the total world increase.

These are ample evidence that China is on a green, low-carbon, and circular economy development path fitted to its national characteristics. Because of the pandemic, China's GDP in the first quarter dropped by 6.8 percent, affecting the employment of tens of millions of people. But despite the **daunting** (使人畏缩的) challenge facing its socioeconomic development, China aims to turn the crisis into an opportunity and find a breakthrough in change.

China will continue to apply the new development philosophy, which promotes the construction of new types of infrastructure, strengthening the development of a new type of urbanization, facilitating industrial upgrading, and developing energy conservation, environmental protection, new energy and circular economy industries.

The country will continue to actively adopt policies and actions to fulfill its climate change commitments and make greater contributions to global climate governance and to promote a high-quality green recovery.

(选自 https://www.chinadaily.com.cn/a/202007/27/WS5f1e1da0a31083481725c1cd.html.)

 Questions for Discussion

1. What does China do about climate change?

2. What do China's remarkable results of fighting against climate change prove?

Passage 3

China Remains An Engine For Global Economic Growth

The fundamentals of China's long-term sound economic growth have not changed and will not change. China will keep deepening reform and expanding opening-up, and provide a better business environment for the investment and development of Chinese and foreign enterprises.

China is dealing with the COVID-19 epidemic and socio-economic development in a coordinated manner, striving for a decisive victory in building a moderately prosperous society in all respects and **eradicating** (根除) poverty.

China will comprehensively implement major policies and measures aimed at ensuring the six priorities of employment, people's livelihoods, development of market entities, food and energy security, stable operation of industrial and supply chains, and smooth functioning at the community level, and ensuring stability in the six areas of employment, finance, foreign trade, foreign investment, domestic investment, and market expectations.

In today's world, the interests of all countries are highly integrated, the human race is a community with a shared future that shares weal and woe, and win-win cooperation is the trend of the times. China will be unswervingly(坚定不移地) committed to pursuing the path of peaceful development, making economic globalization more open, inclusive, balanced and beneficial to all, and promoting the building of an open world economy.

(选自 https://www.chinadaily.com.cn/a/202007/16/WS5f0fb68ea310834817259da2.html.)

 Questions for Discussion

1. How is China coping with the COVID-19 epidemic and socio-economic development?

2. What will China be committed to in the world where all countries are closely related?

Chapter 9 Intercultural Communication Competence

Passage 4

Brewing Civilization

Tea is more than a drink. It's a significant component of shared cultures and individual lifestyles, and the ancient beverage is playing an even greater role in the world today.

Imagine the average day of a caffeine addict in a coffee culture like Italy or the United States. It may be a pot of java drained by family or co-workers in the morning to get the day going; a to-go **espresso** (浓咖啡) as an afternoon pick-me-up; and, if time allows, perhaps a sit-down **cuppa** (一杯茶) during a coffee date with a friend. Coffee's aroma, flavor and preparation endow it with an undeniable gastronomic appeal. But, ultimately, the drink is a ritual **refuel** (加燃料) to counteract fatigue and get through the day.

For millions of people in countries like China, the United Kingdom, India, Japan, Pakistan, and Sri Lanka, tea is a source of relaxation, spirituality, tradition and pleasure. It isn't merely a drink. It's very much a way of life. Across the world, at any given moment, millions of people are enjoying the beverage for various reasons.

China is the perfect place to begin an in-depth examination of tea's place in global society. The country's diverse climates produce hundreds of varieties. Nearly every province has its own distinctive type of tea, such as West Lake **Longjing** (龙井), Suzhou **Biluochun** (碧螺春) and Huangshan **Maofeng** (毛峰).

In the Cantonese culture in southern China, people often greet one another by saying oh yum cha, which means, "Let's go drink tea." Tea is used for social reasons because it invokes so many cultural connotations.

Tea can involve a great deal of etiquette, tradition and **serenity** (平静). In November, the **United Nations General Assembly** (联合国大会) adopted a resolution that designates May 21 as **International Tea Day** (国际茶日). The resolution suggests observing the day through education and activities to raise public awareness of the importance of tea for rural development and sustainable livelihoods. As a major producer and consumer of tea, China will work to promote a steady and healthy development of the global tea industry and to deepen cultural exchanges involving tea.

(选自 https://www.chinadaily.com.cn/a/202007/21/WS5f162c43a31083481725adc8.html.)

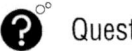 Questions for Discussion

1. What can people enjoy when they drink tea?

2. What cultural connotations does tea invoke?

3. Why did United Nations General Assembly adopt a resolution that designates May 21 as International Tea Day?

Exercises

I. True or False

Directions: *Decide whether the statements are true (T) or false (F) according to the chapter.*

1. Our lives are influenced by decisions made by others and events that take place somewhere in the world. (　)

2. The concept of "communication competence" was first put forward by American psychologist Brian Spitzberg. (　)

3. Without explicit cultural identities, the two parties in intercultural communication can still communicate or understand each other well. (　)

4. Without motivation to communicate with others, it probably doesn't matter what knowledge or skills you possess. (　)

5. It's more important to acquire knowledge about cultural differences than to acquire specific knowledge concerning certain cultures. (　)

6. Cultural context is the factors which influence speech acts in an actual situation, including participants, setting, utterances' degree of formality, medium of communication, topic and register. (　)

7. The objective of learning a foreign language is to have the same mastery over a language as a native speaker. (　)

8. With confidence in Chinese culture, we can proudly carry forward China's civilization in intercultural communication and see how it is seen from the

perspective of the interlocutor. (　)

9. The international community should advocate the concept of comprehensive, common and cooperative security, so that our global village can become an arena for competing with each other. (　)

10. It is significant to solve the contradictions brought about by industrial civilization and realize the sustainable development of the world with the aim of harmonious coexistence of man and nature. (　)

II. Matching

Directions: *Match the words with the following definitions.*

A. contradiction

B. ethnocentrism

C. humanity

D. empathy

E. exclusive

F. civilization

G. stereotype

H. interaction

I. inclusive

J. solidarity

1. ____ a fixed general image or set of characteristics that a lot of people believe represent a particular type of person or thing

2. ____ a mutual or reciprocal action

3. ____ belief in the intrinsic superiority of the nation, culture, or group one belongs to, often accompanied by feelings of dislike for other groups

4. ____ a lack of agreement between facts, opinions, actions, etc.

5. ____ the state of being a human being, rather than an animal or an object

6. ____ the ability to share another person's feelings and emotions as if they were your own

7. ____ including a wide range of people, things, ideas, etc.

8. ____ the state of having an advanced level of social organization and a comfortable way of life

9. ____ not able to exist or be a true statement at the same time as sth. else

10. ____ support by one person or group of people for another because they share feelings, opinions, aims, etc.

III. Translation

A. Directions: *Translate the following paragraph into Chinese.*

Listening and speaking are both important aspects of human interaction and communication. However, different cultures place different weight on these two parts. Chinese culture, due to its orientation of analogical thinking and the ethnic of concern and responsibility for others in human relationship and communication, tends to lay more emphasis on the part of listening. In the interaction in a Chinese context, the meanings or messages of a statement mainly lie in the listener's inner articulation, whereas in the interaction in many Western cultural contexts, meanings or messages mainly lie in the part of the speaker—the speaker is mainly responsible for transmitting the meanings or messages. However, the difference is relative. It is important to remember that this is only a difference in degree rather than in kind.

B. Directions: *Translate the following paragraph into English.*

来到天坛，登高一望，满眼绿林，可以看得很远很远，在这雄伟和伟大之中，忽然感到人的渺小。其实，天坛并非证明天的伟大和人的渺小的，更不是让人匍匐在苍天之下诚惶诚恐。天坛让你感受到融入天地之中的乐趣。人虽然是一个微小的存在，在时间和空间上都是有限的，但当你将自己的身心融入到天地中，就会超越个体生命的有限存在和有限意义，获得生生不息的信心和力量。

Key to Exercises

Chapter 1 Intercultural Communication

Exercises
I. True or False
1. F 2. T 3. F 4. T 5. F 6. T 7. T 8. T 9. T 10. F

II. Matching
1. C 2. D 3. E 4. B 5. A 6. I 7. F 8. J 9. G 10. H

III. Translation

A. 跨文化交际通常是指在多种文化内对某一观点或概念进行的研究。这种研究是以兴趣为基础的,其目的是通过跨文化分析进行文化间的比较。

内文化交际是指同一文化内其成员之间的交际。总的来说,同一种族、政治倾向、宗教或者具有同样兴趣的人们之间的交际是内文化交际。

B. The Silk Road is an ancient traffic route connecting China and Eurasia. As this trade route focuses on the trade of silk, it is called "the Silk Road". As a channel of international trade and a bridge of cultural exchanges, the Silk Road has effectively promoted the economic and cultural exchanges and development between the East and the West, and exerted a far-reaching impact on the process of world civilization. Nowadays, under the new historical circumstances, our country proposes the "the Belt and Road Initiative", namely the Silk Road Economic Belt and the 21st-Century Maritime Silk Road. One Belt and One Road focuses on win-win cooperation and emphasizes the mutual benefits and common development of relevant countries. As soon as this initiative was proposed, it received a positive response from the related countries along the road.

Chapter 2　Communication

Exercises

Ⅰ. True or False

1. F　2. T　3. F　4. T　5. F　6. T　7. T　8. T　9. T　10. F

Ⅱ. Matching

Directions: *Match the following words and expressions with the correct Chinese.*

1. E　2. G　3. F　4. B　5. D　6. C　7. I　8. J　9. H　10. A

Ⅲ. Translation

A. Cyber language was born with the Internet. It is almost a natural law in communication that any new media, whether print newspapers, radio broadcast or television, will create a unique language that suits its style. In the era of the Internet, communication is redefined by keyboards and screens, a striking contrast to the traditional way through word of mouth or paper and pen. When it is hard to detect emotion or mood on the other side of the screen, memes and emoji are born to help people express their feelings.

B. 业务通信的主要类别对于执行基本操作及有效地运行和管理业务至关重要。如果没有有效的沟通流程和工具，运营一家企业必然困难重重。商界的竞争非常激烈，大多数公司都停留在通信技术的前沿，以确保他们在内部和外部接收，并向其受众或客户传递清晰的信息。企业有内部沟通流程、外部沟通流程、营销与销售沟通、正式沟通、非正式沟通以及各种不同的沟通方式，在不同的角色和层次上进行企业沟通。随着邮政、电话、互联网和移动电话的发明和主流接受，企业的通信方式发生了巨大的变化。具体来说，互联网和移动电话对内外部商业沟通模式的广泛变革负有责任。

Chapter 3　Culture and Language

Exercises

Ⅰ. True or False

1. F　2. T　3. T　4. F　5. T　6. T　7. F　8. T　9. T　10. F

Ⅱ. Matching

1. B　2. C　3. A　4. E　5. F　6. D　7. I　8. G　9. J　10. H

Ⅲ. Translation

A. "Three friends of winter" refer to the pine, bamboo and plum. In traditional culture, certain human characteristics are attributed to plants and animals based on their natural qualities. The pine and bamboo remain green all year round even in the coldest season, and the plum blooms in early spring when snow and frost are still frequent. These three plants are cold resistant and retain their beauty even in harsh weather, just like good friends keep each other's company during an icy winter. This term is often used to refer to loyal and steadfast friendship, and also represent the fine qualities of high-mindedness and detachment.

B. 当"地球村"的概念随着21世纪的到来而出现时，跨文化交际的发生比以往任何时候都要多，而且从未像今天这样重要。作为跨文化交际的同义词，它指的是一种全球性的交际形式，用来描述在一个由不同宗教、社会、种族和教育背景的个人组成的组织中自然出现的各种各样的交际问题。跨文化交际研究是近年来通过跨学科的互动发展起来的，即行为科学、人类学和语言科学。

Chapter 4 Cultural Patterns

Exercises

Ⅰ. Multiple Choice

1. B 2. A 3. D 4. C 5. A 6. C 7. B 8. D 9. B 10. C

Ⅱ. Matching

1. E 2. I 3. H 4. G 5. J 6. F 7. D 8. C 9. B 10. A

Ⅲ. Translation

A. The ideal of rural life reflected in art and literature is the important feature of Chinese culture, which is, to a large degree, attributed to the feelings to the nature from Taoism. There are two most popular topics in the traditional Chinese painting. One is the various scenes of happiness about family life, with the old men often playing chess and drinking tea, the men harvesting in the field, women weaving and sewing, and children playing outdoors. The other scene is all kinds of pleasures about country life, in which the fishermen are fishing on the lake, the farmers are cutting wood and gathering herbs in the mountains and the scholars are chanting poetry and painting pictures sitting under the pine trees. The two themes can represent the life ideal of Confucianism and Taoism respectively.

B. 白描是中国传统的艺术表现形式之一。它具有用墨线绘制的图像轮廓。这种画风多用于画人物和花卉。着墨不多，但这种技法可以达到很生动的效果。起源于早期的"白画"；一般运用同一墨色，通过线条的长短、粗细、轻重、转折等表现物象的质感和动势。白描也是叙事文学中非常重要的表现方式。它主要指的是用一种朴素简练的笔墨，不加烘托渲染，描绘出鲜明生动的形象。

Chapter 5   Verbal Communication

Exercises

Ⅰ. True or False

1. F   2. F   3. T   4. F   5. T   6. F   7. T   8. F   9. T   10. F

Ⅱ. Matching

1. D   2. G   3. A   4. H   5. B   6. J   7. C   8. I   9. F   10. E

Ⅲ. Translation

A. 跨文化交流是一门跨学科的研究科目，它综合了社会心理学、社会学、文化人类学、社会语言学以及传播学等学科。研究不同文化之间交流的学者，最重要的研究课题之一就是不同文化背景的人在交往的时候，如何尽可能地减少误解。低语境的交流就像计算机程序，一切都按照编好的程序进行，否则就运行不了。美国的文化就是低语境的，美国人表达自己思想的时候尽可能简单明了，以有利于传播或交流。与此相反的是高语境的交流，这种交流就像生活在一起的孪生兄弟姐妹之间的交往。因为他们能够心领神会，谈话时只需要使用简短的句子和言辞。

B. Social scientists tell us that cultures differ from one another, that each culture is unique. As cultures are diverse so languages are diverse. It is only natural then that with difference in cultures and differences in languages, difficulties often arise in communicating between cultures and across cultures. Understanding is not always easy. Learning a foreign language well means more than merely mastering the pronunciation, grammar, words and idioms. It also means learning to see the world as native speakers of that language see it, learning the ways in which their language reflects the ideas, customs, and behavior of their society, learning to understand their language of the mind, Learning a language, in fact, is inseparable from learning its culture.

Chapter 6　Nonverbal Communication

Exercises

I. Multiple Choices

1. C 2. D 3. C 4. C 5. D 6. B 7. C 8. A 9. B 10. B

II. True or False

1. T 2. T 3. F 4. T 5. F 6. T 7. F 8. F 9. F 10. T

III. Translation

A. 非言语交际中出现的错误往往比言语交际中的错误更难避免。比如说，会谈时目光交流多少次才是恰当的，在不同国家就差别很大。和日本人谈判时，我学会了在谈判桌上要不时地与对方的目光错开，不能一直盯着对方。东南亚人也对直视感到不舒服。在东南亚要学会不去直视对方，而在地中海地区、西亚和拉丁美洲谈生意时，你得忘掉这些。这些感情外露的人认为"眼睛是心灵的窗户"。他们直视你以表示他们对谈话感兴趣，还表示诚实和真诚。如果你不直视对方，你就会被认为是不真诚——甚至是不诚实的。

B. The color of red in Chinese culture usually means good luck, longevity and happiness. Red can be found everywhere during Chinese Spring Festival and other joyous occasions. Cash is often put in red envelopes and sent to family members or close friends as gifts. Its popularity can also be attributed to the fact that people associate it with Chinese revolution and Communist Party. However, it does not always equal good luck and joy in that the name of the dead used to be written in red. Using red ink to write names of Chinese people is seen as an offense.

Chapter 7　Intercultural Communication Barriers

Exercises

I. Word-filling

1. feeling 2. superior 3. judgement 4. attitude 5. race

6. economic 7. associative 8. different 9. difficult 10. conceptual

II. Multiple Choices
1. D 2. D 3. B 4. C 5. C

III. True or False
1. F 2. T 3. T 4. F 5. T
6. F 7. F 8. T 9. F 10. T

IV. Translation

A. Zigong asked, "Is there any teaching that can serve as a lasting principle for conduct in one's whole life?" Confucius replied, "Surely that is to be considerate! Do not do to others what you do not want others to do to you." Do not impose on others what you do not want yourself. That is the "way of being considerate" advocated by Confucius. It calls for using one's own mind to infer and understand other people's minds. In today's words, it means to put oneself into others' shoes or to think from their positions. Its philosophical basis lies in the similarity of people's basic natures. It is an important principle put forth by Confucians to govern inter-personal relationships, and is now extended to international relationship management to counter power politics. Its essential elements are benevolence, equality, and tolerance.

B. 我们要致力于推进合作共赢的共同开放。这次疫情告诫我们，各国是休戚与共的命运共同体，重大危机面前没有谁能够独善其身，团结合作是应对挑战的必然选择。我们要坚持合作共赢理念，信任而不是猜忌，携手而不是挥拳，协商而不是谩骂，以各国共同利益为重，推动经济全球化朝着更加开放、包容、普惠、平衡、共赢的方向发展。

Chapter 8　Intercultural Adaptation

Exercises

I. True or False
1. T 2. F 3. T 4. T 5. F 6. F 7. T 8. F 9. F 10. T

II. Matching
1. D 2. G 3. I 4. A 5. B 6. H 7. F 8. J 9. E 10. C

III. Translation

A. 当人们去不同国家旅游时，他们会经历文化冲击。这个术语描述了当环境和文化与旅行者的所熟悉的环境和文化不同时，他或她会有困惑感。陌生的环境、陌生的语言和陌生的习惯都会让人产生不安和困惑的感觉。不仅仅是那些在国外旅行和生活的人会受到文化冲击,任何环境的变化都会带来这种感觉。例如,如果一个人第一次离家去上大学,那么新的环境和新的经历可能会对这个人造成冲击。

B. Intercultural communication ability is a necessary ability in contemporary society. With the rapid development of world economy and the deepening of educational globalization, the communication between people from different nationalities, countries and races has reached an unprecedented level. Different cultural backgrounds lead to different behavior habits or ways of speaking, which inevitably leads to a lot of conflicts and contradictions in communication. Since people live in different social backgrounds, and their education methods, behavior habits, social customs, values, history and culture are different, there will be great difficulties and obstacles in communication. If we want to reduce unnecessary cultural conflicts in communication, we need to improve our intercultural communication ability.

Chapter 9 Intercultural Communication Competence

Exercises

Ⅰ. True or False

1. T 2. F 3. F 4. T 5. F 6. F 7. F 8. T 9. F 10. T

Ⅱ. Matching

1. G 2. H 3. B 4. A 5. C 6. D 7. I 8. F 9. E 10. J

Ⅲ. Translation

A. 听和说都是人际交往和沟通的重要方面。然而,不同的文化对这两方面的重视程度不同。中国文化由于在人际关系和交际中具有类比思维的倾向及对他人的关心和责任的民族性,更倾向于重视倾听。在汉语语境的交往中,一个陈述的意义或信息主要在于听者的内在表达,而在许多西方文化语境中,交际的意义或信息主要在于说话人——讲话者主要负责传达意思或信息。然而,这种差别是相对的。重要的是要记住这只是程度上的差异,而不是性质上的差异。

B. Arriving at the Temple of Heaven and climbing high, one can see the green forest all over the place, and suddenly feel the insignificance of human beings in the midst of such magnificence and greatness. In fact, the Temple of Heaven is not a proof of the greatness of heaven and the smallness of man, nor is it a place for people to crawl under heaven struck with awe. The Temple of Heaven allows you to feel the joy of blending into heaven and earth. Human is a tiny existence, limited in time and space, but when you integrate your body and mind into the heaven and earth, you will transcend the limited existence and limited meaning of individual life, and gain endless confidence and strength.

References

[1] BIERI J. Cognitive Complexity and Personality Development [M]. //J Harvey (Ed.). Experience, Structure and Adaptability. New York: Spriner, 1996.

[2] BYRAM M. 跨文化交际能力的教学与评估 [M]. 上海：上海外语教育出版社, 2014.

[3] CHEN GUOMING Intercultural Communication Competence: Some Perspectives of Research [C]. Paper presented at the Annual Meeting of the Eastern Communication (Philadelphia PA, April 1990).

[4] GUDYKUNST, W. B. Intercultural Communication Theories [M]. //GUDYKUNST, W. B. (Ed). Cross-Cultural and Intercultural Communication. London: Sage Publications, 2003.

[5] HYMES, D. On Communicative Competence [M]. //J. B. Pride and J. Holmes (eds) *Sociolinguistics*. Harmondsworth: Penguin, 1972.

[6] JANE WOODIN. Interculturality, Interaction and Language Learning—Insights from Tandem Partnerships [M]. NY: Routledge, 2018.

[7] JIA YUXIN. Experiencing Global Intercultural Communication [M]. Beijing: Foreign Language Teaching and Research Press, 2019.

[8] LUSTING, MYRON W. and JOLENE KOESTER. Intercultural Competence: Interpersonal Communication Across Cultures [M]. 5th ed. Shanghai: Shanghai Foreign Language Education Press, 2007.

[9] LARRY A. SAMOVAR, RICHARD E. PORTER. Communication Between Cultures [M]. Beijing: Foreign Language Teaching and Research Press, 2000.

[10] LARRY A. SAMOVAR, RICHARD E. PORTER. Intercultural Communication: A Reader [M]. 8th ed. Belmont, Calif: Wadsworth Publishing Company, 1997.

[11] MARTIN S. REMLAND, Nonverbal Communication in Everyday Life [M]. 2nd ed. Boston: Houghton Mifflin, 2004.

[12] NAN M. SUSSMAN, 庄恩平. 跨文化沟通 [M]. 北京：外语教学与研究出版社, 2014.

[13] RAN AN and XIANPENG WEI. A Study of Intercultural Adaptation in the Context of Micro-environment: an Observational Case of an Intercultural Classroom [M]. Intercultural Adaption (I): Theoretical Explorations And Empirical Studies. Shanghai:

Shanghai Foreign Language Education Press, 2012: 165-167

[14] SPITZBERG, B. Interpersonal Communication Competence (SAGE Series in Interpersonal Communication) [M]. London: Sage Publications, Inc, 1984.

[15] SUMMER, W. G. Folkways: A Study of the Sociological Importance of Usages, Manners, Customs, Mores, and Morals [M]: Ginn, 1906.

[16] WISEMAN, R. L. HAMMER, M. & NISHIDA N. Predictors of Intercultural Communication Competence [J]. International Journal of Intercultural Relations, 13: 349-370.

[17] 曹盼盼. 跨文化交际中川菜菜名地域文化英译探析: 基于《美食译苑》和《中国川菜》的对比 [J]. 南阳理工学院学院, 2020 (1): 66-70, 86.

[18] 窦卫霖. 跨文化交际基础 [M]. 北京: 对外经贸大学出版社, 2007.

[19] 丁毅伟. 跨文化交际中的语言对比与翻译 [J]. 江苏外语教学研究, 2002 (1): 76-79.

[20] 杜平. 跨文化交际教程 [M]. 北京: 中国人民大学出版社, 2015.

[21] 关世杰. 跨文化交流学: 提高涉外交流能力的学问 [M]. 北京: 北京大学出版社, 1995.

[22] 胡文仲. 跨文化交际学概论 [M]. 北京: 外语教学与研究出版社, 1999.

[23] 贾玉新. 跨文化交际学 [M]. 上海: 上海外语教育出版社, 1997.

[24] 李雅芳. 如何实现国际传播中的"无障碍"阅读: 以北京周报社的传播实践为例 [J]. 中国翻译, 2015 (5): 11-12.

[25] 刘法公. 汉英文化差异与汉英翻译信息障碍 [J]. 外语与外语教学, 2000 (2): 45-50.

[26] 刘凤霞. 跨文化交际教程 [M]. 北京: 北京大学出版社, 2005.

[27] 贾玉新, 等. 跨文化交际新视野 [M]. 北京: 外语教学与研究出版社, 2019.

[28] 萨莫瓦, 等. 跨文化交际 [M]. 北京: 外语教学与研究出版社, 2000.

[29] 许力生. 跨文化交际英语教程 [M]. 上海: 上海外语教育出版社, 2004.

[30] 余卫华, 谌莉. 跨文化交际教程 [M]. 杭州: 浙江大学出版社, 2019.

[31] 叶朗, 朱良志. 中国文化读本 [M]. 北京: 外语教学与研究出版社, 2008.

[32] 鄢小凤, 陈文娟. 跨文化交际障碍分析与对策 [M]. 北京: 中国书籍出版社, 2013.

[33] 严明. 大学英语跨文化交际教程 [M]. 北京: 清华大学出版社, 2009.

[34] 庄恩平. 跨文化商务沟通案例教程 [M]. 上海: 上海外语教育出版社, 2004.

[35] 郑兰英. 翻译中理解障碍问题分析 [J]. 中国科技翻译, 2003 (5): 6-8.

[36] 祖晓梅. 跨文化交际 [M]. 北京: 外语教学与研究出版社, 2015.